John Eleuth... ...nd the wheel o... ...er. His own Li... ...or repairs that ...

Dave Schultz ... half in, half out of his car. Du Pont pulled up next to the Toyota. As Schultz stood and smiled, du Pont picked up the gun from the front seat.

Schultz took a few steps toward the Lincoln. He said, "Hi, coach."

Schultz likely saw the gun in du Pont's grip come out of the window, and raised his arms instinctively. His elbow, though, was no protection against a bullet.

When Nancy Schultz heard the shot, her immediate thought was that it might have come from her husband's rifle; he sometimes took target practice on du Pont's vast estate.

Then she heard David scream loudly.

FATAL MATCH

BILL ORDINE AND RALPH VIGODA

AVON BOOKS  NEW YORK

HV
6533
.P4
O73
1998

FATAL MATCH is a journalistic account of the actual murder investigation of John E. du Pont for the 1996 murder of David Schultz in Newtown Township, Pennsylvania. The events recounted in this book are true. The scenes and dialogue have been reconstructed based on tape-recorded formal interviews, police department records, and published news stories. Quoted testimony has been taken verbatim from trial and pre-trial transcripts and other sworn statements.

AVON BOOKS, INC.
1350 Avenue of the Americas
New York, New York 10019

Copyright © 1998 by Bill Ordine and Ralph Vigoda
Published by arrangement with the authors
Visit our website at http://www.AvonBooks.com
Library of Congress Catalog Card Number: 98-92451
ISBN: 0-380-79105-6

First Avon Books Printing: August 1998

AVON TRADEMARK REG. U.S. PAT. OFF. AND IN OTHER COUNTRIES, MARCA REGISTRADA, HECHO EN U.S.A.

Printed in the U.S.A.

WCD   10 9 8 7 6 5 4 3 2 1

*For Debra, Natalie, and Yolanda
and for Tasha, Jessica, and Rachel*

Acknowledgments

Late in the afternoon on January 26, 1996, our editor at the *Philadelphia Inquirer,* Dick Cooper, popped out of his office and said to us, "There's something going on at the du Pont estate. Can you check it out?"

We spent the next eighteen months checking it out; the result is this book.

Though we saw almost everything firsthand, the book couldn't have been written without the work of our colleagues at the newspaper. Many were involved in the coverage of the tragedy, and the stories they wrote for the paper were crucial in helping us fill in the gaps. Other *Inquirer* reporters had, in earlier years, written about du Pont's association with law enforcement and athletics.

Our research for the history of the du Pont family was aided immensely by two books: *The du Ponts: From Gunpowder to Nylon* by French journalist Max Dorian and *Alfred I. du Pont: The Man and His Family* by Joseph Frazier Wall.

And, of course, our thanks to our agent, Mark Kelley, for his confidence in the project, and to our editors at Avon Books: Coates Bateman, who shepherded most of this through, and Yedida Soloff, who put on the finishing touches.

PART ONE

Fallen at Foxcatcher

Don't let my kids come home. David's dead. John killed him.

NANCY SCHULTZ

This is holy property here! This is a forbidden city!

JOHN DU PONT

One

David Schultz, Olympic hero, was dying very quickly.

He was flat on his stomach in his driveway, next to his blue Toyota Tercel, near the steps of the porch of his house. His arms were at his side, his bearded face turned to the right.

On his hand, perhaps as a reminder of a task, the word "Kids" was written in ink.

Above his right shoulder blade was a fresh bullet hole visible through his shirt. Another was evident near his right hip, just above his waistline. Blood, in a slowly widening stain, melted the snow.

He was making some sounds, nothing loud, nothing labored, just small noises, as though he had the wind knocked out of him and was struggling to breathe. His eyes were open, but not moving, not focused.

"David, it's going to be okay," said his wife, Nancy, kneeling beside him.

She had already dialed 911; the cordless phone was still in her hand. She had run out of the house with it.

"The ambulances are on their way," she added.

She noticed the blood pooling around her husband. She thought to turn him over, to put pressure on the wounds to stop the bleeding before the paramedics arrived. But she couldn't do it by herself. He was too heavy.

"Pat," she said, "please help me roll him over."

Patrick Goodale bent down to help. At that moment, Goodale knew, he was lucky to be standing there, alive. He could just as easily have been lying next to David Schultz.

Seconds before, he had been in the car with the killer, frozen, staring at the barrel of a .44-Magnum revolver that was pointed at his face.

"John," Goodale asked, as calmly as he could, "what are you doing?" He was shocked by the lightning change in demeanor of the man sitting behind the wheel next to him.

The killer looked at Goodale wordlessly, then pushed the control to roll down down the electric window. He swung his arm around, clutching the gun, as Schultz came toward him from a few steps away.

He pulled the trigger.

The first bullet entered Schultz's left arm, slightly above the elbow. It came out his arm and rammed into his chest. The hollow-tip slug expanded as it traveled through his body, nicking the esophagus, passing through his heart, and stopping in Schultz's lung.

Schultz screamed.

"You got a problem with me?" the killer asked.

Then he fired a second time. That bullet went through Schultz's stomach and came out his back with such force that it blew through the Toyota behind Schultz, completely cracking the rear window and leaving a spiderweb pattern on the front windshield. The casing landed on the dashboard, the lead core on the front seat.

Goodale punched the buckle on his seat belt, grabbed at the passenger door, and reached for his own gun—he carried two, one in a holster, another in his jacket. He was halfway out when the killer squeezed the trigger the third time at Schultz, who was already splayed in the snow.

That bullet severed his spine, passed through the right lung, and lodged in the left lung.

Goodale finally gripped his gun and lifted it. The killer raised his, too. Their barrels almost touched.

For a split second the two men simply stared at each other.

Then the killer dropped his gun on the seat. As Goodale got out of the car, crouching next to the door, the killer hit the gas and backed out of the driveway in a rush. The tires spit out gravel. Goodale kept his gun trained on the car, just in case the killer changed direction. He didn't.

Certain he was gone, Goodale helped Nancy gently move her husband onto his back. Nancy placed her palms on David's chest to apply pressure. She was surprised—there was no resistance. David's muscles, normally rock-hard from a lifetime of training, had been shattered by the bullets and left soft and pulpy.

How could this be?

Just a few minutes earlier, Nancy and Dave had been inside the house, finishing a late lunch. She had worked at the elementary-school library that day and not gotten home until almost 2 P.M. When they were done eating, she gathered the dishes. Dave had a little time before going to the gym at three, so he went outside to tinker with the radio in the Toyota parked in the driveway. From both places, inside and out, the Schultzes awaited the arrival of their two children from the elementary school down the road. David would have seen them first.

It was about two-forty-five on a chilly, overcast late-January afternoon.

John Eleuthère du Pont pulled up, behind the wheel of a Lincoln Town Car, a loaner. His own Lincoln had been brought in for repairs that morning. Sitting beside him was Pat Goodale. The two had met for ten minutes at du Pont's mansion about a half hour earlier. They discussed a project on du Pont's four-hundred-acre Foxcatcher estate in Newtown Square, fifteen miles west of downtown Philadelphia. Du Pont then got up—a signal, Goodale knew, that the meeting was over—and asked Goodale to take a ride around the grounds. It had been a rough winter; du Pont said he wanted to assess the storm damage.

Du Pont went into the telephone room and came back carrying a camera, a bird book, and a .44 caliber Smith & Wesson with a barrel that stretched nearly nine inches long. Normally, Goodale knew, du Pont liked to have a smaller, .38-caliber pistol with him.

"I see you're back to carrying your cannon," Goodale joked.

Du Pont grinned.

They drove on one of the estate's interior roads that led to the Schultz house, but were blocked by huge piles of snow. Du Pont made a three-point turn and headed out the main exit, onto Goshen Road. He turned right, drove about a mile, and made another right into Schultz's driveway.

Dave Schultz was half-in, half-out of the car. Du Pont pulled up next to the Toyota. As Schultz stood and smiled, du Pont picked up the gun from the front seat.

Schultz took a few steps toward the Lincoln. He said, "Hi, coach."

Schultz likely saw the gun, in du Pont's grip, come out the window, and raised his arms instinctively. His elbow, though, was no protection against a bullet.

When Nancy Schultz heard the shot, her immediate thought was that it might have come from her husband's rifle; he sometimes took target practice on du Pont's vast estate where they lived in a large home—a house that over the years had become the center of a tight community of amateur wrestlers, assembled through du Pont's wealth, who lived and trained on the grounds.

Then she heard David scream loudly. Even at that pitch, she recognized his voice. She took four or five steps toward the door, picking up the telephone as she went. *There's obviously something wrong*, she thought. *I'm going to have to call 911.*

She heard a second shot just before reaching the door. She looked out and saw her husband's body on the ground.

She pushed open the door and was confronted by a second image, as horrible as the first: John du Pont aiming a gun from point-blank range at David's back.

"John, stop," Nancy shouted.

Du Pont looked up, his concentration broken. The eyes in his thin, pinched face stared at Nancy. Wordlessly, he raised his arm, leveling the gun directly toward her. Nancy drew back into the house. She watched through the glass as du Pont lowered the gun again, at her husband, and pulled the trigger.

As du Pont's hand recoiled from the shot, David's body flinched.

Nancy looked at David; his feet didn't move, his hands didn't move. She thought: *He must already be dead.*

Nancy dialed 911 and stepped outside again. She had to make du Pont leave. "John," she called, "I've got the police on the phone. Get out of here! They're coming. They're going to be here any minute!"

He answered by waving the gun in her direction. Again, she pulled inside. She heard the sound of tires turning on gravel and knew du Pont was driving away.

The 911 operator answered.

Goodale ran up the porch steps and told her to call 911. Without thinking, she redialed. She rushed out to her husband.

"Pat, do you have a gun?" she asked Goodale, apparently not seeing the one already in his hand. She wanted to know, in case du Pont returned.

Nancy bent down. Talking to the operator, she kept her eye on her husband's body. David was still alive. But the amount of blood around him was staggering.

"Thirty nine zero nine Goshen Road," Nancy told the operator. "A man's been shot." She started to get hysterical.

"Ma'am, calm down," the dispatcher said.

"Thirty nine zero nine Goshen Road. A man's been shot."

"With what?"

"A gun or a pistol."

"Okay, was it accidental or did somebody do it on purpose?"

"Somebody did it on purpose. You get an ambulance here right now. Thirty nine zero nine Goshen Road."

"We have them on the way. Can you relax?"

"He's been shot many times."

"Okay, ma'am. You have to give me the information I need. Is the person that shot him still there?"

"Yes, and he's conscious barely."

"No, the person that shot him."

"It's John du Pont."

"John du Pont shot him?"

"Shot him, yes . . . Oh, God. Please hurry."

She turned her attention to David.

"It's okay, David. It's okay, David. It's okay. Don't move. It's okay, David. They're coming. They'll be right here."

The dispatcher said, "Okay, ma'am. They're on their way, okay?"

"Oh, God. I don't hear the sirens yet."

"Do you know what, what the story is? Why he'd do that, ma'am?" the dispatcher asked, referring to du Pont.

"Yes," said Nancy. "He's insane."

Goodale, after helping turn David, ran to the end of the driveway and out to the street to flag down the police; the driveway could easily be missed. Nancy put her husband's head in her lap and continued to talk to him. "I love you," she said. "I love you."

A deep exhaling noise left his body, followed by gurgling sounds. His eyes went fixed. Nancy fought the understanding that he was dead.

Newtown Township police officers Steven Shallis and Mike Savitzki were at headquarters when they heard the broadcast from the dispatcher about the shooting. It took them about four minutes to get to the Schultz house. Goodale was standing in the middle of Goshen Road, waving his arms. As Shallis pulled into the driveway, he noticed dark, wet tire marks along Goshen. Someone had recently pulled out, he thought.

About seventy-five feet away, Shallis saw the Schultzes. David was on his back, his feet pointing toward the street. He was being cradled by Nancy. Shallis rushed over. Dave Schultz's eyes were open, but fixed and dilated. There was no rise to his chest. Shallis took Nancy a few paces away before he and Savitzki began first aid. Shallis opened Dave Schultz's shirt and saw the massive injury. Savitzki inserted a tube into his mouth and began squeezing an ambubag, forcing oxygen into the body. He did that for a minute, adding chest compressions. Shallis checked the neck.

No pulse.

He took out a stethoscope and listened to Schultz's chest.

No sound.

As he did, he kept up a conversation with Nancy and Goodale, getting a brief synopsis of the events. He noted that, considering what she had just witnessed, Nancy Schultz was relatively composed; she was trying to be helpful.

Why, Shallis wondered, would du Pont do this?

"I have no idea," Nancy said.

The paramedics arrived. They took over CPR as a police officer moved Nancy back to her porch. She went inside, looking out the door as they worked on David.

Nancy realized her two children were due out of school soon. *They can't come here*, she thought, *see the chaos, see the blood.* She called the school.

"Whatever you do," she told the secretary, "don't let Alexander and Danielle come home. John shot David, and I think he's dead. Send them home with one of my friends."

Then she called her friend, Laura Short. There was no answer, so she left a message. "Laura, don't let my kids come home. David's dead. John killed him. Please take them somewhere where they can't go by the estate."

She phoned her father, James Stoffel, in Illinois. "Please come," she said.

"Get someone to stay with you," he said, then made arrangements to fly to Philadelphia that evening. He also gave her a strong warning: Don't call the local police. Whatever you do, call the county authorities, not the local police.

She reached a friend, Toni Lyon, who arrived within minutes. The two climbed into Schultz's van and drove to Mercy Haverford Hospital.

There, she wasn't allowed to see her husband. "Is he dead?" she asked over and over. She still held on to a glimmer of hope.

"Is he dead?" She needed to know.

Nancy was led to a room. Finally, a doctor came in. "Are you the wife of the gunshot victim?" he asked.

"Yes."

Softly, she was told David was gone. The bullets had crushed his lung and his heart.

She was led to his room. She had him to herself for a few minutes. The tubes the emergency crew used were still in his body. She leaned over her husband, gave him a kiss, and said good-bye.

Not far away, on du Pont's Foxcatcher Farm, police were already beginning to swarm over the property.

That evening, at Toni Lyon's house, Nancy Schultz took her two children into a room and sat them down.

"Something very bad has happened," she said.

Six-year-old Danielle's ear-piercing screams rang throughout the house: "I want my daddy! I want my daddy! I want my daddy!"

Two

John du Pont retraced his route, up Goshen Road, through the main entrance onto his estate. He drove to his mansion and parked the Town Car outside the front door.

The colonnaded mansion, built in 1925, was du Pont's lifelong home. It was a replica of Montpelier, James Madison's house in Virginia, and a former du Pont family property. Montpelier had been owned by du Pont's grandfather, William Sr., and du Pont's father, William Jr., had there lived as a boy.

The house was the centerpiece of Foxcatcher Farm, the family estate located amid parks, upscale homes, and historic buildings in Newtown Square.

There were forty-plus rooms on three floors in the mansion, plus a basement and attic. On the first floor was John du Pont's library, entered through double doors that reminded one of a bank vault. On the right door was a combination lock, on the left a lever. The room was lined with bookcases; at the back was a section of bookshelves that could be swung forward, revealing a large, heavy steel door. Behind the steel door was a screen door, and beyond that the rear yard. It was, in effect, a hidden escape route.

Du Pont went to this room, his private sanctum, twirled the combination lock, pushed down the lever, and stepped inside. Still holding the revolver, he opened its cylinder and in the three empty ports slid in three new bullets, replacing the ones used to kill Schultz. He put the gun in a leather holster, the kind worn by police, took a few steps up a library ladder, and placed the gun and holster on the top shelf of a bookcase.

On the second floor of the mansion, which held bedrooms and offices, two employees shared an office: Barbara Linton, du Pont's personal secretary, and Georgia Dusckas, an adminstrative assistant who began working at Foxcatcher in 1990.

Dusckas's official title was sports psychologist; she was supposed to work with the athletes who peopled Foxcatcher. But over the years she took on more household duties and did less psychological testing. She saw du Pont every day.

Dusckas was unaware du Pont had returned to the mansion until she heard him call her name. That was unusual. Usually du Pont wouldn't talk to someone unless he was in the same room. Dusckas walked out of her office. From another part of the house, du Pont gave a cryptic instruction.

"If the police come to the door," du Pont called out, "don't let them in."

Dusckas wasn't quite sure what to make of the remark.

Du Pont had had a minor mishap with his car the previous day. Perhaps, Dusckas thought, it had something to do with that and he simply wanted to avoid being questioned. Du Pont, she knew, rarely handled his affairs one-on-one. His longtime lawyer, Taras Wochok—known to everyone as Terry—took care of things.

She also recalled a conversation earlier in the day with Wochok. He said that du Pont might be served with a subpoena from representatives of Larry Eastland, a former employee who was preparing a suit to collect nearly $1 million in severance pay he claimed he was owed. So du

Pont could have been referring to that when he told her to keep the police away.

Thirdly, she was unaware of the shooting. There was nothing to even hint of it. Du Pont didn't act alarmed. In fact, he seemed calm.

And besides, in six years of working for du Pont, she had seen and heard far more bizarre things than an order to keep the cops out. She had learned, in her words, to "become desensitized" to du Pont's weird ramblings.

She certainly didn't know that about a mile away, at the corner entrance to the estate, police were starting to converge.

Or that a police tactical team was being assembled.

Or that Pat Goodale was already talking to police about the shooting.

The four hundred acres of Foxcatcher Farm encompassed prime real estate, with woods, streams, an athletic facility with an Olympic-sized pool, a hangar that once housed du Pont's helicopter, a greenhouse and hunting lodge, and dozens of farm buildings. It afforded countless places to hide. Police knew that the extraordinarily security-conscious du Pont had a tunnel under his mansion.

They also knew that he was armed—and with much more than the .44 Smith & Wesson used to kill Schultz. The mansion held a miniarsenal.

That knowledge came from personal experience.

Du Pont was a good friend of the cops. For more than twenty years he owned a 60-by-150-foot pistol range on his estate, one of the most sophisticated indoor target-practice sites in the nation and a popular spot for local law-enforcement personnel. Many of the officers on the force of Newtown Township—which encompassed Newtown Square—were trained and certified at the range. They were encouraged to use it, and they did.

He had been, though, more than a friend. Much more.

He had been one of them.

Du Pont was absolutely fascinated by police work, and because he never actually held a job, it became an avocation. In the 1970s he worked for neighboring Chester County as an assistant special county detective. His salary: $1 a year.

His boss was the county district attorney, William Lamb. Twenty years later, Lamb would be one of the men initially leading the massive team assembled to defend du Pont on murder charges.

Around the same time he was a Chester County special detective, and lasting into the 1980s, du Pont was also an unpaid member of the Newtown police. His Cadillac was equipped with a police radio, siren, and loudspeaker. He was empowered to issue tickets and make arrests. He had a badge and a uniform.

"When I'm on duty," he said then, "it distinguishes me from the baddies."

Then–Newtown Township Police Chief Charles L. Kress was effusive in his praise. Du Pont, he said, was an "excellent" policeman.

"For an individual who is not actively engaged full-time in law enforcement, he probably knows as much, if not more, than the average police officer," he said.

Some Newtown officers had even lived on the estate.

Therefore, many of the policemen arriving at Foxcatcher late in the afternoon on January 26, 1996, were familiar with du Pont and his property. And one fact they were certain about was especially troubling: du Pont had guns. Lots of guns. A Sturm Ruger assault rifle. A Smith & Wesson .357 Magnum. A Winchester double-barrel shotgun. A pocket derringer. A 12-gauge, twelve-shot shotgun with a revolving cylinder, known officially as a Striker 12—and unofficially as a "street sweeper."

Fourteen guns in all, many of them loaded.

And more than seven hundred rounds of ammunition in the home.

And he knew how to use them. He had, in fact, taught policemen how to use them.

Veteran Newtown Sgt. Brian McNeill, one of the first officers on the scene, summed it up: "You get a great marksman, you get a lot of weapons, you've got a problem."

Police had a problem.

The first dilemma was to locate him, something they were trying to do as they escorted workers off the estate, which was—and still is—a working farm. In January 1996, it also encompassed a dairy enterprise.

Steven Shallis, the officer who spent the first, few frantic minutes trying to bring David Schultz back to life, had left the driveway and drove with Pat Goodale back to the main gate, where they met Police Chief Michael Mallon.

Shallis then went on his own to drive down Route 252—the eastern border of the estate—and entered the long drive that led to the dairy farm. He began evacuating the cottages and, with another officer, went to the athletic training facility. It was locked.

Shallis moved behind a tree where he could watch the front of the mansion; his partner was about fifty feet away, staring at the northern side of the house. Shallis stayed put for close to an hour, peering through binoculars at the mansion.

It was nearly 4 P.M., and the winter sky was beginning to grow dark.

Then Shallis spotted movement past a second-floor window. He radioed the information to his superior.

John du Pont was inside.

But so were the two women, and police didn't know if they were being held hostage or not.

They weren't. They could have simply walked out. But there was no reason to. They did not feel threatened. Du

Pont was not acting abnormally. They were unaware that an armed contingent of policemen was nearby, plotting strategy.

Dusckas returned to her desk after du Pont had told her to keep police away. Then du Pont made another request: "Call Pat Goodale."

That had to be done on a cellular phone. A suspicious fire three months earlier had destroyed a powerhouse at Foxcatcher, knocking out the phone lines. Du Pont hadn't bothered to fix it. Goodale, in fact, had installed the cellular phone, placing it in the bathroom to hide it from others.

Using it was a little awkward for Dusckas because du Pont made it clear that Linton was not to know about the phone. It was, he told Dusckas, just for emergencies. It had nine numbers programmed; Dusckas kept a sheet of paper with the nine names in her bag.

She got her list, walked to the bathroom and punched a button to place the call to Goodale's cell phone. There was no answer. Back and forth she went, from office to bathroom, unsuccessfully trying to get Goodale, maybe ten times.

She was holding the phone, standing in the bathroom, when she looked out the window.

"You know," she said to du Pont, "there are guys with guns out there."

"Well," du Pont replied, "don't stand in the window." He moved behind the draperies and peered out.

Until that point, du Pont did not appear agitated. Now, however, his requests to reach Goodale increased.

"Okay," Dusckas said. "I'll get him. I'll get him. Then I'll come and get you."

For the first time, Dusckas became unnerved. Still, her initial thought was that the guys with the guns were somehow connected to Larry Eastland, the former aide to du Pont who was now trying to get a subpoena to him. She figured they were U.S. Marshals, just waiting for either her or Linton or du Pont to step outside.

"Get Mr. Wochok," du Pont said, referring to his lawyer.

Wochok wasn't in his office. Tracey Rea, a paralegal, answered. Dusckas told her that there were men with guns around the house.

"Hang up," Rea said. "I'll try to reach him. Call me back."

Wochok had left not long before to watch one of his sons play ice hockey at a rink in West Chester, about twenty minutes from his office in Paoli. When he got there, his wife, Judi, met him in the parking lot.

"You just got a call from the office," Judi said. "Call immediately."

She said she heard that Dave Schultz had been shot, and there was evidence that du Pont had shot him.

"How is Dave?" Wochok asked.

"I think he's dead," his wife said.

Wochok got back into his car and called Rea. Rea said Dusckas was trying to reach him. She added that she had been listening to KYW-AM, Philadelphia's powerful, top-rated all-news station and heard the first sketchy details of the Schultz murder.

Dusckas, meanwhile, remembered that a painter was in the house, on the third floor. That likely meant the laundry-room door, which workmen used, was unlocked. She asked Linton to lock it. She didn't like the thought of armed men being able to get in.

Then she called Wochok's office. Rea had him on the line. Dusckas held the phone and called du Pont's name.

"Here I am," he answered from the bottom of the stairs.

"I have Mr. Wochok on the phone. Would you like to speak to him?"

"No. Get him over here now."

She talked into the phone.

"Does he want to see me?" Wochok asked.

"Terry," she said, "he'd like you to come over."

"Well," said Wochok, "I'll do my best."

He drove to Foxcatcher, but police refused him entry to the property. He saw three people he knew at the front gate, and one—landscaper Terry McDonnell, a longtime du Pont friend—got into his car to explain what was happening. Wochok returned to the gate, again identifying himself and saying he had to see du Pont. Again, he was refused. No one, the officer told him, was allowed on the estate.

"Who's in charge?" Wochok asked. He was told all commanders were at the police station. That's where he went. On the way, he called his office and was told that Det. Barry Williams was trying to reach him. When he got to the police station he asked for Williams. Instead, Det. John Ryan greeted him.

"Come with me and stay with me," Ryan said. They got into Ryan's cruiser and drove to the fire station, where the command center was being assembled. Wochok got the impression that police didn't want him to talk to du Pont privately.

In the first couple of hours, many possibilities were explored, including having someone go inside to talk with du Pont. Police believed he was frightened, and a friendly face—like Wochok, perhaps—might help resolve the situation quickly and peacefully. But the risk, they decided, was too great.

Inside the mansion, the painter was done and came downstairs to say good-bye. Dusckas, too, had planned to leave by 4 P.M. for an appointment in New Jersey.

"I would like you to stay until Pat arrives," du Pont said.

End of appointment.

Dusçkas walked the painter to the laundry room to let

him out. In that room, Dusckas had her first clue that something was wrong. Typically, du Pont tossed his laundry down the steps and the housekeeper would pick it up. But as Dusckas and the painter walked down, she found one of du Pont's T-shirts on the stairs.

It was soaked with sweat.

Oh, she thought, *the poor man must have really done something because he's sweating.*

Du Pont had a strictly regimented routine. He usually wore a Foxcatcher Wrestling sweat suit and a Foxcatcher T-shirt underneath. He worked out in the morning and afternoon, changing into a fresh sweat suit afterward and tossing the laundry downstairs. A wet T-shirt at that time of day was an ominous signal.

But not as strong as the one Dusckas picked up when she saw what du Pont had put on: a sweat suit with the word "Bulgaria" written across the back.

"When you saw him in his Bulgarian sweats, and there were no other Bulgarians around," she would say later, "you knew, 'Hold on to your seat.' When he was in Bulgarian sweats it always meant trouble."

Bulgaria held a special fascination for du Pont. He traveled to the country frequently. One of the wrestlers at Foxcatcher, Valentin Jordanov, was a Bulgarian—and clearly du Pont's favorite. He sometimes carried a Bulgarian passport that Jordanov had obtained for him. Jordanov's wife was giving him lessons in the language. And du Pont, whose ancestors landed in America from France two centuries earlier, often talked about being of Bulgarian heritage.

In his Bulgarian clothes, du Pont's demeanor changed. Dusckas called it his "executive order" mode. His requests became commands. His bearing became regal. He thought of himself as a Supreme Being.

His identity was altered, too. He talked in the third person—but not as himself. He was the Dalai Lama, the Fuhrer, the Christ Child, the Crown Prince of Russia.

"This is an executive order," he might say. "Get Goodale here. Get Wochok here."

Dusckas tried to do that. But Wochok had run into the police cordon. When Dusckas reached him on his cellular phone, he told her to call back in a few minutes; he was going to the police station. Dusckas waited, then dialed his number.

"Let me tell you what is going on," Wochok said. "Schultz is dead."

"Okay," Dusckas answered. Her immediate reaction was this was just one more situation with du Pont that had to be dealt with. And her first concern was getting Barbara Linton out of the house.

Dusckas and Linton had been clinging to the subpoena theory and were afraid to go out. That theory, now, was shattered. Dusckas knew the men with the guns were not process servers. They were police.

One of them was Steve Shallis. After a relief officer came to take up Shallis's position behind a tree, Shallis had moved toward the front of the mansion, using the thick brush for cover. He stopped close to the kitchen entrance and remained there for another hour. Periodically he saw Linton and Dusckas moving through the kitchen. He took a few of the tactical officers around to the kitchen side of the house, showing them where they would have the best view.

Dusckas, realizing the police were there for du Pont, continued to worry about Linton's safety. And she kept trying to reach Goodale.

It was after five-thirty—more than two hours since first dialing his number—when she finally got him on the cellular.

"How is John?" Goodale asked. Was he agitated? Upset?

"He wants to see you here immediately," she said.

Goodale said that was impossible. "You and Barbara should get out as soon as you can," he added.

Dusckas called back. John Ryan, who was heading the negotiations team, got on the phone. That caused some tense moments for Dusckas. Du Pont was hovering around; though Dusckas never felt in jeopardy, she was afraid du Pont would be set off if he found out she was talking with the police. He wanted Wochok and Goodale—and he wanted them now.

Dusckas told Ryan that Linton wanted to leave. "What color is her coat?" Ryan asked. Dusckas told him, and outlined exactly how she would exit the house.

At 5:45, Linton walked out. Shallis rushed up, put his right arm around her, and hurried her down the sidewalk, into the arms of a dozen SWAT members.

Inside, du Pont asked, "Now are we the only two in the house?"

"Yes, we are. Barbara just left. The painter has left. So it's just you and me."

"Okay."

"Even if Pat comes," du Pont added, "would you mind staying here with me?"

He touched Dusckas's left arm—an extraordinary gesture from a man who seemed to loathe any physical contact outside the wrestling arena.

He then said something that gave an indication of his immediate plans.

"Do you mind staying? We have a lot of food and supplies in the house, and we'll be okay in here. We'll have to take turns sleeping so that while one sleeps the other one can watch."

Dusckas was confused. She still didn't know the circumstances of the shooting. And she was getting irritated. She wanted to talk to Goodale, but Ryan kept getting on the phone.

"I don't understand what is wrong with Pat," she said to du Pont.

She walked into the lunchroom, realizing she had no chance of making her appointment in New Jersey.

So she called her hairdresser to cancel.

Du Pont followed her. He asked a question that seemed odd.

"Did I get their attention?" he asked.

"Yes," said Dusckas, not exactly sure what he meant. "Because they're all out there."

At du Pont's request, Dusckas brewed coffee and brought him a cup. He was back in his executive-order persona.

"Get Pat up here now," he said.

Then he added, "Make sure they know that Valo visits me at eight o'clock every evening and that Valo can have access to come up here."

Valo was Valentin Jordanov. He had left earlier in the day to drive a group of visiting Bulgarian wrestlers to Kennedy Airport in New York, but was expected back in the early evening. Usually, he came to visit du Pont each night.

Also, du Pont told Dusckas, see what other wrestlers could come.

Then, his face suddenly red, a giggle escaping him, du Pont uttered five words that chilled Dusckas:

"In fact, invite Schultz up."

That was the last signal she needed. The red face, the inappropriate giggle—she had seen it before and she knew what it meant. Du Pont was going over the edge. His sickness was taking over.

She knew suddenly and clearly: it was time to get out of the house.

Just one problem. Du Pont had asked her to stay, and she agreed. If there was one thing she also knew from six years of working with him, it was this: Du Pont always got what he wanted.

She called the firehouse. She spoke with John Ryan.

"If you feel you can walk out of the house, do so now," he said.

"I can't right now," said Dusckas. "It'll take me fifteen or twenty minutes."

She was eager to leave, but couldn't tell du Pont. Not that she feared him, specifically. But the situation, she felt, was getting out of hand. Inside the house was a man whose dementia was rising rapidly. Outside were sharpshooters with rifles pointed toward the house.

It was not a pleasant combination.

While Dusckas was thinking about her escape, du Pont was still asking if Pat Goodale was coming.

"Yes," Dusckas said finally. "Pat will be up in a few minutes."

She hated to lie, but didn't know what else to do.

Du Pont seemed to relax. The two of them were in the center hallway of the mansion, and du Pont was prattling.

Suddenly, there was the sound of a horn. It wasn't the fire horn, which was the only sound that normally pierced the quiet enveloping the mansion. It sounded more like a car horn.

Du Pont heard it. "I'm going to go look to see what that is," he said. He handed his coffee cup to Dusckas. "You take this down to the kitchen."

Perfect, thought Dusckas. She went downstairs into the kitchen, put the cup down, and walked out the door. It was about six-forty-five. David Schultz had been dead for four hours.

Outside, voices from the bushes called to her. A couple of police jumped out and grabbed her. Dusckas took care to remain out of sight of du Pont. She felt bad leaving him the way she did. But she realized the situation was out of control, and she had no way of resolving it.

That was up to the authorities.

And the authorities were preparing for the long haul.

Three

Word of the shooting spread rapidly to surrounding townships. At 3:25, beepers started alerting police who had special training in sieges, hostage situations, and other emergencies. By 4:10, about twenty-five officers reported to the Newtown police station for a briefing, including four negotiators and a command staff of four. Eventually, twenty-three separate police departments would send men.

One of the people waiting for them was Pat Goodale. On and off the property over a three-year period, Goodale was intimately familiar with Foxcatcher. He explained the layout of the grounds, drew floor plans of the mansion, and made rough sketches of the surrounding buildings and foliage.

Not all the officers needed that information, though. Many were familiar with the estate.

Perhaps, it was later suggested, too familiar.

Chief Mike Mallon and Goodale drove toward the mansion, stopping some distance away. They could see du Pont's Town Car parked out front. Goodale said there were men at the powerhouse, so they went there and told the workers to leave immediately.

Goodale wanted to get to his car in the parking lot near the mansion. Mallon sped past the front of the big house, Goodale got out, and drove his car to the dairy farm. Then they went to the Newtown firehouse. Situated on the highest elevation around, the firehouse afforded the best spot for police communications and cellular phone service without interference. It became the command center.

Goodale talked to the officers, then drove back to the estate with some of them, pointing out the best places to put their teams.

One group of police set up directly behind the pool house, which gave them a view of the mansion. Another was sent to the Olympic Foxcatcher National Training Center, du Pont's $600,000, state-of-the-art wrestling facility. There was some concern about that building because it had once housed du Pont's firing range; police worried it might be a storehouse for ammunition. That, though, proved to be unfounded, and the facility became the headquarters for those officers on the estate.

One sniper team went to a hill behind the mansion, one set up directly in front of it. Another contingent hunkered down at the kennel, and another at the powerhouse. Officers set up blockades at the parking lot.

The manpower was incredible. When everyone was deployed—about seventy-five in all—it looked like this: a SWAT group of thirty men surrounding the home, a contingent of police encircling the SWAT team, and more police securing the perimeter of the grounds. There was a warren of tunnels under the house, primarily large ducts for the heating and electrical systems, many with exits beyond the house. One long one, about four hundred feet and big enough to walk through, stretched from the mansion to the powerhouse. All had to be guarded.

Sgt. Paul Trautmann of Springfield Township and two officers crept up to the back of du Pont's Town Car and let the air out of the tires on the right side. They would repeat the exercise on the left side early Saturday morning, rendering it all but useless.

Officers hid behind trees and crouched near bushes. The

weather conditions had started out badly enough—dark and gloomy, clouds blotting out the moon—and soon turned rotten with pouring rain and freezing temperatures. "Raining sideways," said Trautmann. The cops wore army ponchos, blankets, and anything else they could use to keep warm. Some were in camouflage. Some wore dark clothing. They were equipped with body armor, Kevlar helmets, semiautomatic weapons, and sniper rifles with high-power scopes and night vision.

They just sat tight. Knowing du Pont was alone made it easier to do that; no innocent people were involved.

"We're prepared for the long term, as well as the short term," said Newtown Police Lt. Lee Hunter.

Meanwhile, the first vanguard of media had already arrived, drawn by the news of the shooting crackling over police scanners. By that night it became the top story across the country, although it wasn't until the next day that police were organized enough to give news briefings. That left reporters groping to make stories out of sketchy information, giving fifteen minutes of fame to anyone who had even a remote connection to du Pont.

Storm the house? It was never given a thought. Police were all too aware of the firestorm of criticism that came down on authorities following such well-publicized events as the Waco and Ruby Ridge confrontations that had turned fatal.

"In this situation, waiting and patience are better than blazing guns," said Springfield Township Lt. Jack Francis, who directed the joint tactical squad. "It's that simple."

"Our goal," added Hunter, "is to resolve this situation through negotiations."

Trouble was, there was no easy way to negotiate. The fires a few months earlier had knocked out the phone lines. Du Pont had never bothered to fix them. And no one pushed him on that point.

"It's his house," Dusckas explained. "However he wanted to do it really didn't create a hardship on us because we were doing things that he requested."

To get messages in and out, she or Linton would use the phone in the wrestling facility, about one hundred yards away, where secretary Beverly Collier worked. Sometimes, Collier would send a note to the mansion. Other business was conducted through FedEx or the mail.

"It was very serene, very nice," Dusckas said. "A world without phones was very nice."

Except when you're trying to negotiate with a man who just shot somebody to death. Then, no phones is a pain.

Police knew they couldn't rely solely on the one cellular phone in the house to try to talk du Pont into surrendering. So one of the first pieces of business was getting phone repairmen into the main tunnel between the mansion and powerhouse. That's where the phone cables were damaged.

About 8 P.M., workers from Bell Atlantic were brought to the estate. Their job was to wire du Pont's phones in the mansion so when he picked one up, it would immediately ring at the command center. He could make no other outgoing calls on those phones.

Police escorted the phone crew to the tunnel, and remained throughout the job of rewiring. No one could discount the possibility that an armed du Pont would try to make an escape underground. But the heater in the powerhouse was so noisy that police worried they would not be able to hear anyone in the tunnel. The noise also made communications with the command post difficult. So the supervisor asked for permission to turn it off. It was granted.

Police didn't know it at the time, but that casual move would play a major part in ending the standoff. Because soon after the heater was shut down, it started to get cold inside the mansion.

Around nine o'clock police began to set up a portable generator; by eleven a bank of bright lights illuminated the home, front and back.

Near midnight, police switched on the public address system in one of their vehicles near the mansion. Trautmann read from a script given to him by negotiators.

"Mr. du Pont, this is the police. Will you please pick up the phone? Pat Goodale wants to talk to you." He repeated it four times over the next twenty minutes.

There was no response.

But if du Pont wasn't taking calls, he was making them. About ten minutes before nine he called Jordanov's house. Jordanov, of course, wasn't there. After dropping off the Bulgarian wrestlers at Kennedy Airport, he had returned to chaos.

Du Pont heard the answering machine click on.

"Hello, Valo, this is Eagle," he said, identifying himself by his favorite nickname. "I hope you get back from New York today. I've been looking for you. Would you please come over the house right away when you get this message. It's very important. Come by foot if you have to. Thank you."

Three minutes later, he called again.

"Hey, Valo, the house may look like it's dark when you come, but come to the front door. Ring the doorbell, hit the doorknocker, and don't let anybody stop you. I'll see you when you get here. It's very important that you come. Thank you."

He tried to reach Jordanov repeatedly during the next twenty-four hours.

Pat Goodale remained at the firehouse through the night. Just after midnight the regular phones were hooked up. Police now had a way, other than the cellular phone, to reach du Pont. But he was not answering his phone. Not, that is, until shortly before 4 A.M. Goodale called, du Pont picked up. It was the first time the two talked since Goodale had jumped out of du Pont's car more than thirteen hours earlier.

"Are you all right?" Goodale asked. "Have you eaten? Have you slept?"

Du Pont said he was all right. Goodale thought he seemed calm.

"Will you come out?"

"No."

In fact, instead of agreeing to come out, he told Goodale to come in. And, he said, bring Wochok, Jordanov, and Mario Saletnik. "Wait on the front porch for me."

Saletnik was an official with *Federation Internationale de Lutte Amateur*, or FILA, an international wrestling organization based in Europe. He had been a regular visitor at Foxcatcher.

He'd also been a victim of what had been—until the Schultz shooting—one of the more notorious episodes at Foxcatcher. That took place in December 1994. Du Pont, never a careful man behind the wheel, was driving on the estate and ended up sliding into the pond. It is not at all sure if he simply lost control or drove into the water on purpose. By the time the car settled, according to one version, only the antenna stuck out of the water. Du Pont was uninjured. The car was a mess. Workers had to put inflatable balloons inside it to get it to the surface and yank it out with a cable.

Soon after, Saletnik was in the car with du Pont. The facts of what happened next are slightly murky, but by one account Saletnik made an offhand remark about the pond incident.

"You want to see me do it again?" du Pont is supposed to have said.

This time, he headed straight for the pond. Both men had to wade to the bank. It became a standing joke among the wrestlers. "Hey, Mario," they'd say, "want to go for a swim?"

Now, though, it didn't seem so funny. And as du Pont pressed Goodale to bring Saletnik and others, Goodale danced around the issue.

"I need time to contact them," said Goodale. "You need to come out and we'll deal with this issue here."

"I'm not coming out," du Pont said. "You do what I tell you. Get those people together and come to the house! Do whatever you have to do to get hold of my people.

"Don't you know who you're dealing with?" du Pont said. "I'm the president of the United States. I have negotiated over nuclear arms. I'm not leaving until this is resolved."

Then he hung up.

The two talked periodically throughout the early-morning hours. Mostly it was Goodale calling the mansion, but a couple of times du Pont rang the firehouse. Time and again, he asked for Jordanov.

During a call shortly after 8 A.M., du Pont told Goodale to come to the front door by himself. "I'm not scared," du Pont said. "Tell Valo I love him. I don't want to be a prisoner."

When they talked just before nine, Goodale asked du Pont for help in ending the standoff.

"John, you are in control," he said. "Help me. Can you leave by the side door?"

Du Pont wouldn't talk about leaving. He again wanted to know Jordanov's whereabouts. This time Goodale had been prepared for that question by negotiators.

"Valentin is sick," said Goodale. "He's been taken to the hospital."

Du Pont expressed great concern about that. "Tell Valo I love him," he said.

"Valo says he loves you," Goodale answered.

Du Pont complained that Jordanov was being used by police to get him to surrender. Police, he said, were all over his lawn.

Then, for the first time, he alluded to the previous day's tragedy.

"I don't know what happened yesterday," du Pont said. "No one told me. I've been kept in the dark."

"About yesterday?"

"I have a story to tell you. Come up to the house. We're in charge. You have federal authority. The local police have to obey us. Leave one of your people in charge."

Goodale tried to get him to talk about the killing, but du Pont changed the subject each time.

"Are you aware that Dave Schultz was killed on your property yesterday?" Goodale asked.

"Get those people I've asked you to get and come here and we'll talk about that," du Pont responded.

He again asked for Jordanov. And he wanted to talk to Wochok.

Goodale said he was going to have to give the phone up to the police.

"I need you to come out the kitchen door," he said. "My men are at the kitchen door. I'm concerned about you."

"Well," said du Pont, "I'm concerned about you. Come up and see my condition."

"I may have to give the phone to the police negotiator."

Du Pont became angry, threatening.

"I'm not talking to the police," he said. "If it keeps up, if police are involved, I'll start to play with some of my toys. You know I have them." He threatened to create a "fireball." Goodale assumed he was referring to sticks of dynamite in du Pont's possession.

At 11 A.M., they talked again. Goodale told du Pont that Chuckie—Chuck King, a stablehand on the estate—was concerned about the horses, which had been out in the field throughout the bitterly cold night. Now rain was beginning to fall and King wanted to get them inside. Goodale asked du Pont if that would be okay.

"Yes," du Pont said.

"I located Terry Wochok."

"Have him come here."

"We're concerned about you. Have you seen television?"

"No. I have no TV. It's disconnected. Am I all over it?"

"Yes. Yes, you are."

That was true. The du Pont story was news around the world. Because of international wrestling organizations and competition, du Pont and Schultz were probably better known in some European countries than in America. Schultz, in fact, was a hero in some nations. He was just as used to receiving accolades from an audience in Iran as he was from an audience in America.

Broadcast-news trucks from up and down the East Coast lined the road outside the gates of Foxcatcher. The dozens and dozens of reporters included representatives from newspapers around the country. Tabloid television was there; a rich eccentric charged with murder was too good to pass up. Someone who said he was from the *Far Eastern Economic Review* was taking notes. ESPN and *Sports Illustrated* had reporters on the scene. CNN carried continuous updates.

"We're all just on our toes, waiting for something to happen," said Michael Raphael, a reporter for the Associated Press, which had the du Pont story marked "top national budget." Reporters hungered for the scraps of information given out by police at the periodic news briefings held in a church near the estate.

Anyone who walked by was fair game for reporters. Some shrugged and refused to speak. Others were more than happy to talk. Vicki Welch, who had lived on the estate until 1984, strolled from camera crew to camera crew, repeating the wild story of du Pont and his armored personnel carrier. One Christmas Day, she said, du Pont drove the APC up her driveway. He was bruised and bloody, she said.

"He lifted the hatch and poked his bloody head out," Welch said. "He asked, 'Can Tim come out and play?' "

Her husband, Tim, was a Newtown police officer.

Tim Welch wasn't the only township officer who had lived on du Pont's property. Another, Sgt. Richard Fairlamb, was especially friendly with du Pont. He, in fact, was involved in a rather unusual piece of police business less than two months before Schultz's death that had some wondering if his action had unwittingly contributed to setting du Pont down a murderous path.

But Fairlamb's cozy relationship with du Pont wasn't unique. In fact, as more and more stories emerged during the standoff about du Pont and the police, Chief Mallon felt the need to set the record straight.

"John du Pont is a property owner in the township," Mallon said. "If he calls the police, we respond, we act. Beyond that, there is no relationship."

That, though, clearly wasn't true.

Du Pont was a good friend to police. He not only allowed Newtown officers to use his shooting range; he often gave them pointers. He bought the Newtown department radios and bulletproof vests. For years he sponsored police training courses and donated cash and equipment to law-enforcement agencies. He cosponsored one of Pennsylvania's first arson-investigation schools. He invited police to lavish Christmas parties and private deer hunts on his property.

His days of using his badge and patrolling Newtown Township, however, ended in 1982 when Edward Corse became a township supervisor. He was concerned about du Pont's police work, especially since he was not a certified officer.

"I knew that he had done this," Corse said. "I guess the township fathers at the time felt there was nothing wrong with it. When I got on the board, we said it would never happen [again], and it never did."

Over the years, du Pont flew his helicopter on police business, using it to conduct surveillance, to help police reconstruct crime scenes, and to locate stolen cars, missing children, and criminal fugitives.

In 1979, du Pont told a newspaper reporter, he was working twenty to thirty hours a month on volunteer police work.

Halbert E. Fillinger, who has spent more than thirty years as a coroner in the Philadelphia area, said du Pont used to pick him up in a French-made Gazelle helicopter and ferry him to homicide scenes and murder trials.

"He used to make his facilities available, had a helicopter, and was always ready to sponsor a police course," said Fillinger in the days following the Schultz killing.

Fillinger added that he had heard stories about du Pont's odd behavior.

"You heard comments that John would be acting funny lately, but frankly, I never got the impression it was anything serious," he said.

William Ryan, a former Delaware County district attorney, said he never had reason to believe that du Pont was anything but eccentric. "I had heard enough stories over the years to lead me to conclude he was a goofy guy," Ryan said, but nothing to suggest that he was dangerous.

He knew du Pont as "a big supporter of law enforcement, not only in Newtown Township, but around the Philadelphia region."

In recognition of his time, effort, and money, a formal ceremony was held in 1985, with former president Gerald R. Ford and Pennsylvania State Attorney General LeRoy S. Zimmerman presenting du Pont with a large plaque commemorating "his dedication to law enforcement."

Du Pont also had some unusual equipment, like the armored personnel carrier. He had purchased that in California for $50,000 from FMC Corporation in San Jose; FMC got permission from the army, which said there was nothing illegal about a private citizen owning an APC, as long as it didn't have the .50-caliber machine gun that was normally attached to the top. That was fine with du Pont—although nearly thirty years later he would spend enormous sums to get that machine gun.

Newtown officer Steven Shallis remembered his first meeting with du Pont in 1982 or 1983, when he was assigned to escort du Pont and his APC to a parade for a local fire department.

"I went to the main gate," Shallis said. "I waited for several minutes. The ground started rumbling. The next thing I know there was a tank at the main gate of the du Pont estate. The tank came to a stop. The back portion came down."

Du Pont exited the APC holding a martini glass.

Once, before a parade, Du Pont suggested that somebody sit on top of the vehicle and throw candy to the crowd along the parade. A volunteer, John Bourne, was recruited for the task, but as du Pont drove down the street he hit a boulder, sending Bourne flying. Bourne sued, and was awarded $35,750.

Shallis's dealing with du Pont for the next dozen or so years was mostly limited to an exchange of pleasantries at du Pont's firing range. After the range was dismantled, he wasn't called to the property until Jan. 26, 1996—the first officer to find David Schultz in his driveway, mortally wounded.

But other officers had been at Foxcatcher on and off in the months before the shooting. One incident in particular became fodder for suspicions about how police handled du Pont—or, perhaps more appropriately, how du Pont handled police.

In October 1995, wrestler Dan Chaid, who had been living at Foxcatcher since 1987, had complained to police that du Pont threatened him with a gun. His relationship with du Pont was deteriorating, and he was in the gym one day, Chaid said, when du Pont walked in, pointed the gun to his chest, and screamed, "Get the fuck off my farm."

Du Pont had come to dislike Chaid intensely, viewing him as disruptive and—even more heinous to du Pont's thinking—immoral because he had a child out of wedlock in April 1994.

On January 29, three days after Schultz's death, Chaid filed a federal suit against du Pont. And that night he appeared on ABC-TV's *Nightline*, telling the country how the gun episode had scared him so much that he packed his things and left for California. Chaid complained to police, he said, but claimed he wasn't taken seriously by them, or by the Delaware County District Attorney's Office—the office that would eventually prosecute du Pont. Law-enforcement officials, Chaid complained, had an "Oh-that's-just-John" attitude.

In November 1995, a month after the gun episode, there was a bizarre event at the Schultz house that seemed to be precipitated by Chaid's exit from the estate. Before going to California, Chaid had parked his van in the Schultz driveway, intending to pick it up a few weeks later. That annoyed du Pont no end.

On November 10, Chaid returned briefly to Foxcatcher to retrieve the van. When du Pont found out he had been on the property, he was livid. Around midnight, he drove to the Schultz house.

Besides being extremely angry, he was also so drunk, Nancy Schultz later recalled, that he could barely stand.

The Schultzes helped him into the house, sat him down, and gave him coffee.

"He was searching for Dan Chaid," Nancy Schultz said. "He wanted to know where we had hidden Dan Chaid. He was walking through our house saying, 'Where's Dan? I know he was here.' "

After sipping the coffee, he wanted to go back to his mansion. David Schultz was supporting him with both arms as he walked him to the door. As Schultz reached out to open it, du Pont slipped from his grip, smashing his head on a windowsill.

Schultz looked at the wound. "John," he said, "you're going to need some stitches." He said he'd take him to the hospital.

Nancy Schultz picked up the phone to call the hospital to alert the emergency room. "Tell them I'm the Dalai Lama," du Pont said. "They'll treat me better that way. No, wait. Tell them I'll build them a wing like I did at Crozer [Chester Hospital]. They'll treat me better that way."

"I don't think you need to build a wing on a hospital, John, just to get stitches," Nancy said.

Du Pont then changed his mind. He wanted to go home.

"Okay, John," Dave Schultz said. "I'll drive you back."

As he was being put in the car, Nancy Schultz noticed a rifle on the seat. She took it back into the house. Du Pont started to yell. "I want my gun. I want my gun. Give me back my gun."

Dave Schultz went back into the house. "He wants his gun back, but I'll take the bullets out."

He returned the rifle to du Pont, who was sitting in the backseat. Du Pont was trying to get out. "Give me my bullets," he shouted. "I know you took my bullets."

"John," said Schultz, "you certainly don't need a weapon right now and you don't need a gun and you don't need bullets. Let's take you home and take care of you." A physician and family friend, Paul Gostigian, was called. He stitched up the cut and suggested someone watch du Pont through the night.

Dave Schultz and Rob Calabrese, another Foxcatcher wrestler who had his own home on the estate, took turns.

The next day, du Pont looked horrendous. "John," Calabrese said, "you look like you've been hit by a base-ball bat."

Du Pont didn't remember how he had been injured. Could it have been from a baseball bat? In his mind, it made sense. He adopted the baseball-bat story. He em-bellished it. He called Terry Wochok, his lawyer, saying he had been assaulted. Wochok called Fairlamb of the Newtown police. Fairlamb told Lieutenant Hunter about du Pont's concern. Hunter called Wochok and suggested that du Pont come to the station and give police a written statement. Du Pont refused. He wanted police to come to him.

In the meantime, Hunter interviewed the Schultzes to find out what had occurred. There was no baseball bat. But du Pont was insistent that he was attacked. And, he said, he believed he knew who attacked him.

Hunter, who became chief of Newtown police in July 1996, was familiar with du Pont. He first met him—like many other Newtown officers—on the shooting range when he joined the force. Later, the two rode together one Mischief Night for about two hours. After that, Hunter said, they simply had a wave-and-hello relationship.

On November 24, 1995, he drove to Foxcatcher. At their meeting, du Pont was extremely serious. Hunter asked about giving a statement. "I don't give written statements," du Pont said. "I'm John du Pont."

He told Hunter he was driving around Foxcatcher at seven-thirty in the evening on November 10 when he de-cided to go to the Schultz home and look for Chaid. The next thing he knew he was back home, stitched up. He heard no one, he saw no one.

But, he added, Schultz and Calabrese had told him he was attacked with a bat by Chaid.

Hunter returned to the police station, typed up a page based on his five-minute interview with du Pont, and signed it.

Then he drew up a second page. It was marked "Confidential Information." It noted the thoughts of the same man—but, seemingly, a different person.

"During my interview of Mr. du Pont," the report read, "he kept referring to the seriousness of this investigation because he feels that Chaid is a player in a very secretive international conspiracy to have him removed as an international wrestling coach. He told me that the state and FBI were also working on this case and that if it was not solved, an arrest was not made soon, then the entire Russian army would be in Newtown Township fighting the ultimate war with the Americans and this would not be good for the residents of Newtown Township."

At that point during the interview, Hunter stopped him. Hunter said he had some different information about how the injury occurred.

But du Pont continued, elaborating on the international conspiracy. It was also meant to kill the Holy Child. And he, du Pont said, was the Holy Child. And the Dalai Lama. And the head of the Buddhist church.

As a Supreme Leader, du Pont continued, he removed all phones, televisions, and radios from his home. And he did not read newspapers. Those things were for followers, he said, not leaders like himself.

He seemed to be off in another world inside his head. But he was lucid enough to remember one thing Hunter said: someone had contradicted his story about being attacked.

After Hunter left, du Pont called Wochok. He wanted

that other report. Wochok got in touch with Fairlamb. Fairlamb had been on the force for more than thirty years. Until 1992, he lived at Foxcatcher. He considered himself a friend of du Pont's. Fairlamb got a copy of the report Hunter wrote based on his November 16 interview with the Schultzes.

"Mr. and Mrs. Schultz assured me that Mr. du Pont was not hit at their home by a bat or anything else and that his injury was his face impacting on the windowsill in their living room," read part of that report. "As I was getting up to leave the Schultz residence, their ten-year-old [sic] boy came into the living room and Mr. Schultz asked him how Mr. du Pont got hurt last Friday night. He told me that Mr. du Pont was very drunk, fell against the windowsill, and cut his face."

Du Pont, Wochok told Fairlamb, would like to see that. That was no problem.

Fairlamb, in fact, delivered it personally a few days later.

Du Pont now had in his hand a statement from the Schultzes that made him look like a fool.

And a liar.

Four

On Saturday morning, January 27, workers from a nearby Wawa convenience store showed up at the command center with seventy cups of coffee and hot chocolate. By noon, the sightseers were out in force. Traffic was backed up on Goshen Road, a normally sleepy country road bordered by woods on one side and du Pont's estate on the other. Police finally decided to seal it off.

Because it was the middle of winter and the trees were bare, there was one spot along Goshen Road where one could peer through the fence and get a glimpse of the columned mansion on a hill. A policeman in a car used a bullhorn to disperse the curious who gathered there.

"Get back. Children should not be here. This is a dangerous place. The road is being closed."

Newspaper photographers also found the location perfect for getting pictures of the mansion with their zoom lenses. And that made police realize that a marksman in the mansion with a telescopic sight could just as easily zero in on journalists and others on Goshen Road. That increased their anxiety.

But the people moved away slowly, talking about the biggest spectacle in memory in Newtown Square. And everyone, it seemed, had a prediction.

"It's going to be like another Waco thing," said one

man, who brought along his eight-year-old son to gawk. "He could be in there for months."

"I think he's going to kill himself," the son said.

"I wonder who's getting the money after this?" asked an elderly gent, who stopped at Foxcatcher with his wife on their way to do some food shopping. Then, he added, almost as an afterthought, "It's a beautiful property, isn't it?"

Not to the police who spent a long night on that property—a long, cold, bone-chilling night. Temperatures had dropped to the twenties, and the windchill made it feel much worse.

During the standoff, officers spelled each other, moving in and out of the athletic facility, which served as their tactical command post. The facility includes a wrestling gymnasium and an indoor swimming pool, showers and locker rooms.

They changed their soaked clothes for warm, dry sweat suits. Warm, dry sweat suits with the word "Foxcatcher" written across. Later, when the clothing wasn't returned, du Pont's lawyer accused the police of looting and souvenir-gathering.

Meanwhile, as police were waiting out du Pont on the estate, off the estate at the firehouse command center they were making arrangements to record his phone conversations. That couldn't be done without a court order, though, and it wasn't until 11:30 A.M. that Superior Court Judge James Cavanaugh signed an order giving authorities permission; by 1:00 P.M., the equipment was in place.

Just before the recorder was turned on, Goodale and du Pont had one last talk. Goodale said Wochok was not there. Then he turned the phone over to Sgt. Robert O'Donnell, one of the negotiators.

"We're trying to see how we can resolve this situation," O'Donnell said.

"Well," du Pont answered, "when they have time to

get here, and Mr. Wochok gets here, then I think we can resolve something, but until then, unless you have something, you know, on your mind . . .''

''Well, we want to resolve this situation, we want to make sure you're safe. Mr. Wochok is en route as far as I understand.''

''Well, when he gets here send him to the big house.''

''Well, it may be that he talks to you by phone first.''

''Well, look, I'm not going to discuss it with you any longer. I was having my negotiations with Pat.''

Actually, Goodale never again talked to du Pont. He wouldn't even see his former employer for more than a year—not until Goodale took the witness stand during du Pont's murder trial in January 1997.

Wochok, meanwhile, was not allowed to talk to du Pont—at least from the command center. Citing attorney-client privilege, he refused to allow his conversations with du Pont to be taped. So authorities kept him off the phone—despite du Pont's repeated requests to talk with him. Several more hours would pass before a deal was worked out and du Pont was able to get a call from his attorney.

O'Donnell was spending time on the phone with du Pont, but he wasn't getting very far.

''How can we resolve this situation, so that you're safe and the situation is resolved?'' he said. ''The ball's more or less in your court.''

''The ball is not in my court,'' du Pont said. ''All right, the ball's in my court. I hold the ball, and the fact is that (when) Mr. Wochok and Mr. Saletnik get here, you call me.''

''I will do that. But in the interim why don't we talk and try to resolve this?''

''No talk.''

''We're concerned.''

''I said no talk.''

Du Pont started to lapse into broken English. It was a curious pattern that those around him had noted during the past few years. His explanation was that he used pidgin English in his many dealings with Eastern Europeans, and it sometimes entered his own speech. But people believed it was more in keeping with du Pont's belief that he was a Bulgarian, not an American. He also insisted, at times, that he wasn't a real du Pont, but had been born in Eastern Europe and was adopted.

"There's a lot of people that have you as their main concern right now," O'Donnell said.

"That's right, the whole world does. The fact is that, no talk until I talk to them."

"I'm willing to talk as long as you want to."

But du Pont didn't want to talk at all.

"No, no, no, no, no," he said. "I no talk."

O'Donnell was having trouble keeping du Pont from hanging up. He told him he had met him on the firing range a few years back. It didn't work. Du Pont kept turning back to the same theme: Get me Wochok. And get me Saletnik. And get me Jordanov.

And then he hung up.

O'Donnell called back.

"It's Bob. How are you doing?"

"What do you want?"

"Basically, to resolve the situation."

The conversation then started taking a different turn. Du Pont never wavered from his demand to talk to Wochok. But he seemed off on a delusional path.

"I will talk with Mr. Wochok," du Pont said. "And he will probably get my ambassador here in order to resolve this situation."

After another minute, O'Donnell asked, "Can you tell me why you want to speak to your attorney?"

"Why do I want to speak to him?"

"Yes, sir."

"His Holiness is under siege here," du Pont replied, "and the thing is I want to get the thing resolved and get the lights off the lawn here, and a few other things that are annoying me. There is holy property here."

"That can be resolved. I mean, we can take the lights out the first thing."

"Well, why don't you do that, take them out of here and then the thing is we'll go from there and see what happens."

"We can't do that unless you come out, sir. You understand the situation."

"I am not talking to you anymore until you have somebody else to talk with me. Thank you very much."

"Why not stay on the line, and we'll try to resolve this?"

"It's now good-bye."

O'Donnell was persistent. He called again.

"Don't make a nuisance out of yourself," du Pont said.

"If I don't call back, how am I going to give you the information about Mr. Wochok?"

"When you have information, you call. Otherwise, don't call."

"Okay, but in the interim . . . Mr. du Pont? Mr. du Pont?"

O'Donnell picked up the phone again. So did du Pont.

"Mr. Wochok is here in the building," O'Donnell said.

"Let me speak with Mr. Wochok."

"That I will do, sir. I've gotten the approval to do that. I need to know if you'll come out if you speak to him."

"I no make deal."

"I know you're a man of your word."

"I no make deal. I speak with Mr. Wochok."

"Well, what can I tell my bosses about your present situation?"

"That's your problem. Let me speak with Mr. Wochok.

He may be able to straighten you out and help you with your problem.

"Where is Wochok?" du Pont asked. "In the building," said O'Donnell. "Well, what building are you in?" said du Pont. "We're very close to you," O'Donnell said, "but I can't say exactly where."

"Why not? Why not?" du Pont demanded. "This is holy property here! This is a forbidden city! You should have no right to be here in the first place. I'm concerned about you being on the property. There's lights out around the house, there's lights in the driveway that didn't used to be there. You sneaked them in here, and I want them out of here."

Terry Wochok arrived at the command center in the late afternoon. He made a deal with Chief Mallon: his conversation with du Pont would not be recorded or monitored. However, one of the negotiators could remain in the room to at least record Wochok's words.

That settled, Wochok called du Pont.

Wochok told him that police had the estate sealed and the home surrounded. No one could get in.

"We're concerned about your safety," he said. "It is of the utmost importance that you come out. The police are not going to leave."

Du Pont refused to budge. Instead, he directed Wochok to call Mario Saletnik, the FILA official.

"No one will be allowed in," Wochok said. "They won't let him in. You need to come out. This has to end. It is not helping anything. Think about what I told you."

Du Pont wanted the lights turned off. He wanted the police to leave.

"The police will not go away," Wochok said. "I'll discuss your concerns with them. Come out."

Du Pont also made another demand. He wanted Wochok to contact the Bulgarian ambassador.

"I'll get back to you," Wochok said.

Du Pont, expecting that Wochok was on a mission to round up international help, called the firehouse a few times, hoping to talk with his lawyer. But a new negotiator, Det. Barry Williams, answered the phone.

"We're willing to allow him to call you back only to discuss coming out of that house, okay?" Williams said. "I hope you understand that, sir. I have lived in this area all my life. I know your reputation. I know a lot of your friends. They have a strong faith in you. They think you keep your word. I want you to bargain in good faith like we've been showing you. Believe me, sir, we're going out of our way to assist you right now."

Du Pont said he'd wait for Wochok to call him.

Williams then got to the heart of the matter.

"Are you aware of the fact that a man was shot and killed on your property yesterday?" he asked.

"I thought you were going to have Mr. Wochok on the line."

After a few seconds, du Pont hung up. Williams called back.

"You are aware of the fact that something occurred on your property yesterday, correct?"

"Yeah, listen, I've got some diplomatic papers to go over now."

"That's fine."

"I'm president of the Soviet Union."

Again, after a few more exchanges, du Pont put the phone down.

Again, Williams called. And he got pushy.

"We have some incidents to discuss," he said.

"Not yet. I got these diplomatic papers to take care of."

"I don't want to talk about your diplomatic papers. We have to discuss the man who was shot and killed on your property yesterday."

"Look, you discuss it with Mr. Wochok."

"Your hanging up on me, I don't appreciate that."

"That's the way it's going to be."

"You have to stop."

"Look, you're involved with a war between the Soviet Union and . . ."

"I don't want to hear about the Soviet Union. We have to discuss an issue that a man was shot and killed on your property yesterday."

"Well, I want you to discuss that with Mr. Wochok."

"That's fine and good, but we have to discuss that; we don't want to discuss about the thing with Russia or Bulgaria."

"I told you I will not discuss anything until I have a chat with Mr. Wochok."

"Okay, if you talk to Mr. Wochok you're going to discuss the incident, and to come out of the house. That's the only two issues you're going to discuss. Do you understand that?"

"I'm going to discuss international things."

"You're not going to discuss your international things."

"You better call the president of the United States."

Williams kept trying to get du Pont on the subject of the killing. But du Pont parried every attempt. He talked about the international work he had to do. He told Williams he had no right to order around a head of state. The real issue at hand, he said, was an international war that was about to break out. He needed, du Pont said, to work on that, and the phone calls were getting in the way. He controlled missiles, he said.

"They're not aimed at you at the moment," du Pont told Williams. "But they might be."

Williams tried a different tactic. He appealed to du Pont's ego.

"All I've got to do," he said, "is hear your name and think of all the things you've done for the community.

You've done some fantastic things. You've helped the community of Newtown Township, the police officers from Marple and Newtown.''

Du Pont wasn't buying it. ''Praises will get you nowhere, right at the moment, because I've got something else, it's a very hot issue. And I got to take care of that first. So when Mr. Wochok is finished with his assignment, please put him on the phone.''

Wochok did finally get on the phone, about 9:15 P.M.

''I spoke with Mario and the Bulgarian government,'' he said. ''These people cannot talk to you at this time. Bulgarians will not interfere with a United States government domestic matter. Mario said he can't help until the issue is resolved.''

He told du Pont there was a warrant for his arrest. No one would be allowed near the house. Come out, he said, and you'll be met by two officers who will bring you to me.

Again, du Pont would not discuss leaving home.

Wochok knew du Pont about as well as anyone. And he knew at that point police were just going around in circles. Du Pont was tired of talking.

In fact, he was just plain tired. He wanted to get some rest. Negotiators decided to let him. Sleep deprivation, they felt, could have led to further deterioration of his emotional stability. They weren't going to solve anything at that point anyway. So by nine-thirty on Saturday night negotiations—such as they were—broke off.

The next day was Super Bowl Sunday. But for more than a hundred law enforcement officials, it was beginning to look like the parties were going to have to start without them.

Five

Except for three years of law school at Notre Dame, Terry Wochok had spent all his fifty-seven years in and around Philadelphia. He grew up at Franklin and Parrish in North Philadelphia. It was an ethnic neighborhood: Germans, Jews, Ukranians, African-Americans. One of his regular mates on the local basketball court was Bill Cosby.

"He was a real peacemaker, even then," Wochok said. "There'd be trash talk starting on the court, and he'd step in and calm things down."

He attended LaSalle High School, a parochial school in Philadelphia, and La Salle College, also in the city. After graduating in 1962 he left for South Bend, Indiana, and Notre Dame University's law school. He came back with more than a law degree; in his last semester he met his future wife on a blind date. He and Judi were married in August, 1966, on the same day that Luci Baines Johnson married Patrick Nugent.

"I remember watching their wedding on TV in the morning and thinking mine wouldn't be quite as elaborate," he said.

Not long after receiving his law degree he started working for a firm in Philadelphia. Then, for two years, he worked for an insurance company.

In 1968 he joined the Philadelphia District Attorney's

Office. Richard Sprague, who twenty-eight years later would become du Pont's first lead defense attorney, was first assistant district attorney, the number two man in the office. Wochok remained with the D.A. until January 1974. During that time he spent a year as a special Assistant U.S. Attorney in the drug-enforcement division, and also took a leave of absence for six months in 1973 to run an ultimately unsuccessful district attorney campaign for Arlen Specter, now a United States senator.

He met John du Pont in 1972, and the two saw each other casually from time to time after that. Du Pont occasionally would call, and ask Wochok, "Can you come out, I'd like to talk to you about a few things?"

Sometimes du Pont would ask for advice, other times he just wanted to talk. During the Specter campaign, du Pont asked Wochok to gather some information for him. Du Pont was apparently pleased with the speed and quality of the work. Wochok came to believe that all of it—the conversations, the sought-after advice, the assignments—was a kind of extended interview. Du Pont had an attorney who handled his affairs, but was looking for another, someone closer to his own age.

"In a sense, what he was doing, he was trying to make sure he was comfortable with me in terms of telling me what he was involved in, the kinds of things he did, the kinds of interests he had, and whether or not I was a person who shared those interests or could be helpful in carrying out whatever wishes he had," Wochok said.

Over time, du Pont became increasingly comfortable with Wochok and sent more legal work his way. Wochok had just left the district attorney's office and joined a firm in Lansdale, Montgomery County, north of Philadelphia. The triangular drive from his Philadelphia home to his office to the du Pont estate—a journey that covered three counties—became more frequent, and more taxing.

In the summer of 1975 Wochok told du Pont he had

an opportunity to join a firm in Media, closer to his home and to du Pont's. Did du Pont think he'd have enough work to make the move feasible? Yes, said du Pont, he'd continue to have a substantial amount to keep Wochok busy. Wochok relocated his practice, and two years later, in 1977, also moved out of Philadelphia. His life was becoming centered around one client.

In the beginning, he would talk with du Pont every day, sometimes several times. Some years there was little to be done other than housekeeping; other years dealing with du Pont took much of his time.

Wochok said a big part of his job was "keeping other people's hands out of John's pockets."

Not that du Pont was averse to giving away his money. He was, in fact, quite generous. Proposals came in all the time, and he would review them, rejecting some, agreeing to others, and putting the rest in a pile to be explored. Wochok handled all the legal affairs, including lawsuits that became almost annual occurrences. From 1981 to 1990, for example, du Pont was sued nine times in Delaware County, where he lived. And he filed a couple of suits himself. A number of court actions—both by him and against him—were for breach of contract.

One of the first things Wochok did, in 1975, was help du Pont get Foxcatcher Farm qualified as a nonprofit corporation, used as an athletic training facility. The name Foxcatcher was a link to du Pont's father, William Jr., who had grown up at Montpelier in Virginia. At the turn of the century, William Jr. acquired and trained a pack of foxhounds. When he married Jean Liseter Austin in 1919 and settled on the estate in Newtown Square—a gift from Jean's parents—William du Pont began calling it Foxcatcher.

William du Pont, who left his wife for a tennis player in 1940, when John was two years old, died New Year's Eve, 1965; the farm—and an estimated $80 million worth of inheritance—passed on to John. He was twenty-six. Fitness conscious, he cleared running trails for himself. Interested in swimming, he built a six-lane, indoor Olympic-sized pool. Intrigued by the arcane sport of pentathlon, he added a target range in 1971, modeled after the FBI range at Quantico, Virginia.

The shooting area was eventually changed into the Foxcatcher wrestling room. The whole enterprise was officially incorporated soon after.

It wasn't long before Wochok found himself devoting nearly all his time to du Pont. In 1980 he was doing well enough to begin his own firm in Paoli, not far from the du Pont estate. He remains there today.

Throughout the early years of their relationship, Wochok said, du Pont was vibrant and alive, a caring person, dedicated to sports, dedicated to his own development.

He was also dedicated to bachelorhood, it seemed, until he married Gale Wenk in September 1983, two months before his forty-fifth birthday. It was a disastrous union that ended almost as soon as the vows were completed and came at a time that marked the beginning of tremendous upheaval in his life. Within months of his marriage, two beloved aunts died. One, his mother's sister, was Anna Austin, who lived nearby in Beaumont, a 1912 mansion built by du Pont's maternal grandfather William Austin. The other was Marion du Pont Scott, who lived at Montpelier and had been married to the cowboy actor Randolph Scott.

The cataclysmic event of the 1980s, though, was yet to come. That was the death of his mother in 1988, leaving du Pont alone. Wochok points to that as hastening du Pont's downward spiral, which included alcoholism, drug abuse, mental disease.

During their twenty-five-year relationship, Wochok likely got to know du Pont better than anyone. So there were few things about du Pont that could shock him.

One surprise, though, came when the phone rang at 6:50 in the morning on Sunday, January 28, 1996.

Jesus Christ was on the line.

And he was getting low on smokes.

Du Pont had been out of contact since the previous evening. He had tried using the regular phone to call out, but it had been rigged by police to prevent that. So he picked up the cellular phone and dialed Wochok's home number.

"I am Jesus Christ," he said. And he issued a warning: if Jesus Christ died, it would be the end of the world.

Du Pont also said he was low on food and water. He wanted cigars and pipe tobacco. He wanted to go to the gym to exercise. He had the ability to create chaos.

And he wasn't coming out. "Call me back at nine-thirty," du Pont said. "Better yet, make it ten o'clock."

Wochok was doubly surprised by the call because he thought the cellular phone service had been disabled. He drove to the command center and reported his conversation. At nine-thirty negotiators resumed making calls to du Pont. But he wouldn't pick up his phone until 10 A.M. That's the time he told Wochok he would accept calls, and he was adamant about sticking to it.

With permission of authorities, Wochok called du Pont. As had happened the previous evening, a negotiator recorded Wochok's side to get some idea of the questions coming from du Pont.

As usual, du Pont asked the whereabouts of Jordanov. He also said he wanted a maid and butler to come to the mansion.

"Valo is at his house," Wochok said. "I met with police as soon as I got here and asked for the maid and butler. They said no, no one goes into the house."

It was more than thirty-six hours since his heat had been shut off. Du Pont had started a fire, but didn't have logs. To keep the flames burning, he tossed in copy after copy of a small paperback, a collection of essays that had been ghostwritten for du Pont and published for him by a vanity press.

The name of the book was *Never Give Up*.

But the warmth of the fire wasn't enough. He wanted to go into the tunnel to fix the boiler.

"Be careful. Be careful if you're coming out," said Wochok. He envisioned du Pont getting shot.

"There could be someone back there. The police control that. They will not listen to me. Remember, if you fire the first salvo, it will be returned. If you fire first, fire will be returned."

Det. John Ryan immediately notified the officer in charge of the command center, who passed along the word to the tactical team on the estate that du Pont might be coming out.

"If you come out, you will be subject to being taken by police," Wochok said. "If you want to come out, arrange to do it orderly so that you talk to me. Stay safe. Now listen, if you do want to come out, I can arrange for that. Think about what you are going to do. If you want to come out, call me back."

Du Pont was getting more and more uncomfortable. He wasn't quite ready to leave. But his resistance was clearly cracking. That was good news for negotiators.

From the beginning police had a strategy: Be patient, negotiate, wait him out, negotiate, hang on, negotiate—and wait for a break.

Veteran negotiators knew it took a lot of guts to just sit back and do nothing.

People from around the country were offering to help. One of the better known—the Reverend Robert Schuller, the host of the weekly *Hour of Power* televangelism program—opened his sermon from his Crystal Cathedral in Garden Grove, California, with a personal appeal to du Pont.

"If you did what they suspect you did, if you did that, John, you came under a spell that is not you," he said. "It is demonic. John, walk out, and if I can help you, call me."

Schuller said he had known du Pont for about ten years and had visited Foxcatcher. Du Pont and his mother, he added, had once visited the Crystal Cathedral.

And he said God had told him that du Pont's mother wanted him to surrender.

"Just lay down those weapons, open the front door, raise both hands, and walk between those pillars, and do it now," Schuller said.

Police, though, knew it wouldn't be that easy. A man of great pride like du Pont would have a hard time simply surrendering. They had to, if they could, give him a dignified way to end the standoff.

"You always have to give them respect and dignity," said Thomas B. Cupples, a retired FBI agent who was called in to advise the du Pont negotiating team.

The lack of heat, in the language of negotiators, was a "precipitator." "It gives us something to negotiate," said Cupples. "Sometimes it might be water. It might be food. It comes down to basic human needs."

When du Pont talked about coming out and going into the tunnel to fix the heat, police saw that as a signal: he might be willing to take some risks to resolve the problem. Du Pont, they felt, probably had had enough, but needed a way to save face.

In his next talk with Wochok, in fact, he again said he wanted to fix the heat. But he also said he believed he could walk through the tunnel without fear of police. It was private ground, and police couldn't touch him there.

And he again complained about the lights on the lawn, threatening to shoot them out with missles.

"I'd advise you not to do that," said Wochok.

He asked Wochok if he had contacted the Bulgarian

embassy yet. He said he wanted to go the playhouse, one of the buildings on the estate, to visit Buddha. He said he wanted to talk with Wochok again at 4 P.M.

That didn't happen. Instead, du Pont resumed a conversation with negotiators. Sgt. Anthony Paparo of the Upper Darby Township police was now manning the phone. It was the policeman's first experience as a negotiator. He kept his tone polite and deferential.

"How are you doing?" Paparo said. "My name is Anthony. How would you like me to call you, Mr. du Pont, John, what? What's better for you?"

"Anything you want at the moment. What's on your mind?"

"I just want to talk to you, that's all, just talk to you. Is it okay to call you Mr. du Pont?"

"You can call me Dimitri. That's my other name. That's my Bulgarian name."

"Okay, that's going to be a little difficult for me, so I'll stick with Mr. du Pont, if that's okay."

"Whatever. That's my American name."

Du Pont brought up the problem he had with the lights. But it was more than the brightness that bothered him. "They seem to be creeping in," he said, "and I'd like them removed."

"Okay, they haven't been moved in any way, shape, or form closer to the home," Paparo said. "They're in the same spot."

Du Pont was insistent. "They were moved in last night. Some new ones moved in last night."

Paparo didn't know it, but du Pont's complaint about the lights was eerily similar to a fear he had about trees on his property. There were mechanical trees, he believed, that would surreptitiously move toward the house, reach in with their branches, and steal valuables. The items, du Pont thought, were then passed back from tree to tree in the woods, where a person waited to receive the loot.

Paparo gently changed the subject from lights to heat. "How are you feeling?" he asked. "Are you cold?"

"Of course."

"Okay, do you need anything to make you warmer?"

"I would think a load of firewood . . ."

"Okay."

"Why don't you turn the heat on?" du Pont asked. Then, he became demanding.

"I want the heat turned on . . . Get the heat turned on over there."

"I don't know if we can send a maintenance guy onto the property to do that," said Paparo.

Du Pont then made a suggestion that startled Paparo.

"Would you allow me to go over and take a look at the thing?" du Pont asked.

"You want to go over and take a look at it?"

"Yes."

Paparo realized he had an opening. But he also knew he couldn't let du Pont just fly out the door.

"One of the things I would have to do which would be a concern," he said—thinking fast, but talking slowly—"I have to let the people know that are out there that you're going to do that and would have to make arrangements of how you're going to do that, so that you don't get hurt or no one gets hurt."

"Well," du Pont replied, "no one would be hurt. I would just go over myself."

"Okay, I'd have to make arrangements with them to let them know you're going to do that."

"Well, you discuss that with Mr. Wochok."

"Well, the problem is, Mr. Wochok is not able to do that. You have to go through me so that I can tell my bosses what you're doing, so they're not jumping out of their pants when you come out of the house to do something simple as just turning the heat on."

"Oh, I see, I see."

"You follow me?"

"Yes."

"Okay, I mean if you tell me what door you're going to be able to come out and where exactly you're going to go, I can make arrangements so that they know that, so that they don't get a little antsy."

"All right, well I can let you know. We'll see if I can survive here in the meantime without it."

Paparo was afraid the opening was starting to close. He needed to keep du Pont thinking about the cold.

"Well, it's about twenty degrees out there," he said. "It's going to get pretty cold tonight."

"Yes, I guess that's my problem."

"Well, I'll tell you what I'll do. I'll talk to my bosses about you going out to turn the heat on. Could you call me back in about ten minutes?"

"No. You can call me back."

"Okay, that's great, sir. I'll call you right back."

"And why don't you also tell them that at 1500 every afternoon," said du Pont, using military parlance for 3 P.M., "I will walk out in front of the house and show myself and go over to the Fox"—a statue—"which is right at the bottom of the steps."

"Okay, hold on, because it's three o'clock now, and I don't want you to go out now because I haven't told anybody yet."

Things were happening quickly, and Paparo didn't want to lose him. Then du Pont said, "Starting tomorrow."

"Starting tomorrow?" said Paparo. Maybe he wasn't coming out after all.

"Yes, at 1500 I'll go out in front of the house, down to the Fox for a few moments, and go back inside."

Paparo was bargaining for some precious seconds, trying to coax du Pont out at the same time he was alerting his superiors.

"Can I write this down?" he said. "I don't want to

mess anything up, okay? At 1500 hours you're going to walk out and go to where?''

''Just down the steps to the front of the house, and go back in the house again.''

''What's that, just for exercise?''

''It's a little bit of everything.''

''Okay, do you need exercise? I mean.''

''Yes I do. I have a gym over here that I normally work out in, and I'm entered in a tournament in Sofia, Bulgaria, and I like a partner to work out with me. That would be Mr. Jordanov.''

He was starting to slip away. Talking about wrestling in Bulgaria? The guy was wanted for murder, for goodness sake! Paparo quickly turned him back to the topic of heat.

''Okay, you want to go to the greenhouse now and do the heating thing?''

''Well, you talk to your bosses first and call me back.''

Paparo knew he couldn't hang up. He might not get du Pont back.

''Okay, believe it or not they're on another line for me and they told me that's okay, just tell me which door you're going to go out. They're saying that's fine, you can go to the greenhouse and turn the heat on.''

''All right, I'll go out the garden door.''

''Okay, where is the garden door located?''

''On the temple side of the house?''

''Where's the temple side of the house, sir?''

''On the north side.''

''North side? Okay, how are you going to be dressed? And you're not going to be carrying anything, right?''

Paparo's job now was to make sure du Pont didn't come out with a gun and turn the standoff into a bloodbath.

''No, I won't be carrying anything,'' du Pont promised.

Paparo needed to be sure, so he asked bluntly, "Are you going to be armed?"

"No," said du Pont.

"Okay, please don't come out armed, okay?"

"No, I won't."

"Okay, and I'll tell you what. I'll call you back after you get back."

"Okay. When am I free to go?"

"They're telling me you can go right out now."

"All right, I will be dressed in black. With my Bulgarian colors showing the flag."

"Okay, and then I'll call you back as soon as you get back. How long will it take you to do that?"

"It shouldn't take me very long at all. I just have to check on one or two things over there, and I'll come right back."

"I appreciate you working with me on that. I really appreciate it."

Then du Pont threw another curve.

"May I speak to Mr. Wochok, please?"

The question was unfailingly polite. This, from the same man who during the course of two days of negotiations was often, in the words of negotiator John Ryan, "demeaning, demanding, and very condescending."

Du Pont, said Ryan, was very emphatic when he wanted police to do something, such as get Wochok to the phone, or move the lights. And when police tried to steer the conversation to the shooting, or to his surrender, du Pont became manipulative, lapsing into another identity—"His Holiness is under siege" for instance—and changing the topic.

To those who were close to him, that was not unusual behavior. Georgia Dusckas said du Pont had a "remarkable ability to change states so rapidly." She was so used to it, she said, that she described du Pont as having three personalities.

The most frightening was what she called "the giggler." She first noticed it a half year or so before Schultz was killed. She saw it last just before walking out of the mansion a few hours after the shooting, when du Pont told her to invite Schultz—who was already dead—to the mansion.

As "the giggler," she said, du Pont would become red-faced, would laugh to himself, and hold a conversation with an imaginary person.

"I could speak to and look at him directly and he could look at me eye to eye," she said, "and then his eyes would shift a little bit and he would have a conversation out of the side of his mouth with somebody, and it wasn't me."

It wasn't anyone else, either, because nobody else was in the room. That side conversation, barely audible, could last as long as ten minutes. And it always ended with one word: "Yeah." Du Pont would say, out loud, "Yeah," and return his full attention to Dusckas.

The second du Pont was one who had no respect for authority; he was his own authority. He ignored responsibility. And he had a mean streak, a hair-trigger temper. He could tear somebody apart verbally. But usually within minutes, Dusckas said, he would apologize.

Then there was what Dusckas called "the regular du Pont," a gracious, polite man, charming with his guests, almost Victorian in his manners. That was the du Pont who was a pleasure to be around.

And that, apparently, was the du Pont who now was talking to Anthony Paparo. "May I speak to Mr. Wochok, please?"

"I believe he left the room," said Paparo. "Let me see if I can get him back."

"Thank you very much."

Paparo made a suggestion. "Why don't you go out," he told du Pont, "and we'll have Wochok call you as soon as you get back." Du Pont had an answer for that: "Why don't you go and get him, and I'll hold in the meantime."

Paparo turned to small talk to keep du Pont from hanging up. He asked about du Pont's artwork and antiques. He tried to get him to converse about his sports trophies. He brought up the Olympics. Du Pont was unresponsive.

"Is Mr. Wochok around?" he asked.

"They're still trying to locate him, sir. I'm just basically trying to make conversation with you, that's all."

"You don't have to."

"Well, sometimes I talk a lot. I like to talk. You know, I mean, I have hobbies. Do you have any hobbies besides your sports and all?"

Du Pont gave off a danger sign: broken English.

"I no talk," he said.

"All right," said Paparo. "Somebody just came in the room. They can't find Mr. Wochok. Do you want to go take care of the . . . ?"

"I go," said du Pont. "I go. I go try fix heat."

"All right, you go try to fix the heat and then I'll call you back in about fifteen minutes. And if you get back before then, you give me a call, and I'll have Mr. Wochok here. I promise."

"Okay. Thank you."

John du Pont put down the phone, went downstairs, and walked out of his mansion for the last time.

Sgt. Paul Trautmann was providing protection behind the mansion for a group of officers trying to get the generator for the portable lights to work. They tried hand-starting it eight or ten times. Suddenly, he received a radio message that du Pont was about to exit.

The generator was quickly forgotten. Trautmann ordered the men to pull back, and called in a couple of officers as reinforcements. They began moving along a row of hedges, toward a large tree that could provide cover.

Trautmann was still in a trot when du Pont—in his Bulgarian sweat suit, with a long chain and card of some sort dangling from his neck—walked out, took a few steps in one direction, then turned and began walking down a path. Trautmann got to the tree and watched. He waited until du Pont got about thirty yards away from the mansion. It was a point, Trautmann thought, where du Pont couldn't get back to his door without the policeman getting in his way.

Trautmann raised his gun, pointed it at du Pont, and shouted, "Put your hands in the air!"

Du Pont stopped. He raised his arms. He looked right at Trautmann.

Then he seemed to look past him, as if measuring the distance to his back door. He put his hands down and began running.

Trautmann hesitated for a second, long enough to see that du Pont held no arms, and had no holster or weapons tucked into his clothes. He jumped out from behind the tree and went toward du Pont. "Stop," he said. "Put your hands in the air!"

Du Pont complied briefly, then continued his run. Trautmann caught him. He grabbed him with his left hand, spun him halfway around. "Let me go," du Pont said. "Let me go back inside." The rest of the team arrived and got du Pont on the ground, handcuffing his hands behind his back. Trautmann stood up. Other police emptied du Pont's pockets. There was a set of keys and a passport in a jacket with Cyrillic writing on it.

It was 3:25 P.M. The standoff was over, forty-eight hours after it began. At the command center, negotiators let out a cheer. They hugged and clapped.

"I think most of them want a hot shower and bed," said Tom Cupples, the ex–FBI agent advising negotiators.

Said Chief Mallon: "No shots were fired; no one was hurt. I'd call that a successful resolution."

Du Pont was lifted from the ground by policemen. He was put in a black van and driven off his estate to the Newtown police station for arraignment.

The laminated card still hung down the front of his Foxcatcher T-shirt.

It was a pass to the 1995 World Wrestling Championships in Atlanta.

Six

John du Pont knelt in the van for the short drive to the low, brick building that housed the Newtown police station. He looked absolutely dazed as he was taken inside, his cuffed hands bouncing off his back as he walked.

Du Pont was led by two officers into Lt. Lee Hunter's office, a ten-foot-by-twelve-foot room with a metal desk, a few chairs, a filing cabinet, a typewriter and typewriter stand.

Det. Charles List, of the Delaware County Criminal Investigation Division, was seated behind the desk. Du Pont was put in a chair across from him.

"You are charged with the murder of David Schultz," said Det. John Slowik.

He read the laundry list of charges: criminal homicide, first- and third-degree murder, voluntary manslaughter, involuntary manslaughter, aggravated assault, simple assault, recklessly endangering another person, and possessing instruments of crime.

Slowik also read him his rights.

"I want my passport," du Pont said, referring to the Bulgarian document.

The request was ignored.

Terry Wochok came into the room. List was typing biographical information onto a sheet.

"Name?"

"John E. du Pont."

"Date of birth?"

"November 22, 1938."

"Place of birth?"

"Eastern Europe. I left eastern Europe as a young boy to become the American Dalai Lama."

"Height?"

"Five feet eleven inches."

"Weight?"

"Sixty-eight kilograms." One hundred forty-nine and a half pounds.

"Color of eyes?"

"Hazel."

"Marital status?"

"Single."

List moved on to the portion of the report where he filled in the details of the arrest. "I want my passport," du Pont said again. He asked for it four times.

Slowik left the room and returned with Sgt. Joseph O'Berg, who would do the fingerprinting. One of the members of the tactical squad came in to unlock the handcuffs.

As he finished, List heard du Pont direct a question toward Wochok.

"What about a presidential pardon?" du Pont said.

"Just finish the processing and we'll talk later," Wochok said.

Du Pont was taken to another room. Steven Shallis, who two days earlier had bent over the body of David Schultz, checking for a pulse, took the mug shots. He had du Pont stand against the wall and took two pictures from the front. He asked him to turn to his side, then shot a profile. Du Pont was cooperative, although he and Shallis did not have a conversation.

O'Berg finished the fingerprinting. Afterward, du Pont asked to use the bathroom so he could wash his hands.

He signed his name to the fingerprint cards.

List got a call. It came from the mansion, where a police bomb squad was making a sweep to check for explosives. They came to du Pont's library, with the large, vaulted double doors. It was locked.

"We'd like the combination," List said to du Pont.

"No."

"Look," List said, "we've got a search warrant, and we're prepared to blow through the wall if we have to."

"I'd like to speak to Mr. Wochok in private."

Det. Joseph Ryan, another member of the county Criminal Investigation Division, was part of the team searching the mansion. He left the estate and drove to the police station to see Wochok.

"We don't want to do any damage to the house," he said. "Would you give me the combination?"

Wochok went into a room to talk with du Pont. "You can trust this person," he said, referring to Ryan. "I've dealt with him all weekend."

Wochok came out of the room. Du Pont wanted to talk to Ryan privately. Ryan went in, sat down, and introduced himself. He explained again that he needed to get into the library and wanted to do it the easy way.

Du Pont leaned toward Ryan and whispered, "All you have to do is turn the dial and push the handle down and the door will open."

"Well, if that doesn't work, can I have the combination?"

"No, you go try that. If that doesn't work, you come back. I'll give you the combination." Ryan realized he was being dismissed.

"Well, can you give me the combination just in case that doesn't work?" he asked. He didn't want to have to come back to the police station if he could help it.

"No, you go do that," du Pont said.

Ryan left, returned to the library and turned the dial. It

just kept spinning. He was still locked out. He drove back to the station.

Ryan told Wochok what happened. Wochok talked to du Pont, and the two of them approached Ryan.

"I did what you told me, and it didn't work," said Ryan. "I need the combination."

"I do it automatically," du Pont replied. "I don't know if I know the combination."

"Then we're going to have to force our way in," Ryan said.

Du Pont's face took on a look as if he were trying to remember something. In a few seconds he leaned over and whispered a series of numbers into Ryan's ear. Ryan wrote them on a piece of paper. Du Pont also explained how to spin the dial to start the process of unlocking the door.

In other rooms in the mansion, searchers were finding all kinds of guns and more than a dozen boxes of ammunition. In the master bedroom, a Smith & Wesson .38-caliber revolver, an antique revolver, and a small, pocket derringer were taken out of a desk. On the bed was a Browning high-powered 9-millimeter pistol. Next to the desk was a Winchester double-barrel, 12-gauge shotgun.

In the bathroom closet, part of the master bedroom suite, police found a fully loaded semiautomatic assault rifle. In the bedroom closet was a lever-action .30-.30 rifle. A machine pistol rested on a small dresser. In an armoire drawer there were M-80 explosives. Several hunting rifles, two of which were antiques, were in the telephone room.

Ryan got back to the mansion, went to the library, and tried the combination. The doors swung open.

Inside, more guns were picked up throughout the room. A 9-millimeter Luger, loaded. A 12-gauge shotgun. In a cabinet was another Browning high-powered 9-millimeter pistol. There was a Smith & Wesson .357 Magnum and a Smith & Wesson .38-caliber revolver, a .22-caliber target pistol, a rifle with two loaded magazines and a laser sight.

On the top shelf of a bookcase, immediately to the right of the doorway, was a leather holster holding a .44-caliber Magnum. Det. William Welsh opened the cylinder and saw that all six ports in the chamber were loaded with hollow-point bullets. Three of the ports were completely clean. The other three had residue, indicating the gun had been fired and new bullets put in.

It was the murder weapon.

Du Pont was done at the police station around 5:15 P.M. He was escorted through a side door and into a makeshift courtroom at the adjoining municipal building. District Justice Robert W. Burton, who had been on call for the day, conducted the five-minute proceeding.

Du Pont said nothing and stared straight ahead as he heard the charges read again. Because it was a first-degree murder case, no bail was set.

Wochok didn't make a statement either, but he did tell the judge he now had cocounsel: Richard Sprague, one of Philadelphia's leading criminal lawyers and a man with a national reputation. The two had worked together more than two decades earlier in the Philadelphia District Attorney's Office. During his seventeen years as a prosecutor, Sprague had convicted more than four hundred murderers, including United Mine Workers president W.A. "Tony" Boyle, found guilty of ordering the killing of UMW rival Joseph Yablonski. He was known for thoroughness in preparation, inventive strategy, and incisive cross-examination—but with a style that he admitted would not win him a popularity contest.

In 1976, Sprague was chosen as special counsel to a congressional committee investigating the assassinations of President Kennedy and Martin Luther King. A year later he went into private practice; his client list included onetime Philadelphia mayor Frank L. Rizzo and famed defense lawyer F. Lee Bailey.

Joining Wochok and Sprague was du Pont's old friend William Lamb, a former district attorney in neighboring Chester County, politically connected Republican and senior partner in a West Chester law firm. The trio came to be called "Dream Team East" after the West Coast core of lawyers hired by O.J. Simpson.

Burton set a preliminary hearing for 9 A.M. Thursday, Feb. 1, before District Justice David Videon at the Newtown Square District Court. Du Pont was put into a Newtown police car and driven to Delaware County Prison.

He entered prison at 5:45 P.M. There, he was placed in isolation from the rest of the prison population after inmates greeted his arrival with chants of "Du-pont, du-Pont, du-Pont."

"I just felt that it was the safe and prudent thing to move him into a cell alone," said new district attorney Patrick Meehan, whose office would be prosecuting the case.

Like his Foxcatcher estate, du Pont's new home—locally known as Broadmeadows Prison—was set amid rolling hills in rural Delaware County. There, of course, the similarities ended. Du Pont was placed in Cell Number 2, an eight-by-ten-foot space that included a sink and toilet, a metal bed frame with a mattress, an overhead light, and a wall of bars with a Plexiglas window so food trays could be passed through. One corrections officer was assigned solely to watch du Pont's cell.

Under a policy that took effect three days after du Pont's arrival, he was to be charged $10 a day for room and board, medical visits, and over-the-counter medication.

"He's a triple-A credit rating, and I'm sure, with his bank account, he'd probably be able to pay the $10 rate for everybody there," said one prison official.

After du Pont's arraignment, Nancy Schultz appeared at a news conference in the basement of the Newtown Square Presbyterian Church. She sobbed as she praised her husband as an athlete, coach, mentor, and family man.

"I have no idea why John committed this senseless and brutal killing of my husband," Schultz said.

While she spoke, her daughter, Danielle, then six, held a pink tissue, and her son, Alexander, who was nine, touched his mother's shoulder several times.

"My family must now turn its focus and energy to my children, who had a very close relationship with their father, and who are struggling to understand how and why this tragedy happened, and how they will possibly fill this void in their lives."

Her family, she said, was "devastated and saddened by Dave's brutal and unexpected loss. He was not only a world-class athlete, coach, and mentor, but a devoted and loving father to our children and husband to me for the past fourteen years.

"Dave will be missed so much by family, friends, and the wrestling community around the world. Dave had a passion for his sport and an enthusiasm for life that was unmatched."

She said she had received messages from around the world from people "whose lives Dave touched." And she thanked those who had provided support to her during the weekend.

She also expressed the feeling that du Pont would pay for his act.

"I am confident," she said, "that the police and authorities will conduct a thorough investigation and bring him to justice."

As she learned during the next days, weeks and months, however, that would be an often frustrating task for the D.A.'s Office.

In fact, du Pont stopped cooperating as soon as he got

to prison. All new inmates are required by state regula-
tions to undergo an intake and classification process that
includes a general questionnaire regarding personal background, and medical history, a physical exam that consists
of a tuberculosis test and a chest X-ray, and a compre-
hensive placement interview. There was also an optional
blood test for venereal disease.

One of the questions on the interview asks if the inmate
thinks he might be in jeopardy if placed in a particular
area within the prison.

Du Pont flat out refused to go along with any of the
procedures. Without answers, prison officials couldn't
move him. Without knowing whether or not he had any
communicable diseases, he was forced to remain in an
isolated cell in the prison's six-cell Health Services Unit,
normally reserved for inmates with serious physical, emotional, or mental conditions.

Once inside that cell, he stopped shaving. He refused
haircuts. He refused most prison food, except for tea and
crackers. He stopped brushing his teeth.

Lawyers for the prison went to court a week after du
Pont's arrival to get an order that would force him to
comply. They and du Pont's attorneys tried to work things
out. That didn't happen, and prison officials returned to
court. Other inmates, they said, heard of du Pont's actions
and copied it, refusing to answer questions or go through
the medical procedures. On a number of occasions, they
added, inmates who needed to be housed in the medical
wing couldn't be because du Pont occupied a cell.

Sprague parried every attempt to move du Pont.

He was so successful, that Cell Number 2 remained du
Pont's home for the next eight months.

PART TWO

The Collector and the Wrestler

No one ever said "no" to John.
TERRY WOCHOK

If John wants to play, I can play.
DAVID SCHULTZ

Seven

On May 15, 1940, Gimbel's Department Store in New York City took out a full-page ad in the *New York Times*.

"The sale begins today at 9:30 A.M.," the copy read. "Do not delay! There's going to be a mad scramble for this first shipment of Nylon stockings. There won't be enough to go around."

For more than a year, since nylon was introduced at the 1939 World's Fair in New York, the public had read and heard about the miracle properties of this new product. But it wasn't until May 15, 1940—dubbed Nylon Day by retailers—that the stockings were sold over the counter.

And Gimbel's was right: there weren't enough to go around. About three-quarters of a million pairs of the stockings quickly sold out nationwide.

Mattie Kinkaide, who was a hosiery buyer for Strawbridge & Clothier in Philadelphia in 1940, was interviewed in 1990 for a story on the fiftieth anniversary of nylon. "We did a fabulous business," said Kinkaide, who was eighty-six when she gave the interview. "We would have sold many more had we had more. It was a sellout."

The introduction of nylons was hailed chiefly for two reasons. One, the material promised to cut down on runs that plagued silk stockings. Models chosen to test nylon stockings in 1939 reported that they endured "unbeliev-able hours of performance."

That, however, also caused a problem for E.I. du Pont de Nemours & Company, the Delaware company that had invested about a decade and $27 million in developing the product.

DuPont was uncomfortable with the "miracle yarn" label for nylon, and tried to reduce the public's anticipa-tion with a campaign urging women not to expect the impossible. But it did nothing to stem the demand. Stores were besieged with requests for the stockings after leggy models, dresses purposely hiked a few inches above the knee, displayed nylon stockings at DuPont's pavilion at the World's Fair.

The second reason for the intense interest in nylons had to do with a combination of politics, economics—and vanity. Silk came from Japan; it was, in fact, that coun-try's chief export to the United States. When Japan began its military campaign against China, America called for a silk boycott. But the tremendous demand for silk stock-ings by American women rendered it ineffective.

In 1939, for example, retailers estimated that the daily purchase of silk stockings in the United States averaged 1.6 million pairs—about $475 million spent on the prod-uct annually. Boycott supporters hoped that nylon would supplant silk and that, of course, is what happened. In an amazingly short time, silk stockings became almost ob-solete.

The official introduction of nylon—DuPont said it se-lected the meaningless word from 350 candidates "be-cause it was simple and euphonious"—was made in October 1938. That announcement culminated an effort that began in 1928, when DuPont hired a Harvard teacher, Wallace H. Carothers, to begin a research program to pro-duce synthetic fibers compounded wholly from chemicals. About three years later, the members of Carothers's team, investigating why certain molecules united to form other molecules called "polymers," pulled a taffylike material out of a test tube. They found that when it cooled, it was strong, pliable, and elastic.

In the lab, the product was known as fiber "66." But difficulties in bringing fiber 66 out of the lab and into commercial production were enormous. Not only did new equipment have to be designed, but an entire manufacturing plant was built in Seaford, Delaware. By the time nylon was introduced, almost 250 engineers and chemists had been involved in the project.

The kind of money and manpower DuPont put into fiber 66 was typical of the company, where research and development always was a high priority—and where the emphasis on discovery was embedded in the firm's culture. It had always been the company's ability to adapt to change, to expand, to explore new avenues, that enabled it to survive and grow.

For that, thanks must go to the man whose name—E.I. du Pont de Nemours—has adorned the company letterhead for nearly two hundred years. A retiring gentleman whose life crossed from the eighteenth to the nineteenth century, he lived with a stern belief in personal responsibility, and founded his firm not solely with an intention of making money, but of making things better.

It would also be appropriate to offer a bow in the direction of Thomas Jefferson, whose deep and long-lasting friendship with E.I. du Pont's father, Pierre Samuel, laid the groundwork for the beginning of what would become one of the oldest and wealthiest commercial enterprises in the world.

Eleuthère Irénée du Pont—John Eleuthère du Pont's great-great-grandfather—was born on June 24, 1771, in Paris. His roots in the City of Lights had been established by his grandfather, Samuel du Pont, who arrived there in

1735, leaving behind his village of Rouen to seek his fortune as a watchmaker.

Samuel set up his shop on Rue Harlay, and before long was courting Anne Montchanin, the sister of one of his competitors. They married in 1737; within a year a son was born, but lived just a few months. Their second child, Pierre Samuel, was born in December 1739. Sickly and small, undernourished and suffering from rickets, it was only through his mother's unfailing attention that he survived infancy.

One thing that was not underdeveloped, however, was his mind. At the age of three Pierre Samuel was learning to read and write. At five he had a tutor, who recognized his genius. At twelve he put on a public exhibition of his intellect, translating Latin authors, discoursing on law, reading poetry.

Then he died.

Or, at least, he was pronounced dead by a doctor who was treating him for a high fever resulting from smallpox. But after being laid out on a funeral bier, he moved, then uttered a few words.

A miracle? Anne Montchanin du Pont thought so, convinced her son was destined by God for greatness. But Samuel had other ideas. He had long wanted his son to follow him into watchmaking, and became almost tyrannical in his pursuit of that end. His control over the boy became absolute; Pierre Samuel was placed at a table in his father's shop and forced to learn the trade. As with everything else, he excelled. But he never liked it.

In 1756, Anne died; Pierre Samuel was seventeen. His relationship with his father, never good, became hateful. In the aftermath of a fight, he left his father's home, becoming an apprentice to another watchmaker. It was the only trade that could afford him a living. But he longed to use his mind, not his hands.

That opportunity came after a chance meeting with a

Parisian doctor. Impressed by the young man, the doctor urged du Pont to consider medicine. Du Pont attacked it with a passion; a quick study in anatomy, it wasn't long before he could—at a time when no exams or licenses were required for the profession—call himself a physician.

At night, though, it wasn't the pursuit of medicine that occupied him. He wrote poetry and plays. This foray into writing gave him a pass into the salons of writers and artists, where he mingled with the intelligentsia and found their exchanges as exciting as anything he had ever done.

Sometimes, though, he needed to escape the city. Du Pont would ride the forty miles to a small town called Nemours to spend time with his former neighbors, the Doré family. It was on one such visit that he learned a Doré cousin, Marie Le Dee, was about to enter into an arranged marriage with a villager three decades older. Outraged, du Pont offered himself as a husband instead. Madame Doré gave him two years to earn enough money to be able to support a wife.

Almost immediately, he quit the watch trade. He thought of a military career; Britain and France were at war. But the Treaty of Paris in 1763 ended that. So he turned to writing. He wrote poetry and essays; one treatise on the financial situation of France ended up in the lap of François Arouet Voltaire, who was impressed enough to initiate a correspondence. Pierre Samuel was twenty-three when he penned *Reflections on the Wealth of the State*, a pamphlet that offered radical ideas on finances. He advocated one flat tax to replace the series of taxes that was crippling the people of France.

His ideas—but not his name—reached the court at Versailles. Officials of the king tracked down the anonymous author and brought him to a royal reception. Du Pont's rise in politics had begun; he eventually became an economic advisor to the king, and his fame and fortune followed.

He returned to Nemours to claim Marie Le Dee. They were married in Paris on January 28, 1766. In late 1767 a son, Victor Marie, was born. Another son, born in 1769, lived less than a month, but a third came into the world perfectly healthy in June 1771. His name, Eleuthère Irénée, meant freedom and peace.

Soon after, Pierre Samuel purchased a small farm near Nemours. It was to become the family's country retreat.

He also wrote another pamphlet, this on politics and economy. The English translation was read with rapt interest by both Thomas Jefferson and Benjamin Franklin. In 1776, when Franklin arrived in France to negotiate treaties between France and the fledgling United States of America, one of the first individuals he asked to meet was Pierre Samuel du Pont. Du Pont was an ardent supporter of American independence, and he and Franklin spent countless hours together over the next two years.

In 1784, at the age of forty-one, Marie Le Dee du Pont died. Victor was seventeen, an outgoing teenager full of charm. Irénée, at thirteen, was more sober, more reflective. At their farm, Pierre Samuel called them together and made them promise to always be there for the other. The two were to fulfill that pledge countless times over the years.

While the boys continued their education, Pierre Samuel was in Paris, helping formulate a commercial treaty between France and Britain. He frequently consulted Thomas Jefferson, who replaced Franklin in Paris in 1785; the friendship that grew between the two men lasted the rest of their lives, and played a large role after the du Ponts moved to America at the turn of the century.

That same year, 1785, he was made a noble by Louis XVI. Oddly, his name on the king's order was spelled

"Dupont," although shortly afterward Pierre Samuel began to sign his name "du Pont."

Victor, meanwhile, still in his twenties, joined the diplomatic corps and was selected to go to New York as a member of the French legation. Irénée, with his love of natural science—a love that marked the early years of John du Pont five generations later—was apprenticed to Antoine-Laurent Lavoisier at the Royal Arsenal in Essonnes.

Irénée spent more than three years under the tutelage of Lavoisier, a brilliant scientist and the father of modern chemistry. As Commissioner of Powders, he changed France's gunpowder from the worst to the best in the world.

But Lavoisier was also in a bad position—that of a high-ranking government official—when the Bastille was stormed on July 14, 1789. The French Revolution had begun; four years later, in an atmosphere of distrust and an era of factional infighting, the Reign of Terror was unleashed. Anyone suspected of treason, no matter how far-fetched the evidence, was arrested; thousands were guillotined. The upper class was particularly vulnerable. Lavoisier was one of the nobles who lost his head.

Pierre Samuel du Pont kept his, but just barely. Out of government, he had become a printer and political pamphleteer. Considered a troublemaker, he was jailed twice, in 1793 and 1797. The second time, Irénée, who had worked with his father in their print shop, joined him in prison. Irénée was cleared, but Pierre Samuel was sentenced to be deported; he was saved only by some old, well-placed connections.

By this time, Irénée was married—his wife, Sophie Madeleine Dalmas, was sixteen at their wedding—and the father of two daughters; a son, Alfred Victor would arrive in 1798. That same year Irénée's brother, Victor, ended his bachelorhood.

Pierre Samuel had also remarried, not for love but for money, of which he had a rapidly dwindling supply. Two tours of prison life had also convinced him that his family's future lay not in France, but in the exciting place called America. Always a dreamer, he envisioned a colony where French refugees could live in liberty, working the soil, looking out for each other's welfare. He even had a name for it: Pontiana.

But the timing couldn't have been worse. France and the United States were at each other's throats; war seemed imminent. Victor du Pont, now a veteran diplomat in America, wrote to Tallyrand, the French foreign minister, convincing him that any conflagration would be disastrous to both countries. Tallyrand softened France's stance toward America, inviting an envoy to come and talk. Shipping embargoes ceased, prisoners were freed, tensions cooled. In that eased atmosphere, Pierre Samuel du Pont drew up plans to get his extended family across the ocean.

His second wife, Françoise du Pont, and her son-in-law, Bureaux de Pusy, left first in 1799, establishing a household in Bergen Point, New Jersey. On October 2 of that same year, thirteen members of the du Pont family—seven adults and six children—plus three nurses and two prisoners who decided America had to be better than Devil's Island, boarded the *American Eagle* for passage to their new home.

Three months and three thousand miles later, they landed briefly at Block Island, Rhode Island on New Year's Day, 1800, then left the ship for good two days later at Newport. Within a month they were all together at Bergen Point, and a new American company, Du Pont de Nemours Father & Sons & Company, was opened at 91 Liberty Street in New York City. Alexander Hamilton was hired as counsel to the firm. They had a letter of welcome from old friend Thomas Jefferson. They planned to become brokers, to open shipping lines, to get into the import-export business, to invest in real estate. One of their most ambitious projects was to colonize one million acres of land in Virginia.

Then, one fall day in 1800, Irénée went hunting. The story of that daylong outing plays a major role in the du Pont family history—even if researchers have questioned some of its facts. For instance, his partner on the expedition was Colonel Louis Toussard, who left France to join the American Revolution. Toussard's role seems suspect to some historians, who point out that he had lost an arm in the war, an injury that might have kept him from shooting a clunky hunting rifle.

Whether the story is more legend than gospel, though, is besides the point; certainly, there is enough truth to it that the result would have been the same: the founding of a gunpowder factory along the small Brandywine River near Wilmington, Delaware.

The tale goes like this: Having exhausted their supply of ammunition, Toussard and du Pont were forced to purchase more in a country store. There, du Pont was surprised by the terrible quality of American powder. For quality, one had to buy gunpowder made by the British. Later, he asked Toussard to arrange a tour of a gunpowder factory, and the two had a walk-through of the Lane-Decatur firm in Frankford, Pennsylvania, now part of the city of Philadelphia. Du Pont, who had spent years among the best powder manufacturers in the world, was surprised to find how outdated were the methods of the Americans.

Du Pont's idea to get into the business was met coolly at first by his father. One reason was the family's ardent pacifism; it was hard to reconcile that belief with a product that was associated with war and killing. But other du Ponts were enthusiastic. And Pierre Samuel was perhaps convinced of moving forward by the thought that the gunpowder would primarily be used for the myriad landclearing projects under way for America's expansion.

Gunpowder's money-making potential, however, would not be realized through blazing a path for land development. It would be war that turned the du Pont company into a wildly profitable business—and resulted in some harsh condemnations for later generations.

Pierre Samuel, after looking at his sons' calculations, saw just how lucrative it could be—especially if the government became a steady customer.

So on December 17, 1800, Pierre Samuel sent a letter to his good friend Thomas Jefferson—President-elect Thomas Jefferson. The letter, as quoted by French journalist Max Dorian in his 1961 book about the du Pont family, read:

> *One of my sons, whom Lavoisier instructed [and] who is one of the best powder-makers in France, where the best powders in the world are made, will set up here a fine manufactory for this material . . . I dare to allege that he will make bullets that go a fifth or more greater distance than English or Dutch bullets. And in light of this promise, I beg you not to let out any contract for supplying your powder magazines before you have compared what we are making with others.*

In February 1801, Irénée and Victor returned to France to drum up financial support—Irénée for the gunpowder company, Victor for the remainder of the du Pont businesses. Irénée was ready to return in July; he had received promises of funds and sophisticated equipment designed by the engineers at Essonnes. Beyond that, the French, eager to break the British hold on supplying munitions for America, gladly passed on their secrets for making top-quality powder.

At the suggestion of his father, Irénée searched for a spot near the new capital of Washington, D.C.—in Maryland or Virginia—for his venture. But nothing was suitable. Pierre "Peter" Bauday, who would become du Pont's business manager, had him look at a ninety-six-acre plot of land on the west bank of the Brandywine River in Wilmington. The purchase, from Quaker Jacob Broom, was completed in the spring of 1802. Within a year du Pont's family was living on the site as construction for the gunpowder works forged ahead. In July 1803, the first batch of saltpeter, the key element in gunpowder, was made. And in early 1804, this advertisement appeared in a New York newspaper.

E.I. du Pont de Nemours
Gunpowder Manufactory
Wilmington, Delaware

This new and extensive establishment is now in activity and any quantity of powder, equal if not superior to any manufactured in Europe, will be delivered at shortest notice.

Samples to be seen at
V. du Pont de Nemours, New York.

Potential customers, though, had to look fast. By 1805 Victor was bankrupt, his New York office boarded. After an attempt to work in upstate New York, he also settled on the Brandywine, near what was called the Eleutherian Mills. There, with Irénée's backing, Victor opened a woolen mill.

Pierre Samuel, meanwhile, had been in France since 1802—while there he helped negotiate the Louisiana Purchase—and would not return to America for thirteen years. When he did come to the Brandywine in 1815, he was astounded. From America, he wrote to his wife—whom he would not see again—a glowing letter of what he had found. The factory was "gigantic, inconceivable that only one man was able to design and execute such a thing . . . Irénée is a great man, with talent, courage, perseverance ten times greater than I had ever dare hoped."

He should have added Irénée's sense of world events and how they might affect the business. The winds of war had been blowing, and Irénée saw conflicts breaking out with either Great Britain or France. Figuring the need for gunpowder would be greater than ever, he proposed putting the company's profits into expansion. Bauday, the business manager, was vehemently opposed, preferring to increase his own windfall and paying some of the profits to investors. Du Pont, as head of the company, got his way, purchasing the Hagley Farm, a short distance down the Brandywine from Eleutherian Mills.

Du Pont, of course, was proved right. The War of 1812 brought an order for 200,000 pounds of gunpowder. That was increased to 500,000 pounds the next year. The company became recognized as the preeminent manufacturer of gunpowder in the United States.

But du Pont's reputation among his investors was bloodied by the rift with Bauday, who took every opportunity to savage his boss. Although it gave the company large orders, the American treasury was unable to pay its bills; with the expansion at Hagley Farm, du Pont's debt mounted. He was sued by his stepsister, the first in a two-century-long line of family squabbles to end up in court. In fact, despite increasing production, money problems haunted Irénée almost until his death in 1834.

"I owe more than $60,000, chiefly in notes at the bank, so that my debts amount to far more than my profits from the powder," he once wrote to a friend in France. "The signatures that must be renewed every sixty days put me in exactly the situation of a prisoner on parole who must show himself to the police every month."

But the argument with Bauday did have one outcome

that du Pont found favorable: Bauday sold his shares in the company, leaving E.I. du Pont de Nemours & Company completely controlled by the family.

Pierre Samuel's return to America in 1815 gave him the opportunity to meet a greatly enlarged family. Victor now had three children, including a son, Samuel Francis, who married Irénée's daughter, Sophie, thus becoming the first in a series of du Ponts who married their cousins. Irénée, meanwhile, had by then six of his own offspring, with one more to be born in 1816. One of his children born in America, Henry, came to be known simply as "The Boss," and would rule the enterprise for thirty-nine years.

In 1816, Victor became the first of numerous du Ponts in politics, winning election first to the Delaware House of Representatives, then the state Senate. That year a disaster at the mills was averted, but at a high cost. On July 16, 1816, one of the buildings caught fire, and Pierre Samuel joined an all-night bucket brigade. When he finally got to bed, exhausted and soaked, he never got up. On August 7, the little man who barely made it out of infancy died, a few months shy of his seventy-seventh birthday.

A far greater tragedy occurred nearly two years later, in March 1818, when an explosion leveled the mills and killed forty people. The operation at Hagley continued, but it took a year to restore Eleutherian Mills; during that time, Irénée continued to pay a monthly pension to the dependents of all the men killed.

Victor suffered a heart attack and died in 1827 and was placed next to Pierre Samuel in the family graveyard. Irénée's beloved wife, Sophie, was buried there in 1828. From then on, his interest in his mills waned, and he turned over much of the day-to-day business to his son, Alfred Victor, and son-in-law, James Bidermann. On October 30, 1834, while in Philadelphia on business, his heart gave out. His passing marked the end of the first two generations of du Ponts to set foot in America. They were gone but had established a legacy that continues to this day.

At Irénée's death the title of head of the family—and, therefore, the company—went to his eldest son, Alfred Victor. But it was Bidermann, for twenty years a close aide to Irénée, who ran things.

Just for a few years, that is. Bidermann, husband of Irénée's second child, Evelina, returned to France with his family in 1837, selling all his shares in the company back to the du Ponts. That left E.I.'s six other children in complete control. What they controlled, thanks to Bidermann, was a company that had finally paid off all its bills and loans.

But that comfortable state didn't last long. Under Alfred Victor, the debt piled up. It wasn't long before it became apparent to all—including Alfred, who enjoyed science more than business—that he was not the person to lead E.I. du Pont de Nemours & Company through the middle years of the nineteenth century. Despite the fact that orders had consistently increased, especially after the United States attacked Mexico in 1846, the company found itself owing nearly half a million dollars.

Of the three brothers who were at the top of the company—Alfred, Henry, and Alexis, the youngest son of Irénée—Henry was the clear leader. The great-grandfather of John duPont, Henry took over in 1850 and ruled until his death in 1889. One of his first acts was to stop a price war among DuPont and two competitors. Expansion westward increased business as settlers needed more and more explosives to clear land. Sales skyrocketed when DuPont was tapped to supply powder to both sides during the Crimean War in 1854–55, an indication that the company's product was well-known overseas. And around 1857 DuPont opened a plant in Pennsylvania, its first venture outside Delaware.

FATAL MATCH 93

The Civil War was an absolute boon for DuPont. The company supplied the Union forces and later joined its competitors in a monopoly, dividing the country into sales territories and setting quotas. By the turn of the century, the du Ponts "dominated the explosives industry as completely as the Carnegie Company dominated steel or Rockefeller dominated the oil industry," wrote historian Joseph Frazier Wall in his 1990 biography of Alfred I. du Pont, a great-grandson of the company founder.

But the twentieth century also brought shocking news: the decision by the du Pont elders to sell the company to one of its competitors, Laflin & Rand. Part of the problem was a gap in leadership. Iron-fisted Henry died in 1889 without grooming a successor. His brothers who helped him form a troika at the top of the company had both died long before, Alfred Victor in 1856 and Alexis in an explosion the next year. The heir-apparent had been Alfred's son, Lammot, but he, too, was killed in a company accident in 1884.

Henry had two sons in line, Henry A. and William. William didn't want it, and he didn't want his hated brother to have it either. That left three of Alexis's sons, and the oldest, Eugene, ascended to the du Pont throne with each of the five cousins taking a 20 percent partnership stake.

Peace didn't prevail. According to Wall's book, two other du Ponts, Charles I. and Alfred, clamored for their pieces of the pie. William had a plan. He would sell his 20 percent, to be split between Charles and Alfred. It gave him a chance to take the money, quite a considerable amount, and run. It also cut him off from the company. Neither his son, William Jr., nor grandson, John du Pont, would ever have anything to do with the firm—beyond the handsome wealth it provided.

William further alienated the family in 1892 when he established residency in South Dakota, with its liberal divorce laws, and officially ended his marriage to his cousin, May, so he could marry Annie Zinn, who was awaiting her own divorce to be finalized. It was an eerie foreshadowing of a tactic followed by his son, William Jr., who in 1940 got a Nevada divorce from his wife, Jean Austin, and eventually married a tennis star—a union that would also end in divorce.

In January 1902, Eugene died and the partners were faced with a dilemma. Four of them were either too old or two sickly to take over. The fifth, Alfred—who had purchased his stake from William—was nobody's favorite. So the decision was made to offer the company for $12 million to Laflin & Rand. Alfred almost immediately set about working on a plan to buy the company. He could not, however, come up with that much money, so he turned to his cousin, T. Coleman du Pont, then a successful businessman in Kentucky. Coleman agreed on the condition he be made president. The two brought in another cousin, Pierre. Not only did the trio pull off the deal—offering the elders more stock than cash—but they eventually purchased Laflin & Rand. DuPont was now the biggest manufacturer of gunpowder in the world, and once again three family members stood atop the heap.

The twentieth century heralded unprecedented growth. World War I brought an estimated $250 million into DuPont. Pierre, the financial wizard, set the firm in the direction to become the largest chemical company in the world. The great du Pont estates along the Delaware/Pennsylvania border—such as Winterthur and Longwood Gardens—were built.

To be sure, there were scandals. Alfred fought a long court battle with Pierre when the latter bought out Coleman and became head. Pierre married a cousin when he was in his forties amid rumors of his homosexuality, which were fueled partly by his close relationship with his driver. In the 1930s the U.S. Senate conducted hearings into possible war-profiteering—one senator called the du Ponts the "merchants of death"—and President Franklin Roosevelt attacked the family. No charges were ever brought. Ralph Nader complained in the 1970s the du Ponts wielded so much power in Delaware that it was a threat to democracy. By then, following the death of Pierre and his two brothers, who succeeded him as president, the first non–du Pont had been named as head of the company, although the family retained the majority of stock.

Today, Pierre du Pont IV, who was governor of Delaware and made an unsuccessful run for the presidency, quotes his father as summing up the family this way: "We're just French immigrants who achieved the American dream. We came speaking a foreign language, we built a business in a new country and it succeeded. And that's the promise of America."

Fulfilling that promise has likely impacted nearly every American, and countless millions around the world. Think of the DuPont products in use every day: Teflon, Rayon, Lucite, Dacron, Stainmaster carpet, auto-finishes, paints, petroleum and agricultural products, pharmaceuticals.

And, perhaps the most popular DuPont discovery ever: Nylon.

By the end of 1940, the year nylon was introduced to the public, thirty-six million pairs of stockings had been sold, and DuPont promised it would make enough in 1941 to supply 10 percent of the hosiery market. World War II, however, intervened, and the military acquired nearly all the nylon that was produced; it was used for parachutes, flak jackets, tires, ropes for towing gliders, and other defense purposes. The few nylon stockings that circulated among the public could fetch $20 a pair, and soldiers overseas often found that nylons, shipped from home, were more valuable than currency. Movie stars auctioned off nylons at War Bond rallies for as much as $40,000.

When nylon stockings went on sale again in the fall of 1945, police were needed in some places to control the crowds.

Today, the crowds have thinned, but not the demand. Consumers spend about $3.5 billion each year on sheer hosiery, 99 percent of which contains nylon.

The nylon story, though, does have a tragic footnote. Wallace Carothers, the ex–Harvard teacher chiefly responsible for the ever-increasing display of female legs, never lived to see his invention embraced by the public. A sufferer of frequent bouts of severe depression, he killed himself in a West Philadelphia hotel in 1937.

Eight

John Eleuthère du Pont was born in 1938, three years before Pearl Harbor. But he might just as well have been born an eighteenth-century crown prince of one of Europe's royal houses.

His parents, William and Jean Austin du Pont, were both products of patrician families whose fortunes were built on America's hard industries. The du Ponts, of course, were the country's chemists and explosives makers. Jean's father, William Liseter Austin, was a draftsman who, during a sixty-four-year tenure, rose to become an executive with Baldwin Locomotive Works in Philadelphia, one of the country's preeminent train manufacturers.

The Austin home was in Rosemont on the prestigious Main Line, where the scent of Philadelphia's oldest and most elite money perfumes the air. Jean grew up with horses, and her love for riding developed early. In 1910, at age thirteen, she showed her first pony in the world-famous Devon Horse Show, a few miles from the family home. It was the first of what would be seventy consecutive Devon shows in which she won ribbons.

During her youth, Newtown Square was rural and isolated, covered with farmland. Between 1914 and 1916 Papa Austin bought three adjoining farms, putting them together into one parcel he called Liseter Hall Farm. "We lived in Rosemont and I went back and forth to see my horses and cattle,'' Jean du Pont told a chronicler of New-town Square history in 1980.

It was with this generous dowry of lush land that Jean Austin married into one of America's first families.

The ceremony, held New Year's Day, 1919, had all the trappings of a gala event of American high society on the cusp of the Roaring '20s. Jean's lifelong affection for animals was in evidence at her wedding; her maid of honor carried not only a spray of yellow orchids down the aisle, but also Jean's pet Pomeranian, Peggy.

William du Pont rechristened his new home Foxcatcher Farm, a name reflecting his own passion for horses and fox hunting. He began purchasing more land adjacent to the property, eventually owning eight hundred acres. In 1925 his father, William Sr., the man who sold his stake in the DuPont company a quarter century earlier, built the couple a house. It was a replica of James Madison's Montpelier in Virginia—designed by Thomas Jefferson, the old friend of Pierre Samuel du Pont—where young William had grown up.

"We copied it," said Jean du Pont. "Even the details of the woodwork inside are the same."

During the decades of the 1920s and 1930s the mansion was a grand house suited to the tastes and social stature of the young, wealthy couple. Oriental carpeting, family portraits, and fine china, along with more exotic touches such as an upstairs train room that housed a model railroad, made it an utterly American palace. Soon the barn would hold a collection of antique carriages, including a landau that one day would be used in the movie *Hello Dolly*.

There was the trophy room that would be the primary repository for the thousands of ribbons, loving cups, and other prizes Jean earned for her horsemanship, her meticulous breeding of prize-winning beagles, and her beloved Welsh ponies.

One of the most memorable experiences of the early years of her marriage, she once said, was in 1921 when she won a hunt team class at a horse show in Washington. She received her trophy from Gen. John J. Pershing.

"When we first started showing, the horses were shipped in a railroad car," said Jean du Pont. "Nobody had a van in those days. One summer my husband and I went to nineteen shows. I felt as though I belonged in the circus."

William was president of Delaware Trust Company, but that was just his job. His real love was horses, but not the genteel breeds that fascinated his wife. His passion was for thoroughbreds. And that led to an offshoot vocation: he became recognized across the country as a top designer of horse race tracks, including Delaware Park in Stanton, Delaware.

By the 1930s horses from Foxcatcher were winning races on both coasts. In 1937, Rosemont won the Santa Anita Handicap and Fairy Hill took the Santa Anita Derby. Another Foxcatcher horse, Dauber, captured the Preakness in 1938.

That same year, on November 22, John du Pont was born in Philadelphia Lying-In Hospital, the last of William and Jean's four children. The first child, also named Jean, was born in 1923. Evelyn arrived two years later, and William Henry—who would later strike the "William" from his name—two years after that. John was, by far, the baby. His siblings ranged in age from eleven to fifteen when he came home.

The du Pont estate was, as it is today, a sprawling, private enclave, a world unto itself. More fiefdom than home, its forests and glens were filled with pheasant, deer, and other wild game, and its sparkling streams and ponds teemed with fish.

But life was not quite so idyllic inside the neoclassical manse.

By the time John was born, the cracks in the du Pont marriage were apparent. Jean and William seemed to move in different directions. Jean loved being on the farm, tending to her animals. At times she appeared almost single-minded in her pursuit of horse show ribbons; she and her three oldest children were frequently photographed for the society pages in carriages, astride horses, and with the ever-present beagles.

William liked his independence. Called "Dirty Willie" by his peers for his less-than-careful attention to personal hygiene, he was distant from the family. On outings, for instance, he would ride alone in one car as the rest of the family followed in another.

William already had a yen for lean, sinewy horses. He soon developed one for lean, sinewy athletes. He was first linked to a tennis star, Alice Marble. But it was Margaret Osborne, a Wimbledon women's singles champion and six-time doubles title-holder, who eventually became the second Mrs. du Pont in 1947, seven years after William went to Nevada in 1940 to get a Reno divorce from Jean.

William and his new wife settled on another du Pont estate, even larger than Foxcatcher, in Maryland. In 1952, at the age of 56, "Dirty Willie" became a father again. His new son was named William III.

Save an occasional hunting expedition with John, William du Pont never so much as took a quick look back at his first family. It is strange, then, to read the dedication in a book called *Off the Mat* that John had Larry Eastland ghostwrite for him in 1987:

"To my beloved father, William du Pont Jr., a great citizen, patriot, and winner, to whom I owe my life."

It seemed to be as great a fantasy as his later belief that he was the Dalai Lama.

In reality, du Pont's relationship with his father was nearly nonexistent. It was only after du Pont got his driver's license that his contact with his father increased.

But before he went to see him, du Pont had to make an appointment a week in advance. And once the two were together, the conversation was rarely more than a status report of du Pont's academic progress and other activities. The encounters were more like business meetings than a father-son get-together.

Years later, a psychologist who examined du Pont would say: "It is clear that he still harbors a great resentment for the perceived rejection and coldness he experienced in the relationship with his father."

John du Pont was just two in 1940 when his parents' divorce became final, and he was left all but alone with his mother in the huge mansion. His sisters and brother were away at school, and soon would be leaving the estate for good to begin their own families.

Perhaps in reaction to her failed marriage, Jean du Pont discovered a new passion around the time of the divorce: Welsh ponies. Over the decades she bred, raised, and sold more than six hundred of them; in fact, Liseter Welsh ponies all but became a breed unto themselves.

George Clardy, a longtime hand on the estate, said her routine rarely varied. She would start early in the morning at the barn, asking about the ponies. She'd move on to the greenhouse to see about her orchids. She might then visit other horsebarns, where the hunting horses were kept.

"She was simply a marvelous woman," said John Girvin, a classmate of John du Pont's. "She managed that place with a strong hand."

The hands-on attention she lavished on her horses and flowers, though, was not always duplicated with her young son. Du Pont once described his mother as a woman who was "cold, cunning, and conniving who always got what she wanted."

To him, family life meant being indulged in a fashion

reserved for royalty. And, he would admit to a psychiatrist years later, there was little discipline.

"No one ever said 'no' to John," said Terry Wochok.

Despite his mother's indulgence to his whims, until he was twelve years old, John du Pont was not permitted at the dinner table; he ate with the servants. The prevailing attitude was that children should not be seen or heard.

It wasn't until he reached college in Florida and lived with two families that he realized what he had missed. By then, he was already having trouble with long-term or intimate relationships. Asked once if he ever had such a relationship, he answered, half-jokingly, that he had—with his pet dogs. Most of his boyhood acquaintances were either children of the hired help or were discreetly bribed to share their time with him.

"He never knew what a meaningful relationship was like," Wochok said. "Whatever he needed was provided by a servant—he was driven to and from school by a chauffeur who was paid, at school an older boy was paid to sort of look after him. It's all he ever knew. If you needed friends, you went out and bought them."

Many years later, du Pont seemed to acknowledge that when he said, "The way other people collect horses, I collect people."

Du Pont attended the Haverford School, an elite school for boys on the Main Line where students wore red blazers to classes. Young, gangly John was a marginal student at best, with a stutter that he would take into adulthood.

He had a short attention span, something both acquaintances and employees would notice about him. Plagued by an awkwardness that was often perceived—sometimes not mistakenly—for aloofness, he yearned, like all young boys, for acceptance. He sought that as a swimmer and, ironically, as a wrestler—much as young David Schultz would twenty years later on the other side of the continent.

As would become du Pont's habit, he fell short of the star status that he craved in both sports.

At Haverford School, he was taken under the wing of a history teacher, or "Master" as the instructors there were called. Donald Brownlow taught American History and was du Pont's teacher in twelfth grade. Mentor and pupil became close.

"He didn't have a father to speak of, his father was interested in other things besides his family," said Brownlow. "So John sought out the Masters, and attached himself to them."

Unlike some others at Haverford School, Brownlow would not indulge du Pont. He failed him, requiring the young millionaire to attend summer school and miss a trip to Europe that Brownlow was leading.

"Life was pretty soft for him, and that kind of shocked him," Brownlow said. "He found out that he had to work and learn a little bit, that you can't allow money to do it all for you. He respected me for doing it."

Brownlow's patient but no-nonsense handling of John appealed to his mother. Jean du Pont asked Brownlow to take a more personal interest in her son and spend more time with him. But he was apprehensive of such involvement.

"I told her that John had his mind, and I have mine," Brownlow said.

Even so, Brownlow maintained a lifelong friendship with du Pont.

While du Pont may have missed that summer trip with Brownlow, the two did travel together over the years. Brownlow, a former army intelligence officer during World War II with ties to the international community, introduced du Pont to world leaders, such as Anwar Sadat, the president of Egypt.

Brownlow and du Pont also visited Albert Speer, Adolf Hitler's favorite architect, after Speer was released from

Spandau Prison following a twenty-year sentence for war crimes. At the time, Speer was living in Heidelberg, with his wife and two St. Bernard dogs. Years later, the meeting would generate another twisted tale from du Pont's mind as he insisted that Speer made him the heir to Hitler's Third Reich, and that he and David Schultz were to serve as co-Fuhrers.

"He was a heck of a nice kid and a gentleman, quiet, not obnoxious," Brownlow said. "He got along with other kids although he might not have been palsy-walsy."

His classmates, in a stroke of schoolboy wickedness, voted him both "most lazy" and "most likely to succeed," obvious nods to his intrinsic shortcomings and the likely consequence of the fortune that was his birthright.

About the same time, du Pont was developing a fascination, almost an obsession, with seashells and sea life. As a boy, he would do much as other children do at the shore, wandering the beach picking up shells that caught his eye. But whereas other parents might allow their little ones to keep a few and toss the rest, John's mother indulged his collecting fever to ridiculous proportions.

"Mother didn't chase me or my collections out of the house," he said in 1980. "So, rather than chase me or both out, she encouraged both."

Dozens of young du Pont's treasures become hundreds, and hundreds became thousands, until a whole section of the mansion's third floor was dedicated to his burgeoning hoard.

His mother bought stuffed birds and eggs to add to the collection and naturalists and artists were recruited to create backgrounds and settings. Although much of the meaningful work was done by professional scientists, du Pont was able to dazzle his youthful friends with his own expertise, letting them assume that what they were seeing was very much his own product.

The third-floor museum would later evolve into an actual one, the Delaware Museum of Natural History, incorporated in 1957 when du Pont graduated from high school. It took another ten years before he began planning the construction of a museum, largely made possible by the $80 million he inherited from his father, who died on the last day of 1965. It wasn't until 1972, though, that the museum building was finished, in Greenville, Delaware, near another du Pont property, Winterthur. When it opened, the facility held an impressive collection of millions of specimens, including shells, skins, and stuffed birds, and a world-class library. It also published *Nemouria*, a scientific journal.

"Things came in by the truckload," du Pont said. "To tape them, organize them, categorize them, build exhibits, search them, build an auditorium, a projection system, a lecture system, and all the other things that go with them is a monumental thing that does not happen overnight. Although we have a staff of about twenty people, it took us years to unravel some of these things."

Du Pont's foray into natural science was a story to be repeated over and over again during his life—money spent freely in order to attract honor and respect. In this case, he hired R. Tucker Abbott from Philadelphia's Academy of Natural Sciences to plan and stock his museum. Abbott was the director of shell collections while du Pont was anointed overall director. Du Pont, though, long ago relinquished the title and is not involved with the museum. However, 400 acres of Foxcatcher land—adjacent to John du Pont's four hundred acres—had been deeded to the museum by Jean du Pont.

Du Pont and Abbott, an expert on mollusks, had traveled the world in search of specimens, making expeditions to the Philippines, Samoa, the Fiji Islands and Australia's Great Barrier Reef. From the journeys, du Pont turned into an author—or, at least, had his name attached to three books. The first was about shells. His next was *Philippine Birds*, the third *Birds of the South Pacific*.

However, five years after he hired Abbott, they had a falling-out. As he would do in other, similar situations, du Pont fired his expert.

And as would happen with some degree of frequency, a lawsuit ensued. Abbott pressed for money he felt he was owed, and the matter was resolved out of court.

Du Pont graduated from The Haverford School in 1957 and enrolled at the University of Pennsylvania, but lasted less than a year. He was as bereft of academic zeal there as he was at Haverford, and college social life left him limp. Unlike his older brother Henry, who cut a dashing figure among the ladies—and would marry three of them—John seemed indifferent to girls. Nor did he give any indication that he found males more attractive. It was, as others would say later, as if du Pont were asexual.

His next stop was the University of Miami where he majored in marine biology, seemingly a nice fit for his acknowledged interest in natural history, and participated on the varsity swim team in 1962 and 1963. His time in South Florida also led him to become the largest single contributor to the International Swimming Hall of Fame in Fort Lauderdale.

Buoyed by his Miami swimming experience, du Pont made a leap into the world of big-time athletics when his name helped him get a place on the world-famous Santa Clara Swim Club. This was the powerhouse that produced a legion of superstars like Donna de Varona, Don Schollander, Lynn Burke, and Mark Spitz.

The coach was the legendary George Haines.

"One of my assistant coaches met John at a college championship, and John had asked if he could come out and swim at Santa Clara in the summer," said Haines. "I kind of pooh-poohed it at first. But then I thought about it and said he could, if he didn't think he could buy his way on. He'd have to pay his dues. And I told him that.''

Haines was skeptical. But that soon turned to admira-
tion. Du Pont had an athlete's regimen. He worked hard
and never missed a practice.

Haines could see, however, that du Pont just didn't
have the talent to be a world-class competitor. ''It was
clear that he wasn't going anywhere in swimming,'' said
Haines. ''I had to make sure I'd put him in lanes where
he wasn't going to impede anyone. But he was all right.
He wanted to be with the best athletes. He just loved being
around those people.''

Du Pont was extremely appreciative for the chance. He
told Haines that he didn't have access to much money at
that point, but knew he was in line for a large inheritance.
Over the years, Haines said, du Pont contributed about
$500,000 to the club.

The real swimmers adopted du Pont like a mascot,
dragging him along to their parties and informal outings.
De Varona recalled that du Pont, despite his wealth, often
had no loose change for a soft drink or an ice-cream cone.

In 1969, though, he did have enough spare change to
help a water polo team travel to Germany. The De Anza
Aquatic Foundation in Cupertino, California, qualified for
the World Club Championships in Berlin as the top club
team in the country. But it had no money for the trip. The
team was practicing at the same pool used by the Santa
Clara Swim Club, and du Pont wandered over to talk to
one of the coaches. When he heard the story, he pulled
out his checkbook and wrote a check for $19,000 on the
spot. He was named the team manager and traveled with
the squad to Germany. A picture from then shows du Pont
dressed in the De Anza sweats, posing next to the club
banner.

Bob Lee, an assistant coach, sat next to du Pont on the
flight to Europe.

''I remember asking him, 'What do you do?' '' said

Lee. "And he looked at me and said 'Do?' I said, 'Yeah, do you have a job?' He said he didn't really have a job, but was curator of the Delaware Museum of Natural History."

When the club landed in Paris late, it missed its connecting flight to Berlin. Du Pont walked up to the Pan Am desk and tried to charter a 727.

"I'll never forget this," said Lee. "He opened his briefcase and took out what I thought was a stock certificate. It was a letter of credit from Chase Manhattan Bank for one million dollars. All of a sudden all these people started running around, trying to help. They couldn't charter a plane, but they did hold one up so we could get on."

The team planned to pass through Checkpoint Charlie into East Berlin, which at that time was still a no-man's-land. But du Pont refused to go.

"He didn't want to show his passport because he was convinced they would see his name," said Lee. "And because of who he was he had reason to believe he'd be a target of the Communist government."

The last night of the trip, Lee said, was spent in Barcelona. Members of the team grabbed du Pont, stripped him to his boxer shorts, taped his wrists and ankles together, and dumped him outside on the street.

"I thought he'd be furious," said Lee. "But the next day he said to the head coach, 'Hey, I think the team likes me.' "

Because he was becoming bicoastal, du Pont needed a place to stay during the long California trips. In the late 1960s, flush with his father's inheritance, he purchased both a home in posh Atherton, south of San Francisco, and a twelve-hundred-acre ranch in Watsonville, on Monterey Bay, where he raised Black Angus cattle and had fields of strawberries and artichokes.

The purchase of the ranch in Santa Cruz's Pajaro Valley in 1967 was the largest land deal in Santa Cruz

County history at the time, and Haines tells a funny story about it. Du Pont, he said, was bidding for the property with three other parties. One group agreed on a $7 million price, but asked for time to go to the bank to set up the financing.

"John said, 'I don't have to go to the bank to put the deal together,' " said Haines. "And he took out his checkbook and wrote out a check for $7 million on the hood of a car."

Du Pont's place in upscale Atherton was a ten-thousand-square-foot mansion on three acres that he used as a getaway retreat. He kept himself apart from the party life of high society but sought out the company of local cops, as he did in Pennsylvania. He would flash his Newtown Township badge to impress the California police and offered to help train local officers.

While the police chief there fended off du Pont's offer, officers did accompany du Pont to the ranch for target practice and rides in the armored personnel carrier that would become a fixture at Foxcatcher. And when du Pont did have small social gatherings in Atherton, he never served alcohol. Haines, in fact, said he never, ever saw du Pont drink when he knew him in California. But he would later see tragic bouts of alcoholism in Pennsylvania.

Du Pont showered donations on police groups in the Atherton area, including a contribution toward the purchase of a police dog. He also shared with police his worry about his own safety; one of his sisters had received a kidnap threat, he said, which heightened his concern.

Despite the opulence of the Atherton mansion, and the Santa Cruz ranch, swimming great de Varona—who visited Foxcatcher and met Jean du Pont—felt a twinge of sympathy for someone she sensed was a lonely outsider.

"Here was a man who could buy just about anything,".

she said, "and what he wanted was to be a great swimmer. He wanted what he could not have."

Then, Haines and other du Pont friends in athletics hit upon an idea that might just work in helping du Pont achieve the recognition and acceptance he craved. One of the more arcane and lesser-known Olympic sports is the modern pentathlon, a five-part event that includes swimming, cross-country running, horseback riding, fencing, and marksmanship.

Du Pont had tortured himself into being an above-average swimmer. He had been shooting guns since he first picked up a rifle at the age of ten at summer camp in Maine, and he seemed to have an affinity for it. Because of his mother, du Pont had been around horses since birth. That left running and fencing, two skills that could prove manageable.

In his quest for a spot on the U.S. Olympic pentathlon team, du Pont had a number of advantages. First of all, there was little competition. The disparate skills demanded by the event narrowed the field considerably. Secondly, among du Pont's competitors, none could muster the resources to provide his own training facilities in the way he could.

Foxcatcher Farm was a pentathlete's dream. Du Pont already owned horses, and there was room aplenty for riding and jumping. Cross-country trails were hacked out through the woods. Fencing needed no more room than a good-sized training room. Du Pont would go on to build both a fifty-meter Olympic swimming pool and a state-of-the-art firing range that was a replica of the FBI training facility in Quantico, Virginia.

Years later, in his book *Off the Mat*, du Pont recalled his time of turning the farm into an athletic facility for himself. But he attached a larger purpose to it.

"Even as I cleared running trails and training areas for myself, I knew that someday I would be able to do the same for others. It was more than idle interest. It was my responsibility.''

Du Pont hired the finest coaches available. Lajos Csiszar, a fencing instructor at the University of Pennsylvania, taught him how to handle an épée. Villanova's famous track coach, Jumbo Elliott, helped him with his running. Haines had been his mentor in swimming and he continued his training under Ed Geisz, another Villanova coach.

Du Pont threw himself into his training, trying to make the U.S. squad for the 1968 Olympics in Mexico City. In 1965, he did win the Australian Pentathlon, but the distinction was a dubious one, triumphing as he did in a locale where the competition was scant.

Two years later, du Pont took on more formidable rivals at the U.S. Championships. The deck was stacked in his favor because the event was held on Foxcatcher, where he had the advantage of familiarity with the venue. He finished fourteenth out of twenty-nine.

In 1968, the Olympic year, twenty-two athletes vied for three spots on the U.S. pentathlon team that would go to Mexico. Du Pont finished twenty-first. (Du Pont would realize part of his dream eight years later when he joined the 1976 Olympic pentathlon squad, but it was as team manager. A picture of the club, in USA warm-up suits, is included in *Off the Mat*, although the caption does not mention du Pont's role.)

Although he didn't make the 1968 team, he did make news. Both *Sports Illustrated* and *Life* magazines did stories about his athletic pursuits.

He made the comics, too. For three months in 1968, du Pont appeared as a character in the Steve Canyon adventure comic strip. The idea came from the United States Olympic Committee, according to Milton Caniff, the strip's cartoonist. The USOC wanted to spur interest in the games, thought the pentathlon was interesting, and suggested to Caniff that he talk to du Pont about the sport.

That gave birth to a dashing and rich gadabout named Jeff Newtown—the surname deriving from du Pont's hometown.

But with his failure to make the 1968 Olympics, du Pont, now thirty years old, put an abrupt end to his own pursuit of athletic glory and started casting about for other ways to keep himself occupied. If he couldn't compete, he could become a patron and benefactor of those who could, sort of a Medici to aspiring Olympians. He already had a huge head start: his estate held an indoor Olympic-style swimming pool. Perhaps as inspiration, perhaps as a monument to himself, one wall of the pool facility was decorated with a huge mosaic of du Pont in the varied poses of the pentathlon.

He also had room to run on his property. So in the early 1970s he created the Foxcatcher Swim Club, the first of several Foxcatcher programs designed to grow the best athletes.

"The idea was to have a place where you could have an athletic academy environment," said Wochok. "John's facility was a place where you could have the freedom to have extensive training sessions, where kids could come in at six-thirty in the morning before school, then come back from late afternoon and into the evening after school."

Frank Keefe, who was coaching at the nearby Suburban Swim Club, gladly accepted du Pont's offer to bring his youngsters to Foxcatcher to train and soon became the first swim coach for Team Foxcatcher. When Keefe left to run Yale's program in the fall of 1978, du Pont looked west and hired his old teacher from Santa Clara, George Haines, who agree to a reported $75,000 a year for five years. Haines admitted it was an offer he couldn't refuse.

"He's a perfectionist, and he wants to have a good team here," Haines said at the time. "I think he means it, too. Otherwise, I wouldn't be here."

The mere presence of Haines at Foxcatcher attracted young, talented swimmers from across the country. Families moved to the area to be part of du Pont's grand experiment. With a stunning swimming pool and facilities for aerobic and weight training, du Pont held the promise of providing American youngsters with a luxurious hothouse environment in which to train and be able to compete against the Soviet Union and Eastern European athletes who had the advantage of state-sponsored programs. At one point, 325 swimmers were using the Foxcatcher facilities.

Du Pont eagerly awaited the 1980 Olympics scheduled for Moscow, anticipating the honor that would be his when members of Team Foxcatcher, wearing red, white, and blue, would stride to the victory stand to hear the "Star-Spangled Banner" played as the American flag was hoisted.

It was not to be. The Soviet invasion of Afghanistan prompted President Jimmy Carter to boycott the Moscow Games, and du Pont saw all his efforts go for naught. He became disillusioned, and all but disbanded the club.

"He got discouraged," said Haines. "And he was drinking a lot then. He came over one day, drunk, and he said we're not going to the Olympics, there's no point in having the program anymore. And that was it. This was in January. I talked him into letting me stay until September, when the summer season was over.

"Du Pont was drinking nearly all the time," Haines said. "He was in a stupor a lot of times. His mother came over to me, and said, 'Can't you do something?' I told her I talked to him about it every day. He'd cry and say he would quit, and I'd think I had him talked out of it. But he just continued."

Sometimes the drinking led to dangerous behavior. Haines was fishing on the estate with his son once when du Pont joined them. But he didn't get any bites.

"So he reached behind him and took out this .45 and started shooting at the geese," said Haines. "The bullets were going about four feet from my son. I ran over and grabbed the gun and knocked him down. And I could smell the liquor on him.

"If I had known he was drinking like that, I never would have left California to go to Foxcatcher. It's too bad, too, because he did a lot of good for a lot of people."

Haines returned to California, where a year later he became coach of the Stanford University women's swimming and diving team. He's now retired.

Families who had been counting on du Pont's continued support groped for ways to recover and find other, suitable swim programs for their young athletes. Du Pont did revive the swimming program at Foxcatcher not long after Haines left, but on a very limited basis; Olympic-bound swimmers such as David Wharton worked out there, representing Foxcatcher in world-class meets.

When du Pont stepped away from the swimmers, he turned some of his attention to flowers. He hired orchid expert Van Ewart to work in the greenhouse. That, though, was over in a year. Ewart was unceremoniously booted off the farm. When he came to collect his plants and instruments, he was turned away. In 1981 he sued; it was settled out of court.

Two years later another new arrival came to Foxcatcher: John du Pont's wife.

She lasted less time than Van Ewart.

Gale Wenk, from Olney, a working-class section of Philadelphia, was chief occupational therapist at Crozer-Chester Medical Center, a complex off Route 95 near the Pennsylvania-Delaware border. Du Pont met her in 1982 when he was undergoing treatment of a hand injury. He was forty-four, she twenty-eight.

The relationship began around a table in the therapy room, where patients and workers gathered. Wenk was talking about her work on a committee that was, pushing for passage of a state bill requiring OTs to be licensed. Backers of the bill believed it would lead to better controls in the profession. Du Pont overheard Wenk complaining that the legislative session was likely to end before the bill was heard. He asked some questions about it.

"Let me see what I can do," he said.

Wenk thought: "Yeah, right."

Not long after she heard from the lobbyist that the bill had passed.

"Next time I saw John I asked him about it," said Wenk. "He said, 'I pulled in a few favors.' How true that was I don't know."

For the official bill signing, Wenk planned to go to Harrisburg, the state capital, about a hundred miles away. Du Pont offered to take her. He did—in his helicopter. They were met by a state trooper, who drove them to the Capitol. Then they flew back.

"He was very quiet, kind of shy, almost seemed like he was looking for friends," Wenk said. "What really impressed me was the fact that he just became part of the group with all the rest of the patients. We had had people come in before who were celebrities, and they had to be treated privately. That wasn't the case with him. He would joke around. He really would do anything for people.

"We had a therapist around that time who was a temporary, and we took Wenk out for breakfast on her last day. He asked if he could come along. He just wanted to be involved with her send-off."

It wasn't until months later, though, that they had their first date—if a trip to California can be called a date. Du Pont was due to be discharged from therapy. He came to Wenk just before.

"I want to go to California," he said, "but the doctor told me I can't go unless I continue therapy."

Wenk said no problem, he would have a home exercise

program. Du Pont said he felt he needed a therapist to
come with him.

"I'm a person who always takes a dare," said Wenk,
"so I said, 'I'll go.' He said, 'Are you serious?' And I
said, 'As serious as you are.' "

On his next visit, she said, he walked in with a first-
class plane ticket. They had a pleasant time and began to
see each other regularly.

Wenk lived in Brookhaven, in the same county as—
but a world away from—du Pont. She'd have him to her
town house for dinner, or they'd go out to eat. They met
each other's friends. On December 28, at a Christmas
party dinner at the mansion, du Pont asked to speak to
Wenk's parents. They went into the library; there, he
asked them for permission to marry their daughter.

"The rest of the night my mother didn't talk to me,
almost ignored me," said Wenk. "And the next day was
my birthday, and she didn't even call. I didn't know what
was wrong."

Nothing was wrong; Wenk's mother was just afraid of
spilling the beans. Du Pont wanted to pop the question
when he took Wenk out for her twenty-ninth birthday.

"I guess I was really surprised, but by the end of dinner
I had made up my mind," Wenk said.

The engagement was announced in January 1983, but
not before Wenk agreed to two things: a prenuptial contract, and an agreement to be married in Christ Church
Christiana Hundred, the family church in Greenville, Delaware. She had no problem with the church, and attorneys
hashed out the prenuptial agreement that said, in the case
of a divorce, Wenk would receive $27,000 annually for
each year that the marriage had lasted. That was a little
more than she was earning at the hospital. The wedding
was set for September 24.

The only concern Wenk had was du Pont's drinking.
Three or four times she had seen du Pont drink to excess.

And she thought he popped too many painkillers.

"I didn't really know that much about alcoholism," she said. "I thought an alcoholic was someone who was drunk all the time, and he wasn't. As I look back I realize he was having just enough to keep him on an even keel. If he knew he was going to see me, he'd drink during the day, sleep it off, and by night he'd be fine."

But du Pont was never violent. Just the opposite, said Wenk. On the twenty-fourth of each month she would get a certain number of roses, one for each month until the wedding. And after she shattered her ankle in a car accident, du Pont would cook and clean in her town house and do her grocery shopping.

The couple took trips to England and Scotland and Hawaii. Du Pont was having a ranch house built on the estate; he designed the layout, Wenk was in charge of the furnishings. There were so many details for the wedding that she quit her job in the summer.

But Wenk was, by all accounts, not the woman Jean du Pont would have liked to end her son's bachelorhood.

"You could tell she was very apprehensive about us getting married," said Wenk. "At the time I remember thinking that she thought I was after John for his money."

Wenk also was troubled by the relationship between mother and son. It consisted, she thought, of equal parts affection and resentment. "I think a lot of what he did, he did to please her."

The wedding was a festive event, with a reception for five hundred guests at the Vicmead Hunt Club in nearby Centerville, Delaware. There the couple was greeted by uniformed trumpeters from Valley Forge Military Academy. There were fireworks to mark the nuptials, and the next day the du Ponts jetted to Atherton for still another celebration. The three-week honeymoon trip took them to Australia and a number of South Pacific islands.

Mr. and Mrs. du Pont stopped in Atherton on their return.

Almost immediately the marriage started to crumble.

Du Pont had received a number of calls from Foxcatcher, and it set him on edge. Wenk tried to calm him down. He got even more upset.

Then he shoved her.

"I remember thinking, 'Whoa, what's going on here?'" said Wenk. "But I thought a lot has happened, we just got married, we're moving into a new house. I kind of put it behind me as a freak incident." It wasn't.

Not long after returning to Foxcatcher, du Pont's aunt, Anna Austin died. Du Pont consoled himself with drink. There was more pushing and shoving. The drinking became more open. The violence became more frequent.

At one point, Wenk tried to set up an intervention meeting with some family members and friends. Terry Wochok, she said, told du Pont about it. Du Pont got angry. "Whatever you're planning," he said, "forget it. I won't show up."

Today, Wochok denies Wenk's version of events. "It's just not true," he said.

At the end of October, barely a month after the wedding, Wenk left. When she returned a few days later, it was the start of a pattern: off and on the estate.

"The majority of time I was living in fear," said Wenk. "There was never any predictability. But as time went on the episodes got more violent and closer together."

Du Pont, she said, never apologized. In fact, he never acknowledged he had done anything. He told her that she was simply unable to handle the elevated station in life she had joined by marrying him.

She decided to go back to work, but didn't tell her husband she was interviewing for a job. She was afraid of his reaction.

Before they were married, du Pont and Wenk were at

a party when a friend inquired about Wenk's heritage. When she replied that her mother's background was Russian, the friend turned to du Pont, and kiddingly warned, "Watch out, John, you're marrying a Russian spy."

One night months later Wenk had gone to bed while du Pont watched television in the living room. Just as Wenk was slipping into sleep, du Pont came into the bedroom and turned on the TV. He came across a program that included what sounded like loud, march music.

"I'm tired," said Wenk. "Either turn that down, or go into another room."

"You're just not patriotic enough," du Pont said.

He got out of bed, walked to his dresser, and took out a gun.

"You know what the problem is?" he said. "The problem is you're a Russian spy. You know what they do with spies, don't you? They shoot them."

He moved to the bed, and put the barrel of the gun to Wenk's head.

In retrospect, that might have been a short, quick glimpse of the paranoid schizophrenia, including the delusions about Soviet invaders, that would later haunt du Pont. And like du Pont's later claim that he inherited the Third Reich from Albert Speer, the Russian spy accusation had been embellished greatly from a small grain of truth.

The reference to Wenk's mother being from Russian stock had stuck in du Pont's mind and apparently led to a suspicion his wife was a spy. Wenk first thought he was playing. But the gun against her temple convinced her otherwise. Then du Pont suddenly stopped talking, put the gun away, turned off the TV, and walked out.

Not long after, Wenk invited her parents to the estate to talk with her husband. Du Pont was belligerent, she said, and he walked out to his car. Wenk followed. She opened the car door.

"We have to talk," she said. "You can't run away from this."

Du Pont responded by putting the car in reverse and pushing her out the door. She went back into the house.

"My parents said I had to make a choice," said Wenk. "Either make a clean break and say I wasn't coming back until he got help, or stay and take my life into my own hands."

She packed up. It was March 1984, less than six months after she and du Pont had exchanged vows. When she returned a couple of months later to retrieve her belongings, she found du Pont had invited one of his workers to live in the house with him.

Wochok handled the divorce for his boss. He figured du Pont and Wenk had spent a total of ninety-three days together. But the financial settlement wasn't as cut-and-dried as the prenuptial agreement was supposed to make it. Wenk later said she was coerced into signing it and filed a suit in which she asked for $5 million in punitive damages.

The divorce wasn't official until 1987. And it wasn't until 1991 that Wenk received any money; the court papers were sealed. In 1990 she moved to Carlisle, near Harrisburg, where she resumed her career.

Du Pont, meanwhile, spent a good part of 1984 locked in a brutal dispute with his siblings, including his half brother William III. The rancor was precipitated by the death of his other close aunt, Marion du Pont Scott, just before his wedding. At issue was what would be done with the real Montpelier, the 2,677-acre Virginia estate that had been Scott's home, and the multimillion dollar trust fund that was tied to it.

Scott wanted it turned into a public museum, and left $10 million to the National Trust for Historic Preservation. Du Pont's brother, Henry, wanted to live in it and filed suit to overturn her will.

Scott's will had actually served to overturn the will of her father, William Sr. She had inherited Montpelier from him, and he directed that at her death the estate go to either his son, William, Jr., or junior's five children: John, Henry, Jean, Evelyn, and William III.

John sided with Henry; the other three stuck together. Thirty-seven children of the siblings joined the suit, as did twenty-five lawyers. It wasn't until October, 1984— a full year after Aunt Marion's death—that Henry walked away with $2 million and Montpelier was opened to the public.

John du Pont, meanwhile, became more and more withdrawn. His marriage was over, his brothers and sisters were all bickering viciously. Drink became his best friend.

Then he found something new: the emerging sport of triathlon, a mega-endurance event that combines long-distance swimming, road cycling, and a marathon. Du Pont's estate became available to prepare American athletes for competitions such as the famous Ironman Triathlon in Hawaii. Among the top-flight triathletes who trained at Foxcatcher were Ken Glah and Joy Hansen Leutner. Both enjoyed a fistful of spectacular finishes and championships as Foxcatcher athletes. Hansen Leutner, who lived at Foxcatcher from 1990–92, said it was du Pont who talked to her and convinced her she should not give up after a debilitating illness.

"He changed my life," she said. "He's impacted so many lives."

She was so grateful for du Pont's support during a stressful period that she had her fiancé seek her hand in marriage from du Pont. She saw du Pont, she said, as a "father figure."

Du Pont came to see himself as a father, too—the father of the American triathlon. So much so, that he had himself immortalized in a small way.

He put himself on a stamp.

The stamp is from Redonda, one of the three islands that make up the nation of Antigua and Barbuda in the eastern Caribbean. It is a large, uninhabited rock.

On the $5 stamp and sheet—five Eastern Caribbean dollars being worth about $2.50 in America—du Pont is called "Father of Triathlon in the Americas." He is depicted running, swimming, and bicycling. Across his chest, on a blue running shirt, are the words Team Foxcatcher.

Victor Krievens, a stamp dealer who once worked for du Pont, explained how the stamp came to be.

"John and I were sitting around having dinner," Krievens recalled, "and John said, 'How do you get on a postage stamp?'

"I said, 'John, here are the rules. In the United States, you have to be dead. So we can't put you on a U.S. stamp.' So he asked, 'Where else can I go?' And I said, 'I have a friend who can handle this.' "

The friend had access to numerous governments willing to issue a personalized stamp for cash. Du Pont paid $10,000. A European artist created the drawings, and a design was put together. On June 15, 1987, the du Pont stamp was introduced at a first-day-of-issue ceremony in Canada.

But even as du Pont got a kick out of autographing the sheets and sending them to luminaries around the world— such as former President Gerald Ford—his interest in the triathlon was beginning to fray. He instead started to turn his sights on the world of amateur wrestling, a sport where he had enjoyed some success as a schoolboy.

Wrestling dated back to ancient Greece and the first Olympic Games. It was a sport of combat and individual strength. It was a sport where du Pont could become a leader of strong young men. It was a sport where he could become the self-anointed Head Coach, and perhaps finally be recognized as the champion he always thought he was.

Nine

Du Pont had toyed with the notion of starting a national-caliber wrestling program, and his initial step was to approach Villanova University, where he had maintained strong ties since his days as an Olympic hopeful in the pentathlon.

The college, founded in 1842, fits in neatly on Philadelphia's Main Line, just ten minutes north of Foxcatcher. A Catholic college run by the Augustinian order of priests, the school caters to a student body that is decidedly upscale. Football tailgate parties are more likely to feature tables set with linen and champagne glasses than wieners on the grill.

As an aspiring pentathlete, du Pont was helped in his training by Villanova swim coach Ed Geisz and legendary track coach Jim "Jumbo" Elliott. Elliott had gained international notoriety for guiding the careers of a long string of Olympic luminaries, such as Marty Liquori and Sidney Maree, and du Pont—able to afford the best—wanted to be trained by the best.

Elliott, though, seemed to take on more than a coaching role—at least in du Pont's mind. Du Pont's book, *Off the Mat*, is largely a collection of egotistical prattlings. But the words about Elliott, say those who have known du Pont the longest, ring true:

"Some people are born with the talent of people-reading," du Pont writes. "I have met only a few. Jumbo Elliott was one of them. He not only loved athletes, he was intensely interested in what came out the other end of the educational process, not just at the finish line. His was a talent to read the hidden messages.

"As my coach, he had the ability to look at me and see where I was in life at the moment. He knew how to motivate me, and how to show he cared. I felt his love for me as an athlete and as a human being."

Du Pont was even more straightforward during an interview with a newspaper reporter. "My mother and father were divorced when I was two," he said. "I spent a lifetime looking for a father, and I found one in Jumbo Elliott."

Terry Wochok says du Pont's special feeling for Elliott spurred his close relationship with Villanova.

"Jumbo was kind of a surrogate father for him, and if you look at John's life, it's as if he was searching for surrogate fathers all along," Wochok said.

In 1986, du Pont offered to fund a wrestling team at Villanova. The school's need for a wrestling squad was debatable, and enthusiasm for a wrestling program never seemed more than lukewarm. But Villanova had been extremely interested in building a new home for its basketball team and John du Pont had already helped bankroll a fifteen-million-dollar, sixty-four-hundred-seat arena. How much of the $15 million actually came from du Pont has never been revealed, but it was enough to put his name on the building.

Why a prestigious institution like Villanova would involve itself with du Pont is a now-familiar tale of how universities and their officials are seduced by the allure and riches associated with big-time sports.

Throughout the 1980s, Villanova had been one of college basketball's most glamorous programs, and the Wildcats capped a Cinderella 1985–86 season by beating

Georgetown in a thrilling NCAA championship game. The basketball program and its charismatic coach, Rollie Massamino, made the school one of the hottest tickets on the college scene, and prospective students, many from well-heeled families, were banging on the door to get in.

A new arena meant a great deal to Villanova. A new, more spacious arena meant more paying fans clicking through the turnstiles to watch Massamino's scrappy Wildcats. But more importantly, a state-of-the art facility would attract high-profile visiting teams that, in turn, meant more nationally televised games.

The bottom line was that a new arena could generate millions for the school.

But first, the school needed millions to build it.

John du Pont had the millions, and he had been generous with Villanova; among his gifts were $50,000 to the basketball program and $250,000 for a swimming pool. His checks also helped pay for much of the bricks and mortar that went into the new arena's construction. On Feb. 1, 1986, the John Eleuthère du Pont Pavilion opened its doors.

So when du Pont suggested that he be allowed to fund a new wrestling program, school officials found it hard to say, "No"—and hard to resist the appeal of a multimillionaire benefactor.

Less than a year after du Pont Pavilion opened, the wrestling program was in full swing. Chuck Yarnall was the coach—the title of "head coach" was reserved for du Pont—with Rob Calabrese and Mark Schultz, Dave's younger brother, the assistants. Dan Chaid arrived in the summer of 1987 to help with the program and to train at du Pont's new Foxcatcher facility. Two other wrestlers, Bill Hyman and Glen Goodman, also came aboard.

At Villanova, du Pont had a lofty ambition: to win a national wrestling title within five years. But he had a second, parallel plan that took place off campus: he wanted his own amateur wrestling organization, peopled with the best wrestlers on the planet.

That is how, at the same time the Villanova program was getting off the ground, Team Foxcatcher was born.

Sometimes, in fact, it was hard to tell if Foxcatcher was the offshoot of the Villanova venture, or if it was the other way around.

Du Pont and his coaches cost the university almost nothing. Their contracts paid them each $1 per year. Du Pont supplemented that by contributing $20,000 to $30,000 to their Olympic trust funds, which finance an Olympic athlete's training and are tax-free. (When that arrangement came to light two years later, the National Collegiate Athletic Association raised its eyebrows; it looked like a violation of its rules governing supplemental pay. By then, though, the program had been disbanded).

Amateur wrestlers who had to scrape for spare change for living expenses, while they underwent rigorous training, were suddenly offered thousands of dollars by du Pont in salaries and bonuses, plus free housing. Not many of the wrestlers du Pont sought could pass up that offer.

Du Pont gained access to the wrestlers through his relationship with USA Wrestling, a relationship that began in 1987 with a $100,000 donation. He gave the same the following year, and would raise that to an annual $400,000 from 1989 to 1995.

Mark Schultz, a tempestuous man who wore his emotions on his sleeve, was one of the first to join the Villanova/Foxcatcher fold; his hiring would prove to be an important thread as the lives of du Pont and Dave Schultz were destined to become entwined.

Yarnall, then thirty, was a graduate of Villanova and The Haverford School, du Pont's old high-school alma mater; du Pont had been on the wrestling team there three decades earlier. Calabrese, the 1981 Eastern college champion at 145 pounds at Temple University, would become

a long-term resident on the Foxcatcher estate. And Calabrese's father, a local contractor, went on to build the
training center at Foxcatcher Farm.

Ruminating about his lofty ambitions for the Villanova
program, du Pont tried to mirror the philosophy of his old
track mentor Jumbo Elliott.

"The kids are not just coming to Villanova to wrestle,"
he said during the program's first season. "I don't plan
on running this team like an animal factory. I want the
kids to graduate and become productive members of society."

Mark Schultz had his own ideas about what made a
top-notch wrestler.

"Ninety-five percent of wrestling is mental and everything depends on how bad you want it," he said. "You
need the gymnastic ability of an acrobat, the endurance
of a runner, the strength of a weightlifter, the mind of a
chess player, and the mental attitude of a psychotic
killer."

With du Pont, Massamino, and about two hundred
spectators in attendance, Villanova wrestled at the new
Pavilion on Jan. 12, 1987 for the first time. The Wildcats
beat Widener University, a local school situated nearby in
Chester, Pennsylvania. Du Pont's glowing appraisal of his
club's first home win sounded as if it was being read from
a script.

"The team is showing outstanding possibilities for the
future," he said. "Above all, they've proven themselves
to be good sportsmen and scholars."

The euphoria was short-lived, however. A month later,
Yarnall quit.

At the time, everyone, including the university and Yarnall, remained mum on why he walked away from the
program. Du Pont, school officials said, would function
as head coach.

Later, it was discovered that there had been a confrontation between Yarnall and Mark Schultz. Schultz, who had won an Olympic gold medal along with Dave in 1984 at the Los Angeles games, felt that Yarnall didn't know what it took to be a world-class winner. There was a bitter argument between the two, and there were reports that Schultz pinned Yarnall against a wall.

Schultz denied it, but admitted shouting at Yarnall.

"I never touched Chuck," Schultz said. "I was very frustrated and should never have yelled and been so intense with him. I get ticked off very easily; that's why I'm so good as a wrestler. I sincerely regret this incident ever happening."

Mark Schultz himself would resign in January 1988. Schultz said he wanted to concentrate on his own wrestling career and was aiming for the 1988 Olympic Games in Seoul, Korea.

Later, Schultz admitted he was forced to quit because of accusations that he treated the wrestlers to beers after meets. Not only does Villanova forbid alcoholic beverages on campus and at university-sanctioned functions, but most of Villanova's wrestlers were younger than the twenty-one-year-old legal drinking age in Pennsylvania.

"Sure, I took them out for a few beers," Schultz said. "What's the harm? I didn't care about what the administration wanted. I only cared about my kids."

By then du Pont had lured another champion into his web: Andre Metzger.

Metzger, one of the top wrestlers in the world, had been an assistant coach at Indiana in 1987 when du Pont went after him. But Metzger was already signed with the New York Athletic Club and was happy there.

Du Pont was persistent. He invited him to wrestle in an exhibition at Villanova. He took him around the farm. He eventually offered him a five-year contract, Metzger said, that included du Pont's unique incentive program— bonus money for winning matches.

Among the other items in the deal, according to Metzger:

- A $25,000 salary in each of the first two years, plus an unconditional $10,000 bonus each year.
- A promotion to head coach by the third year and a $70,000 salary in each of the last three years.
- A home in the Main Line area that would be purchased by du Pont and placed in the name of Metzger and his wife with fee simple ownership.

Metzger couldn't resist forever; he soon agreed to join the Villanova program, and switched his allegiance from the New York Athletic Club to Team Foxcatcher. Du Pont agreed to hire Metzger's buddy, Glen Goodman, for $10,000. Officially, Goodman was added to the hefty list of Villanova assistants. In reality, though, his job was to be Metzger's workout partner.

Metzger arrived at Villanova in the summer of 1987.

He departed a year later.

And if Villanova thought Mark Schultz's exit was bad, it paled in comparison to Metzger's sacking, which would lead to a messy and embarrassing accusation.

At the time, Villanova athletic director Ted Aceto merely said that Metzger's firing was precipitated by "philosophical differences." But the real reason, Metzger claimed later in an explosive lawsuit, was that du Pont wanted him to leave his wife and become his lover.

Metzger, then twenty-nine, said that if he accepted du Pont's proposal, du Pont promised to "deed the house over to [his] wife and make a financial settlement with her that would be worth her while on a yearly basis."

Du Pont's advances toward him were so offensive, Metzger said in the suit, that one night, as he was fending off du Pont's overtures, du Pont fell to his knees and grabbed him. Metzger said he locked himself in a room in the mansion.

After he was fired from Villanova, Metzger said, du Pont moved to evict his wife and three children from the house he had provided for the family in Newtown Square.

"Du Pont had promised that the house would be turned over to me," Metzger said. "He said it would be my house."

Metzger sought more than a half million dollars from du Pont and Villanova, which he accused of "gross and reckless" negligence for not providing "greater supervision and guidance" to the wrestlers. The damages sought included $255,000 in lost income and the threatened loss of the house, valued at approximately $300,000.

Du Pont scoffed at Metzger's charges.

"What comment could I possibly have other than to say it's ridiculous?" du Pont said at the time. "My friends and those who know me won't have any questions about this whatsoever, because they know this isn't true. But some people are going to believe what they read in a newspaper no matter what I say."

Du Pont insisted he wanted Metzger fired because Metzger had discouraged two wrestling recruits from attending Villanova. Apparently, Metzger was concerned that Villanova did not have a wrestling room for training purposes, and passed on that concern to the recruits.

He insisted Metzger was never promised a free house. While he did secure a house for him, it was a rental.

Nothing, though, was in writing—except for the May 31, 1988, letter Metzger received dismissing him from Villanova and Team Foxcatcher.

By the time Metzger was fired, Villanova was having its own second thoughts about du Pont and his wrestling program. Officials had come to realize that a bad bargain had been struck when they allowed a rich benefactor to have his own sports program to toy with in exchange for a fat donation to its athletic program. The relationship had created one headache after another, from the beer-drinking to the Metzger dismissal.

Beyond that, there were steady reports from wrestlers that du Pont attended practices intoxicated. Faculty members said they saw him drunk on campus. Du Pont's explanation: he was taking medicine that made him appear woozy.

There was the alleged rough stuff between Yarnall and Schultz.

There was the incident in which du Pont sought to have a scholarship athlete ousted from the program; a university committee unanimously overruled him.

And in early December 1987, there was a traffic mishap not far from the du Pont Pavilion that would hover over du Pont's murder trial nine years later.

Du Pont had left practice at Villanova in midafternoon and was headed for Foxcatcher. He was in a hurry to catch a flight for Wisconsin for a wrestling meet. On the road just outside the Pavilion, du Pont struck a flagman, Lonnie Harris, with his car.

Harris, fifty-seven, was trying to halt traffic for a cement-truck driver when du Pont's 1986 Lincoln Town Car, traveling fifteen to twenty miles an hour, hit him and lifted him onto the hood of the luxury car. As du Pont slammed on the brakes, Harris hit the ground with a sickening thud.

Du Pont, wearing a blue Villanova wrestling jacket, exited the car and tried to lift Harris to his feet. "You're not hurt that bad," du Pont said.

"That wasn't all he said," Harris told an investigator years later. "He said I was so black he couldn't see me. Then he said, 'You black people are so strong, you'll survive.' "

Du Pont identified himself as the Villanova wrestling coach. He stayed at the scene for about five minutes, then left before police or an ambulance could arrive.

That was illegal.

Edward Meagher, who worked for Villanova at the time, said he saw the accident and took du Pont's license-plate number as he left.

"He slammed on his brakes, moved the car over a little, and he slurred the words, 'You'll be all right,' " Meagher said. "I yelled at him as he drove away and took his number."

Du Pont ignored the shouts. He scooted home, pulling into the estate and heading for the helicopter hangar, where Chaid, Calabrese and a du Pont aide, Bob Powers, were waiting. They had been told to be there precisely at three-thirty; the plan was to take the helicopter to Philadelphia International Airport and then board a plane for Wisconsin.

Du Pont got out of the car. He was, said Chaid, clearly drunk.

"He was rather flustered," said Chaid. "He got out of the car, and he said, 'Don't anybody say a word.' "

They flew silently to the airport. When the Learjet took off, climbing high over Pennsylvania, du Pont said, "Now I can tell you. I was pulling out of the Butler annex at Villanova and I hit a guy in my car. I think I killed him."

Du Pont's plane mates were dumbfounded. They didn't know what to say.

They landed in Madison, and were met by Dave Schultz, at the time an assistant coach at the University of Wisconsin. He and du Pont had been introduced a few years before in 1984, shortly after the Olympic games.

While Schultz was on his way to the airport, Nancy Schultz got several calls from Terry Wochok. He needed to talk with du Pont. It was urgent.

Du Pont, Schultz, and the others walked in about ninety minutes later.

"I could tell as soon as they all got there they were all very, very upset," said Nancy Schultz.

Du Pont called Wochok. Nancy Schultz wanted to know what was going on.

"What happened?" she asked. "Is there something I can do?"

Du Pont turned to her. "I hit someone and left," he barked.

There was a discussion around the table. Then they all drove to the wrestling match. Du Pont's presence was announced. He walked out onto the mat and was given a sweatshirt. He was there for five minutes. Everyone got back in the car, drove to the airport, and returned to Philadelphia.

Police, meanwhile, had tried to contact du Pont at his estate, but were told he had just departed. The next day police were more successful. Du Pont was cited for violating a law requiring a driver in an accident to give information and render aid. In explanation, du Pont said he told Harris and a witness that he was the Villanova wrestling coach and had to catch an airplane for the out-of-town match. Because he believed Harris was not seriously hurt, and because he had sufficiently identified himself, he left.

In the end, du Pont paid a $42.50 fine and the matter was laid to rest, according to police. No criminal complaint was filed.

The flagman, Lonnie Harris, had been taken to a local hospital, treated for minor injuries and released. He also received an insurance settlement of about $15,000.

"Neither Mr. du Pont nor anyone connected with him ever apologized for hitting me, or for his racial remarks," Harris said.

Police in Radnor, Pennsylvania, where the accident occurred, insisted they did not give du Pont preferential treatment. The fact that Harris did not file a complaint made it difficult for the cops to do much more than issue the garden-variety traffic citation.

The incident also was embarrassing for Villanova, just one more link in a lengthy chain of embarrassments that was becoming more difficult to stomach. They needed a way out. Du Pont finally provided one.

Du Pont had asked school officials to renovate an athletic annex for use solely by the wrestlers. Villanova officials, he insisted, promised to do it. He said he even saw the architectural plans.

Instead, it seemed to the school like a good excuse to extricate itself from an unpleasant situation.

On August 5, 1988, the school made its decision. In a statement, university president Father John Driscoll announced the program was being terminated. The reason given was that the university didn't have the resources to provide a wrestling room for the athletes—essentially what Metzger had supposedly told the recruits.

Du Pont was incensed.

"I found out Tuesday Villanova was considering dropping the program," he said. "Thursday, the university had a meeting. I found out late Thursday afternoon by a phone call that the university was terminating the program. The university did not consult me about this. They never contacted me to attend the meeting and, after Thursday, when I knew the program was through, I did not attempt to make any contact with them."

The short-lived Villanova wrestling program fell far short of du Pont's grandiose vision of an eventual national championship. When Villanova shut down the operation, the Wildcats had a lackluster 8-22 record.

Four months later, Father Driscoll admitted to the problems that the entanglement with du Pont set off. That entanglement, he said, "could have been dangerous, in hindsight. But we took every reasonable precaution. We had our reputation to protect."

Du Pont hinted that he might sever his ties to the school.

"Without a wrestling program, there's not much for me to do around there," he said.

There was, though, much to be done with his own Team Foxcatcher. All the money he was pouring into college scholarships and salaries could now be directed to wrestlers who competed for his own team.

And USA Wrestling, the sports governing body, was also to benefit, with donations that totaled in the millions.

"You know what the best thing that ever happened to amateur wrestling was?" Dave Schultz once said. "Villanova dropping John's program, that's what."

In the fall, ground was broken at Foxcatcher to expand the wrestling facility so it could become a staging area for the entire U.S. National Team.

USA Wrestling reciprocated the monetary favors by listing du Pont as an official sponsor of Team USA, and putting his name in the title of the U.S. Freestyle National Championships and the Freestyle World Team Trials. He was elected an at-large member of the USA Wrestling Board of Directors.

In addition, he was made the U.S. National Freestyle Wrestling chairman by the Amateur Athletic Union, which has jurisdiction over nonelite athletes. And he became active with FILA, the international federation. He was listed as a FILA advisor, and was honorary chairman of the Masters World Championships, for older wrestlers.

One of those older wrestlers was du Pont. He won quite a few matches—sometimes because it had been arranged that he would win.

According to John Giura, who wrestled at Foxcatcher for six years beginning in 1990, during trips to Bulgaria Valentin Jordanov would arrange for du Pont to wrestle opponents his own age. Part of the arrangements he witnessed, Giura said, included Jordanov telling the wrestlers to make sure du Pont won.

Alex Steinbergh, a Masters' wrestler and businessman from Cambridge, Massachusetts, said he watched du Pont in two matches in Sofia, Bulgaria, in 1995 that were clearly fixed.

Steinbergh said he was in Sofia to compete in the 80-kilogram weight class—176 pounds—but at the weigh-in he tipped the scales at about 76 kilograms (167 pounds). The next category down from 80 kilo was 72 (158), so he was stuck at the higher one.

Du Pont came in in his underwear and got on the scale: 76 kilograms. Steinbergh then noticed something unusual. A sign advertising the 76-k weight class.

"I said to the official, 'Gee, I didn't know there was a 76. I'd like to go in,' " said Steinbergh. "And he said, 'This weight class is by special invitation only.' "

The invitees included du Pont and two Bulgarians. The first lifted du Pont and spun him around before dumping him on the floor. He could have, Steinbergh surmised, pinned du Pont in thirty seconds. But du Pont recovered to win the match. The second match was almost a carbon copy: a helpless du Pont staging a remarkable comeback to walk away with the championship trophy.

"You have a lot of mixed feelings," said Steinbergh, who is a year younger than du Pont. "On the one hand, he supported this tournament and gave a chance to a lot of guys like myself to wrestle again. On the other hand, it was sort of a big joke."

Joke or not, by devoting himself to wrestling on a national and international scale, du Pont seemed to dull the blow he suffered at Villanova. But two other events occurred in 1988 that may have left permanent scars.

The first was his introduction to cocaine.

The second, on August 9—four days after Villanova dropped wrestling—was the death of his mother.

While there had been on-and-off rumors of his drug use, it wasn't until du Pont's murder trial that it was aired publicly.

Part of the airing included this bombshell: du Pont's cocaine partner on at least one occasion was allegedly Mark Schultz.

That was elicited when Rob Calabrese was on the witness stand.

In the summer of 1988, after the Olympics in Korea were concluded, Calabrese said he picked up du Pont and Mark Schultz from the airport and brought them back to the ranch house—the one that had been built for du Pont's blink-of-an-eye marriage.

"We went in and sat down in the living room," Calabrese said. "John went into the bedroom and came out with an envelope and gave it to Mark, and Mark dumped some white powder on the coffee table. He made some lines with it and they did some lines.

"They snorted them."

"Did you see the powder disappear?" prosecutor Dennis McAndrews asked.

"Yes," said Calabrese.

Calabrese said it was the only time he saw du Pont use the drug. However, he had seen Schultz take cocaine up to a half dozen times.

During the trial, a number of wrestlers described du Pont's behavior as being consistent with snorting cocaine.

Trevor Lewis, who lived at Foxcatcher from 1991 to 1995, described du Pont as frequently being "very hyper."

"He couldn't sit in one place for any period of time more than ten or fifteen minutes," he said. "He would get up and down out of his chair and go into the library, probably twelve times a night in a three-hour period. He'd pace up and down the halls.

"He would sit there and he would bob in his chair a

little bit. And he was always wiping his nose with tissues and sniffling and occasionally he had bloody noses and had white powder on the edge of his nose frequently.''

Dan Chaid said du Pont often went alone into his library—the room with the bank-vault doors—and emerged wide-eyed, giddy, excited, and with white powder marks underneath his nostrils.

He said he saw that behavior dozens of times.

In 1990, Chaid said, he confronted du Pont.

''I talked to him about using cocaine, And I told him, 'John, I'm very concerned about you. I'm very worried about you, and I want to get you help. And I think it's time that you do something about this . . . I'll go with you to a clinic if that's what you want to do,' '' said Chaid.

''And he got really emotional. He started crying . . . And he said, 'Please, Dan, don't tell anybody.' He was very concerned about his family finding out. He was afraid that if they found out anything about his drug use, that they would come and try to take his estate away from him. And then he promised me that he was going to try to quit on his own.''

Apparently, he didn't. Chaid said du Pont continued to exhibit similar behavior until 1995. In fact, in the fall of 1995, a longtime friend of du Pont's, Sandy Deveney, had discussed with law-enforcement officials the possibility of arresting the man suspected of being du Pont's supplier.

Wrestlers said they saw that man at least once a week on the estate, although they never knew what he did. He would only stay for a few minutes, sometimes accompanying du Pont into the library, sometimes coming out, himself all hyped up.

''I asked him at lunch one time what he did, and he said, 'Oh, I just do things for John,' '' said Trevor Lewis.

His name was bandied about during the trial, and there was an attempt to get him to testify, but he never did. No one said they actually saw him use drugs, or give drugs to du Pont. But the intimation was clear.

What exact role he played in du Pont's life—and, perhaps, in Schultz's death—remained shadowy. Prosecutors, though, made the drug use a key element in their strategy to find du Pont guilty of first-degree murder—and put him away for life.

The beginning of du Pont's cocaine problem likely coincided with his mother's death. Jean Austin du Pont was ninety-one when she died. Du Pont was a few months shy of his fiftieth birthday.

It was, say those closest to him, a turning point.

"His behavior deteriorated," said Sandy Deveney.

Terry Wochok points to Jean du Pont's death as the prime factor in du Pont's downhill slide. He recalls a family gathering where Martha "Muffin" du Pont—Henry du Pont's third wife and sister-in-law to John—summed up the relationship between mother and son this way: "She was John's mother, his wife, his best friend, his sister."

Jean's funeral was scheduled for August 13. Nearly two hundred mourners gathered in the garden behind the mansion to hear a service conducted by the Rev. Thomas McClellan.

Du Pont, wearing his blue, Foxcatcher T-shirt, stayed inside.

"He was walking back and forth across the windows the entire time that the service was going on," said Sandy Deveney. "He was not out with his other family members."

When the procession left for the cemetery, du Pont remained in the mansion. He refused to go to the burial.

He later told Victor Krievens why.

"The du Pont tradition is that women never attend funerals, and my sister did," du Pont said, referring to his oldest sibling, Jean. "She broke precedent by attending, so I'm breaking precedent by not attending.''

He did, however, move back into the mansion from his ranch house.

Not long afterward the family gathered to divide up Jean du Pont's things. They sat in Chippendale chairs in the trophy room and started bickering, said Krievens.

"They put different colored stickers on things they wanted, and made up lists," he said. "They'd go through a row of books and instead of taking the whole row they'd pick out ones individually. Finally, John said, 'I've got to go to wrestling practice,' and left.''

Du Pont had the place cleaned, he replaced the faded wallpaper, he gutted and modernized the kitchen. In the food-storage area, boxes of canned goods that had expired six and seven years earlier were tossed. So were hundreds of empty jars. In the trophy room, the cases around the walls that contained Jean's thousands of ribbons were taken down, replaced with life-sized posters of the Foxcatcher competitors. Smaller pictures of du Pont and those athletes were placed around the room. It was in this room that du Pont liked to lounge with the wrestlers at night.

Some of the wrestlers moved in for weeks or months.

Kevin Jackson, a gold medalist at the 1992 Summer Olympics, came to Foxcatcher to train before major competitions, staying two or three weeks at a time. On his first visit, in 1989, he saw nothing alarming about du Pont's behavior—although there was a rigid rule about dinnertime. The evening meal started promptly at 7 P.M.

For the wrestlers, life at Foxcatcher was a working vacation. There were more than twenty-five hundred wrestling clubs in the country, according to USA Wrestling, but only one Foxcatcher. Word spread. You could eat for free, train in one of the best facilities in the world for free, live in a mansion for free. You could watch the big-screen television, play Nintendo. You could fish and hunt. You could get stipends and bonuses.

"It was like the Hyatt Regency of hotels," said Adam Derengowski, who trained at Foxcatcher from 1989–92. "It wasn't just a wrestling room. It was a film room, a training room, a weight room, a sauna, everything you needed to excel."

It also had the man many considered the finest wrestling teacher on the planet: David Schultz.

The Schultz family moved to Foxcatcher in July 1989, and it was clear he was the glue of the place, as big a draw as the fancy facility.

"Dave was like our guru," said Trevor Lewis. "We went to him with wrestling problems, technique, personal problems, everything. He was our leader. He was the reason we were there. We were learning from him, and he was somebody we looked up to."

"When you have a guy like that, it's like having an encyclopedia of wrestling," said Derengowski. "He was the master. He was thought about that way around the world."

Having du Pont as a patron was nice, too. Once, when Derengowski was still in college, he couldn't get to a tournament in Las Vegas because of an exam. Du Pont took him out in a private jet, just the two of them and the pilot.

But when Derengowski left in 1992 for a coaching position at Iowa State, du Pont told him he could never come back. He felt betrayed. One thing du Pont demanded, the wrestlers said, was loyalty.

Mark Coleman had just won a national title in 1992 when he called du Pont.

"He said he knew who I was and if I ever needed anything, I could call and ask," Coleman said. Soon, he was on the payroll, too. He lived in the mansion for a month before the 1992 Olympics. "If I needed to fly anywhere, he would pay for it. If I needed to go to a tournament, he'd pay for it."

For du Pont, the reward was the company of the wrestlers. "He loved it when the guys were around," said Jackson.

But the guys slowly began to notice du Pont's odd behavior. At first it was sporadic. Du Pont might launch into a rambling, disjointed speech. He'd see things moving that didn't move. He'd shoot holes in the wall. He'd pick at cuts on his body, claiming they were bugs. Or he might have his guests watch a two-hour video of his backyard.

Because there was no pattern, it was impossible to gauge his mood from one day to the next.

"One day he'd come in totally normal," said Kanamti Solomon. "The next day he didn't know you. He'd say, 'Who are you? Why are you here?' Stuff like that."

The only thing wrestlers knew for sure was that it was getting worse. But they weren't sure what to say—or whether to open their mouths at all.

"I was a little intimidated because of who he was," said Coleman. "If what he said seemed a little weird, I wasn't going to say anything."

Often, they'd turn to Schultz. He was the one who could talk to du Pont. On that point, the wrestlers were unanimous.

"Dave was the mediator for all the fire in John," said Derengowski.

But the fire started to get more and more out of control. At the end of 1992, Terry Wochok initiated a meeting with psychiatrists at the Institute at Pennsylvania Hospital, one of the premier psychiatric facilities in the country. The sole issue on the agenda: can du Pont be involuntarily committed?

The procedure for involuntary commitment had toughened considerably. In the old days it took little more than the opinion of one psychiatrist to have a person locked up. But the courts felt that was too vague, too filled with potential violations of a person's rights. So the concept of "dangerousness" was added.

Wochok would have been required to fill out an affidavit explaining his concerns, and detailing the actions by du Pont. If crisis workers agreed du Pont was potentially dangerous, they would get a warrant and bring him in for an emergency exam. It would have been possible to keep du Pont locked up, and receiving treatment, for years.

During the meeting, Wochok described for the doctors du Pont's increasingly odd behavior. But the psychiatrists decided they couldn't commit him for two reasons: One, du Pont didn't seem to be a danger to himself. He hadn't harmed himself, hadn't threatened suicide, hadn't shown he couldn't take care of himself.

Two: He hadn't hurt anyone else.

By law, one or the other had to be satisfied for involuntary commitment.

They suggested Wochok try to cajole du Pont into seeking help voluntarily. That was impossible, especially since du Pont didn't recognize his problems.

Part of Wochok's misfortune, too, was in geography. In Philadelphia, it was harder to get an involuntary commitment because of the heavy caseload and limited number of beds. Had Wochok gone to Delaware County, du Pont's home, he might have had an easier time convincing a mental-health worker that someone who shot holes in the wall was a powder keg.

There was another intangible. Suppose Wochok were successful, but after a few months du Pont got out, refused to take his medication, and his condition worsened. Now he would no longer trust Wochok, and any control the lawyer had would be irreparably damaged.

The bottom line, said those in the meeting, was that du Pont didn't meet the requirements for involuntary commitment.

At least, not yet.

Ten

While John du Pont attempted to gain acceptance and respect as an athlete and failed, young Dave Schultz found himself—and would go on to earn worldwide acclaim—through sports.

Like du Pont, Schultz also suffered through the disappointment of having his parents separate while he was still young.

Schultz's father, Philip, grew up in Scarsdale, New York, and was studying at the University of Pennsylvania in Philadelphia when he decided to break with his family's plans for a business career and set out on a much different course. After graduating from Colby College in Maine, he migrated to Palo Alto, California, in 1956 to study drama and television at Stanford University graduate school. Except for a brief period in Los Angeles and New York, he remained in the San Francisco area for the next four decades.

At Stanford, Philip, who was an aspiring actor and writer, met Jeanne St. Germain, who had grown up in nearby Menlo Park. She, too, was studying drama, with a specialty in costume design, a field that would become her career. The artistically gifted couple married on July 5, 1958, and moved to L.A. to be near the movie and TV business. That stay was short-lived; neither Philip nor Jeanne enjoyed Southern California much and they returned to the Bay Area. They also tried New York briefly. Their first child, David, was born there on June 6, 1959.

As a small boy, Dave Schultz told his father a story that Philip never forgot—and never shared until after his son's death.

"One time we were walking together and he told me this story about how before he was born, he was up in the clouds with twelve men, apostle-type figures, and they told him that he was being sent 'down there' to accomplish something," Philip said. "So, I asked him if he would accomplish whatever it was. He said, 'Yes, but I won't be here for very long.' And then he just ran off to play."

In 1964, when Dave was four and Mark three, the Schultzes separated. After several years, Jeanne moved with the boys to Oregon and Philip stayed behind in Palo Alto. In 1974, the boys moved back with their father.

Dave Schultz was a chubby, pigeon-toed adolescent nicknamed "The Pudge." Although he had slightly above average athletic ability, his body was shapeless, almost without definition. Even after he became a world-class wrestler, he still had less than a chiseled physique, which made his prowess all that more surprising to opponents.

Young Dave Schultz got his start in wrestling in Oregon while in junior high school. The wrestling room at Southern Oregon State College became one of his favorite spots, and a sports love affair was kindled that would last a lifetime.

"Actually, a teacher recommended that Dave take up sports because of his dyslexia," his mother said. "She felt it would help with his coordination. He never liked team sports, so wrestling became his thing."

When he returned to California, Schultz's infatuation with wrestling intensified.

"He loved it, he just absolutely loved it, he just couldn't get enough," Philip said. "By the time David got into junior high school, he seemed destined to move into this sport. He was not going to do anything else, period.''

By the time he reached high school, Dave Schultz had embarked on a remarkable journey that would lead to the victor's stand at the Olympics. Ed Hart, Schultz's coach at Palo Alto High School, remembered Schultz as a shy youngster who paced nervously before every match. It would become a prematch habit for the rest of his life, and wrestlers everywhere would copy Schultz's ritual.

Hart recalled fondly that Schultz wore his wrestling uniform underneath his school clothes, laced his wrestling shoes around his neck, and carried around a notebook filled with wrestling moves he had learned. It was as if Schultz lived his life just waiting for the moment he could be on the mat again. So enamored was he with wrestling that he didn't think to get what was every teenage boy's dream when turning sixteen—a driver's license.

''Dave made his first international trip to wrestle when he was still in junior high,'' his father said. ''He went to Peru, and he came back sick as a dog; he looked blue. I told him that that was enough, he was ruining his health, especially with all the weight loss in trying to make weight for matches. But he was adamant; he said he was going to continue, and that was that.''

Dave Schultz, like John du Pont, struggled with early learning problems. While du Pont suffered from reading difficulties and stuttering, Schultz battled dyslexia. And just as Schultz locked on wrestling, he used the same drive to battle his way through his learning disability.

Chris Horpel, who would become the head coach at Stanford, saw the burning determination to do everything right when the two first met through still another wrestling coach, Joe DeMeo, who was with the San Francisco Peninsula Grapplers Club. Schultz was fourteen or fifteen, Horpel a senior in college. Despite the age difference, they became fast friends. And it would be Schultz who would change Horpel's life.

"You couldn't help but like Dave back then," Horpel said. "He was like a little puppy dog that just couldn't get enough."

Horpel recalled Schultz as a polite and courteous young man whose enthusiasm outstripped his athleticism.

"In the beginning, the only thing that was remarkable about Dave was his intense desire to learn everything he could about the sport," Horpel said. "For whatever reason, Dave Schultz and wrestling just fit."

Like everyone else who knew Schultz in the beginning, Horpel said that Schultz's lack of muscle tone made his effectiveness on the mat startling.

"Although it only took a short time for Dave to start moving like a wrestler, it took almost his entire career before he looked like a wrestler," Horpel said.

Dave Schultz's rabid enthusiasm for the sport and voracious appetite to learn all he could about wrestling translated into stunning success from the start. By the spring of Schultz's junior year in high school, he placed in the top eight in both the freestyle and Greco-Roman styles at the 1976 Olympic trials. He was just sixteen and such an accomplished wrestler, he was traveling back to Southern Oregon State where it all started to help tutor college wrestlers there.

His performance at the trials qualified him for Olympic training camp. He was forced to miss school to attend, but Horpel lent a hand by trying to tutor Schultz in Spanish.

"I failed miserably," Horpel said later with a smile.

Almost always, it's a gifted and conscientious coach who changes an athlete's life. In the case of Dave Schultz and Chris Horpel, it was just the opposite. The time Horpel spent with Schultz changed the direction of the older man's life. Horpel's degree was in architecture and, when he came across the young Schultz, he was planning on beginning a career designing buildings.

"Working with Schultzy those first two years felt so gratifying that I changed graduate schools to give coaching and teaching a try," Horpel said shortly after Schultz's death. "That was twenty-two years ago, and I am still grateful for his influence on my career choice."

During those Olympic trials in 1976, Schultz was eliminated in the freestyle tournament by an older and much more accomplished opponent, Chuck Yagla. Yagla, a two-time National Collegiate Athletic Association champion from Iowa, pinned the high schooler using his famous "seat-belt" move, a tactic in which a wrestler controls the hips and waist of his opponent from behind and takes him down.

In a harbinger of how he would approach his opponents throughout his career, Schultz did not forget what Yagla had done. Just six months later, Schultz and Yagla met again in a national open tournament. Yagla was not only a defending national champ but had been voted the outstanding wrestler at that year's NCAA tournament.

This time, Schultz used a step-around bodylock, a technique he perfected to counter Yagla's "seat belt," to pull off an astonishing upset. Still in high school, Schultz had beaten one of the best wrestlers in the world.

"He was the researcher," said Stan Abel, Schultz's wrestling coach at the University of Oklahoma.

Throughout his career, Schultz would replicate time and again the tactics used to beat Yagla. He would study his opponent's technique, delve into his psyche, and then, when he was locked in singular combat, would use all that he learned about his adversary against him. The usual result was a picture of Schultz rising from the mat, his arms held above his head in triumph. Then he would extend his hand and embrace the man he had just beaten.

In 1977, Dave Schultz , then seventeen, won the California high-school wrestling championship in the 165-pound weight category and was named state wrestler of the year.

Schultz was so committed to learning everything he could about the opposition that later he learned to speak Russian. Always a bootstrap learner who had to find alternative ways to achieve, he filled a jar with scraps of paper with Russian words scrawled on them. He put the jar in the bathroom and every time he made a visit, he added another word to his vocabulary.

Schultz went to the trouble because as he was growing up, the Soviet wrestlers were collectively the best in the world. He believed if he knew their language, he could better understand the Russian mind-set. The Russians didn't resent him for it. Instead, they respected him, and that respect turned to love. By the time he was a veteran wrestler, the balding, bearded, swarthy Schultz was one of the most welcomed athletic figures in Eastern Europe.

"Wrestling is a sport that, although in this country it doesn't get a lot of attention, it is the most popular sport in many of the Eastern Bloc countries," said Nancy Schultz. "So when we would travel to Bulgaria or Russia or even Iran, David was basically received as a hero. They would tell him that he is one of their own countrymen and that he is always at home and welcome in their countries. There would be crowds gathered. There would be receptions at airports and standing ovations at all the tournaments that we went to."

Dave Schultz's triumph over Yagla was a springboard into the international arena, qualifying him for one of the premiere wrestling events in the world, the Tblisi Tournament in the Soviet Union. The best wrestlers congregated there, including the state-sponsored champions who were cultivated in Iron Curtain countries.

Instead of being overwhelmed by the wrestling masters of Eastern Europe, the teenager from Palo Alto came back from the Soviet Union with a silver medal and the best win-loss record on the American team. Later that spring, Schultz won the National Open in Greco-Roman and finished fourth in freestyle. In just three years, Schultz had skyrocketed from a nervous kid who hoped to gain a little confidence through sports into one of the best wrestlers in the world.

He remained at the top of the sport for the next two decades. It was the kind of success John du Pont could only dream about.

Dave Schultz had something else du Pont never had. A sibling who was also a close friend.

Dave stood in stark contrast to his brother Mark, who, from the earliest age, was muscular, physically well-defined, and extremely coordinated. There was also a difference in temperament. Dave was cordial and easygoing, Mark intense and sometimes inflexible. Still, it was Dave, a year older, who was the leader.

"David became the balance," Philip said. "From time to time, when Mark was even about to judge me, David would get in there, and say, 'You have to accept him the way he is.' Mark was not only powerful physically but also emotionally."

Mark was a gymnast early in high school, but felt it wasn't physical enough. Intrigued with Dave's success on the mat, he turned to wrestling. Mark was a natural and went on to win a California state championship. While Mark relied on force, though, Dave was, and would always remain, the thinking man's wrestler.

Dave was gregarious and friendly with competitors. Even after beating someone, Dave might share some techniques. Mark—who would go on to be a three-time NCAA champion and an Olympic gold medalist—worked up an intense dislike for his opponents. After a win, he would often do back flips to punctuate his victory. Still, the brothers were tied by a bond—and by the shared burning desire to walk off the mat a winner, even when working out with each other.

Their practices were often more brutal than their actual bouts. Once, while they were working out at Stanford University prior to the Olympic Games in Los Angeles, the two started head slapping, then head butting. When it was over, Dave's nose had been mashed and his brother's head knotted.

"We tend to brawl," Dave said at the time. "Sometimes we get a good workout, and sometimes we kill each other."

He passed it off as just something between brothers. "Egos and all that," he said.

While Dave Schultz wrestled both freestyle and Greco-Roman, he gravitated to the freestyle because it rewarded aggressiveness. That meant he could be innovative and tactical in his approach. As he matured, he became the chess master of the wrestling mat. His opponents were often bigger and probably stronger, too. But Schultz's body was always in the right position. Leverage and balance were his allies. And, of course, he had amassed the biggest bag of tricks of anyone in the sport.

After graduating from high school, Dave went to Oklahoma State. Then he transferred to UCLA when Mark enrolled there. When UCLA dropped wrestling, Dave was recruited by the University of Oklahoma. He talked Stan Abel into giving both brothers scholarships. There were plenty of workout brawls there, too, but the brothers fed off each other. Mark especially benefited from his older brother's wisdom.

It was at Oklahoma that Dave was smitten with a tall, green-eyed blonde named Nancy Stoffel. A gymnast, she was lean and willowy, a contrast to Schultz, who was dark, five-foot-nine and a stocky 163 pounds. They met in a running class in 1981, and their romance was destined to conform to the demands of Schultz's busy wrestling

schedule. Almost from the beginning, Nancy's life re-
volved around Dave's sport. What was important to him
was important to her. She was a jock herself; she understood the tunnel vision required to be a world-class athlete.

"Within minutes of meeting him, I knew he was the
kindest and wisest person I had ever met," she said.

When the two were wed in 1982, written on a workout
calendar in the University of Oklahoma gymnasium was
the notation, "Dave and Nancy get married," both a notice to the local athletic community and a reminder to
Schultz himself.

Their first morning as husband and wife, Nancy awoke
to find Dave gone from bed. He was up and off to a
workout. Nancy may have been a jock, but she was a new
bride, too. She cried about it then. Years later, she smiled
when she told the story. It was an early lesson in living
with a world-class athlete. There would be other, more
difficult lessons to learn.

Once, when a group of wrestlers, including Schultz, had
to travel to an important meet, they set off in a car cara-
van. One of the cars belonged to Nancy, but she wasn't
driving. The group stopped at McDonald's and Nancy
went to the rest room. When she came out, everyone—
having lost track of what car Nancy was riding in—had
abandoned her. She had to hitchhike, and when she
stomped into the hotel where the wrestling party was staying, her husband walked up, and nonchalantly asked,
"Where have you been?"

It was that irrepressible impish sense of humor that led
one friend to describe Dave Schultz as "a thirty-six-year
old Huck Finn."

The year he was married, Dave won an NCAA title at
Oklahoma. In 1983 he graduated with a degree in health,
physical education, and recreation. That same year
Schultz won a world championship while also working as

an assistant wrestling coach at Stanford. But it was in 1984 that he was to achieve the ultimate athletic dream.

Dave and Mark Schultz fought their way through the Olympic trials and made it to the Los Angeles Games. There, both won gold medals, Dave at 163 pounds and Mark at 180.5.

It wasn't all glory for the Schultz boys, though, who were becoming known as wrestling's Bruise Brothers. Both Dave and Mark Schultz were criticized for being overly aggressive, and an extra official was assigned to watch their matches. That official was Mario Saletnik of FILA—the same Mario Saletnik who, ten years later, would be driven into a pond by du Pont at Foxcatcher.

At the Olympics, Dave Schultz had to fight off several warnings from referees in his gold-medal match, a 4-1 decision over West Germany's Martin Knosp. Mark Schultz won his Olympic title by beating Hideyuki Nagashima of Japan.

The Schultz brothers were the targets of criticism throughout the Games and Mark had a victory taken away from him. He had pinned Resit Karaback of Turkey just thirty seconds into the match, but fractured Karaback's left elbow by using, officials claimed, an illegal hold. Milan Eregran of Yugoslavia, the president of FILA, protested on behalf of the Turk, accusing Schultz of excessive brutality. Despite the loss, Mark still won the gold by capturing the rest of his bouts in the double-elimination tournament.

Dan Gable, perhaps the best-known American wrestler of all time, was the coach of the '84 wrestling squad. At first, Gable defended Mark Schultz.

"It's a legal hold unless you bring the arm past a certain angle," Gable said at the time. "The Cubans used it on us four, five, six years ago, and we picked it up from them."

However, after watching replays of the bout, Gable had

a change of heart and agreed with FILA officials. When Gable got the telephone call telling him that Mark Schultz had his early-round win taken away, Dave was there.

"What are they trying to do," Dave complained, "turn this into a sissy sport?"

The same day, Dave pinned Sabin Sejdi, of Yugoslavia, wrenching Sejdi's knee. Dave had drawn unfavorable attention from wrestling officials a year earlier when he received a severe warning and had a special judge assigned to him in the 1983 World Cup.

Despite the criticism and the scrutiny, the Schultz brothers continued doing things their way, battering their opponents and easily winning the gold medals. Dave Schultz, in a newspaper interview ten years after his Olympic victory, conceded he "twisted a couple guys' knees" during the L.A. Games, but all with legal moves. He dismissed the complaints, saying, "Some of these guys aren't tough enough.

"I've been made to stop holds because they feel I'm too aggressive," he said. "I'm not doing anything illegal, I'm just going all out."

Greg Ellinsky, an All-America wrestler at Penn State and longtime Schultz friend, said that the criticism of Mark and Dave came more from wrestling's hierarchy than it did from wrestling fans, even abroad.

"After that Olympics when Mark broke the Turkish guy's elbow, Dan Chaid and I were in Turkey in a grand bazaar," Ellinsky said. "A rug merchant was trying to sell us rugs, and he was snapping them out one at a time. Then, he found out we were wrestlers and he pulled out an old newspaper clip of Mark out of a box right there in the market and all he wanted to know was if we knew Dave Schultz."

In the years following the '84 Olympics, Dave Schultz established himself as one of the world's premier wrestlers, finishing first in the World Cup in 1985 and first in the U.S. Nationals in 1986, 1987, and 1988. By this time, he was an assistant coach at the University of Wisconsin.

Whatever criticism Dave Schultz heard earlier in his career for his aggressiveness faded as he became the sport's goodwill ambassador. His engaging personality and ability to take a combat sport and transform it into an art form made him a crowd favorite.

Schultz's quirky ways captured fans' hearts: He wore camouflage clothing and silly-looking hats with pom-poms and would don Russian-styled fur hats when he warmed up.

He was hailed behind the Iron Curtain as an adopted favorite son, and he was better known to children there than to kids in his own hometown of Palo Alto. Wrestler Miron Kharchilava, who as a twelve-year-old in Russia idolized Schultz, recalled seeing Schultz stride into the Tbilisi arena with thirty thousand Soviets on their feet applauding. Years later, in 1992, Kharchilava would meet Schultz at the Foxcatcher estate. Kharchilava was an unknown, but Schultz took time to coach him and work out with him.

"He was the best technician in the world," Kharchilava said. "When he asked me to work out with him, it was the greatest compliment I could have received. Dave didn't care if you were American, Russian, or Italian, he just wanted to wrestle and have fun."

The summer before he was killed, Schultz wrestled in the World Championships in Atlanta where he finished fifth—and received a standing ovation from the Iranian delegation.

When Prince Albert of Monaco contemplated assembling a wrestling team to represent the glamorous, tiny principality overlooking the sapphire waters of the Mediterranean, he invited Schultz to meet him to discuss the idea. David and Nancy soaked up the glitz and sophistication of the international jet set as Prince Albert, the bon vivant son of Prince Rainier, made his pitch. He wanted to hire the world's best wrestlers for an instant Olympic team.

Dave didn't want to offend the prince, but he found it amusing that someone would think they could just lure world-class athletes onto a single team by waving a check.

Of course, that's exactly what John du Pont was doing back in Pennsylvania.

Schultz, lauded at airport receptions and applauded by crowds in places such as Russia, Mongolia, Belarus, Bulgaria, and Czechoslovakia, frequently gave away bits and pieces of his uniforms and more. He parted with his Olympic ring, his Olympic watch, his Goodwill Games medals, his NCAA championship ring, his World Championship medal, his World Cup trophy, all because he felt those items meant more to the people he offered them to than they did to him. When visiting Russia, he smuggled Bibles and diabetic medicine into the country.

Despite all the acclaim, Dave Schultz never made it back to the Olympics. In 1988, he lost to Kenny Monday in the Olympic trials. Monday went on to win an Olympic gold medal in Seoul, Korea, with Schultz as his biggest booster. In 1992, Schultz—increasingly putting his efforts into coaching other wrestlers—was plagued by injuries. He moved up to the 180-pound weight class because he was tired of fighting to keep his weight down and eventually lost to Melvin Douglas, again falling just shy of making the Olympic team headed for Barcelona, Spain. Those disappointments would be part of the motivation that kept Schultz at Foxcatcher, chasing a final shot at the Olympics by 1996.

The first Schultz at Foxcatcher, though, wasn't Dave, but Mark, who arrived in 1987 as part of the Villanova/Foxcatcher package. After Mark's departure in 1988, Dave Schultz, with a family to raise and even low-paying coaching jobs difficult to find, found Foxcatcher's appeal difficult to resist. The Schultzes—Nancy, Dave, their young son, Alexander, and infant daughter Danielle— moved into a cozy stucco farmhouse on du Pont's lush farm in July 1989. An outdoor enthusiast could hunt and fish to his heart's content at Foxcatcher, and Schultz loved to do both. He hunted for deer on what amounted to a private game preserve and with the animals he killed, he'd feed his family and friends. Grilled venison steaks at the Schultz house was a special treat as their home on Goshen Road became known as a sort of fraternity house for the wrestlers who either lived at Foxcatcher or were just visiting and training for a few weeks.

Tony DeHaven, who wrestled and lived at Foxcatcher, was lured there by both Schultz's glittering name and the promise of du Pont's assistance. Du Pont helped pay for DeHaven's college education at Villanova, and Schultz became his mentor.

"Dave came to all my matches in high school," DeHaven said. "He made me feel like I could do anything. He turned my life around.

"He was a genius on the mat, that way he could break things down and then teach you techniques. But he was more than just a wrestling coach. He was the glue at Foxcatcher. He held everything together."

Trevor Lewis, another wrestler who lived at Foxcatcher, said that one of Schultz's favorite tricks was to eat whole cloves of garlic before working out and then torture his wrestling partner with breath that was as intimidating as his fabled moves.

Schultz had a taste for spicy things, and on shopping forays, he'd taste several hot sauces before making his final choice. He also had a diverse appetite for adventure. In addition to hunting, he enjoyed skydiving, scuba diving, and rock climbing. He trained by running through the deep woods at Foxcatcher and climbing its trees.

One friend, Jeff Callard, spent time with Dave Schultz

in Colorado racing mountains bikes and whitewater rafting along the Animas River.

Callard recalled ''getting thrown out of the raft, finally crawling to shore three hundred yards downstream, teeth chattering, thinking how stupid it was and wondering why we didn't die, yet listening to Dave say, 'Let's do it again!' ''

Schultz's life was so entwined with wrestling that he named his son Alexander after the legendary Soviet wrestler Aleksandr Medved and his daughter Danielle after wrestling pal Dan Chaid. Life at Foxcatcher offered Schultz the luxury of spending time with his children in a way few fathers were able. He went to their school, Culbertson Elementary, just a few minutes away, and talked to children there about following their dreams. He passed his Olympic gold medal from tiny hand to tiny hand to prove that dreams can, indeed, come true.

In the evening, he would tell his kids—fondly called Xander and Danny—the latest installment of an ongoing seven-year bedtime saga in which the children had their own make-believe personas, Alexander as Friendable the flying deer and Danielle as Lisa the fox. The whimsical Schultz even sprinkled in guest appearances by friends and relatives.

Life at Foxcatcher appeared idyllic for the Schultz family. However, it also meant coping with the erratic behavior of Foxcatcher's master.

One moment, du Pont would be a friendly Dutch uncle to the Schultz children; the next, he would be speeding past their driveway in his silver Lincoln, heedless of the kids' safety, despite Nancy's protests to slow down. And, of course, there was the chance that at any moment, something would set off du Pont, and he would summarily fire a wrestler and order the athlete off the property.

Handling the official dismissals was Terry Wochok,

who earned the unflattering nickname of "The Axe Man" among the athletes.

Schultz took it upon himself to be a mediator at Foxcatcher, just as he had been the referee at home between his brother and father. However, at Foxcatcher, du Pont's paranoia made Schultz's self-appointed job as peacemaker extremely difficult.

He went to du Pont and pleaded the cases for wrestlers who were being dismissed, such as Chaid, and he argued that Valentin Jordanov deserved a higher salary when he was appointed the Foxcatcher coach.

What made his intervention on behalf of Jordanov so remarkable was that it was Schultz who was the *de facto* coach at Foxcatcher, with neither the title nor the pay. Du Pont, of course, had the official title as head coach, but the nuts-and-bolts job was always held by someone with *bona fide* credentials. Prior to Jordanov, that was Greg Strobel, who left Foxcatcher in 1995 to coach at Lehigh University. Strobel recommended Schultz, but du Pont insisted that Jordanov get the job even though the Bulgarian's grasp of English was tenuous.

Still, Schultz went to bat for Jordanov when the Bulgarian told him that he felt short-changed on his salary.

"He went to John on Valo's behalf," Nancy Schultz said, "saying that he thought his salary should be similar to Strobel's . . . John basically said, 'This is none of your business, and I run this program the way I want to.' "

In the end, Jordanov did get a salary similar to Strobel's $80,000.

Schultz tried to reason with du Pont, telling him that the things du Pont imagined were just that—products of du Pont's imagination. Schultz offered to go with du Pont to an alcohol and drug rehabilitation facility for treatment and even got Nancy's permission to spend the time away from home. Du Pont rebuffed Schultz and, some felt, resented the wrestler's candor.

The relationship between Dave Schultz and John du Pont was unique at Foxcatcher. Schultz was the only one who refused to kowtow to du Pont's delusional rule and, for a while, it seemed that du Pont respected Schultz more than anyone else around him.

Du Pont credited Schultz with being his entrée with the Eastern European athletic community because the wrestler was so well respected there. The millionaire considered Schultz something of a protector in unfamiliar surroundings. Together, Schultz and du Pont traveled the world in private chartered jets. They played pranks on one another in a fraternal way. Du Pont gave the Schultz children gifts of thousands of dollars at Christmas and, in return, Schultz and his wife gave du Pont a sense of belonging that he never had with his own family. Du Pont sat down to Thanksgiving dinners at the Schultz house and the Schultzes were guests with their parents at du Pont's mansion, "the big house," for Christmas.

In fact, when du Pont started having hallucinations, he asked Schultz to get in contact with his father, Philip. Du Pont knew Philip taught a college course on parapsychology.

"David wanted me to call du Pont because he was seeing visions," Philip Schultz said. "I said to David, 'What kind of visions, like Joan of Arc?' He said, 'No, he sees bugs.' I said, 'No, we're not talking Joan of Arc.'"

When Philip called du Pont, the millionaire told him that he saw bugs on his body, and the insects were working their way into his legs. Philip Schultz told him to videotape what he thought he saw and show it to the other people to get a reaction.

"I also told him to see a doctor, and he said, 'No, I'm not going to see a doctor,'" Schultz said.

Du Pont did have the videotape made.

"He showed it to people and David was the only one

who didn't see the bugs," Schultz said. "Everyone else said, 'Well, maybe there I see them.' But David wouldn't do that; he wasn't seduced by John's power and John's need to have other people see things the way he did."

As time went on, Philip Schultz became increasingly concerned for the safety of his son and his family and saw firsthand how du Pont's mood could shift from benign to ugly in a flash, and without provocation.

"I was at the mansion for Christmas dinner a few years ago, and du Pont was very cordial and acting the very gracious host," Schultz said. "We went into the living room, and he gave the children some Christmas money. Then, he told me to get the hell out of his house. He said, 'Get out of here, I don't want to talk to you any longer.'

"I was stunned, I had to say, 'Are to talking to me?' And he said, 'Yes.' I said, 'Don't worry, I'm out.' "

In the year before Dave Schultz was killed, Philip Schultz stayed away from Foxcatcher, and he repeatedly cautioned his son about du Pont's behavior. But by 1995, Dave Schultz was in the midst of a spectacular comeback. At thirty-five, he had placed first in the U.S. Nationals and in the World Cup. At an age when most athletes are simply thumbing through their scrapbooks, Dave Schultz was the favorite in his weight class to land another shot at the Olympics. And what made it possible was that he could train full-time at Foxcatcher. The Olympics were scheduled for Atlanta in August 1996. After that, Dave Schultz figured, he would settle in as a coach with Horpel at Stanford.

Still, Philip Schultz fretted, especially since he knew of du Pont's practice of carrying a gun. Dave, though, was confident as usual.

"David said to me, 'If John wants to play, I can play,' " Philip said.

Then, pausing and making his hand into a gun, Philip

Schultz remembered how that conversation ended.

"I said to David, 'Well, theoretically that sounds good. But suppose you're not equipped to play that game?' "

It was a question that would be tragically prophetic.

Eleven

As his paranoia escalated, du Pont became increasingly concerned about security. In February 1993, he asked to meet with representatives of Aegis Security Associates, a Leesburg, Virginia firm that had done extensive work in Washington. The company sent Patrick Goodale, an independent consultant, to meet with du Pont at Foxcatcher. Goodale, forty-four, had retired from the Marines in 1992 after twenty-five years in security operations and intelligence and was running a shooting range in West Virginia.

Goodale made arrangements to see du Pont in the mansion. He drove through the front gate, up to the big house, and knocked on the door, where he was admitted by a butler. Nobody at any point asked who he was or tried to stop him. He found it astonishing that a man of du Pont's wealth lived in a huge mansion in the middle of a four-hundred-acre estate with no protection at all.

After a meeting with du Pont and a look around the estate, Goodale prepared a long list of possible threats and potential problems: criminal activity, terroristic attacks, kidnapping, natural disaster, the fact that there was no central alarm system, no surveillance, no lighting on the parking lot, no access control. A Newtown patrol car would drive through the estate once or twice a night, but that was it for security. Du Pont had lived on the estate for more than fifty years without hand-wringing worries, but now they became very real to him. Goodale began work almost immediately, initially with two men. They registered their guns in Pennsylvania and were rarely without them. One of Goodale's jobs was to identify all the people with more than casual contact with du Pont. He determined there was a core group of wrestlers to whom du Pont was closest: Dave Schultz, Rob Calabrese, Valentin Jordanov, Dan Chaid, and Trevor Lewis. All lived on the farm.

Despite what he perceived as his closeness with all the athletes, though, du Pont acquiesced when Patrick Goodale suggested that they all be administered lie-detector tests. The questions included "Do you know of any secret entrances in the house?" and "Do you know anyone who is trying to harm John du Pont?" Eventually, most of the people working at Foxcatcher took the tests, sometimes at du Pont's specific request.

Du Pont also had other concerns, he told Goodale. Foremost, Goodale thought, was du Pont's fear that his family—primarily his sister, Jean Shehan, and brother, Henry du Pont—wanted to wrest control of his money and estate. He called his siblings "the lesser du Ponts."

His other worries were somewhat curious. He believed, for instance, that there were secret tunnels under the house that allowed people to come and go surreptitiously. There was, of course, the one four-hundred-foot tunnel leading from the main house across the back lawn to the powerhouse, where the steam boilers and breaker boxes were located. In the tunnel were phone and television cables, steam and water pipes.

He also thought the property was lined with mechanical trees that were controlled by devices placed around the grounds. Unfortunately, du Pont said, his family had never told him where the controls were located, and he wanted Goodale to help find them.

He was also absolutely convinced that people were sneaking into his house and moving around inside the walls. Some of the wrestlers, he thought, were doing it as a prank, making noises to scare him. At one point du Pont had paid one of the wrestlers to go inside the walls and see how easy it was to move around.

Goodale checked it out. The wrestlers assured him they had never been inside the walls, except at du Pont's behest. But it was, Goodale found, possible to get into the walls from three different points and move about inside; he did it himself, traveling from one end of the house to the other.

Goodale wouldn't dismiss the concerns as nonsense. "He considered that the estate had been built by his father to incorporate some very unusual features," he said. "The way he articulated the issue to us, it sounded reasonable, given the vast wealth and unlimited resources [available] to that family."

To alleviate the wall "problem," Goodale proposed a number of options, including a system of sensors, putting simple physical barriers in the walls, filling the wall space with foam.

If none of that was satisfactory, Goodale said, the walls could be lined with razor wire. It was dangerous stuff— used primarily at prisons and nuclear plants—that could slice a person to ribbons.

Du Pont picked the wire. It was installed in the walls and attic.

Goodale had a crew clear away brush around the estate to look for secret tunnels. Du Pont also enlisted the aid of Rudy D'Alessandro, the project manager for J.S. Cornell and Son, a Philadelphia outfit that spent three years doing repair and restoration work at Foxcatcher. Du Pont would often bring Cornell workers to a place he suspected could be a tunnel entrance, and ordered them to dig.

"You could try to say, 'I don't think there is [a tunnel],' " D'Alessandro said.

But unless du Pont actually saw the area exposed, he wouldn't feel reassured.

Walter Fitzgerald, who joined du Pont's work force in 1992 and eventually became maintenance manager, supervised the search for tunnels under a water tower and under the playhouse. Usually, it was a matter of pulling a few bricks or cinder blocks out of the basement and having du Pont come out to inspect.

"We just couldn't go there and say, 'There's no tunnel,' " Fitzgerald said.

At one point, an opening was actually discovered, but it was part of an extensive storm-drainage system.

Still not satisfied, du Pont gave Goodale the go-ahead to bring a piece of ground radar equipment from California. The cost was $77,000. Nothing was found.

Once, recalled Fitzgerald, du Pont had a large hole—ten feet long and six feet deep—excavated in the rear garden. But it wasn't to seek a tunnel.

"He told me that he felt his mother was a chambermaid and his father impregnated her and then she had passed away," Fitzgerald said. "And he felt that his father had buried her in the rear yard. So he wanted us to try to find the bones so he could give her a proper burial."

Of course, no bones were found. But du Pont had boards placed over the hole; the boards stayed for nearly a month. Then a priest came and blessed the ground.

Du Pont also complained to Fitzgerald about how an ice storm that hit the area in the winter of 1994 could bankrupt him. But his reasoning was somewhat skewered. He believed David Schultz and Rob Calabrese had machines that made ice and threw it over the land.

"He told me he would be broke if they didn't stop it because all the people in Philadelphia will be suing him because the ice, they knew, was coming from his property," Fitzgerald said.

When he heard that, Fitzgerald looked at du Pont. He realized du Pont wasn't fooling.

"He was very serious," Fitzgerald said. "He stared right at you with a very serious look on his face. And in your heart you had to believe he felt that."

Du Pont was also sincere when he said the pool balls in his billiard room might contain transmitting devices. He would watch somebody make a shot, and say, "That didn't happen by accident." So they were sent out to be examined. The wrestlers chipped in to buy him another set.

Goodale also arranged for periodic electronic sweeping of the entire house, looking for eavesdropping devices. The cost: $130,000.

For his services, Goodale charged $300 to $400 a day. His top associates were paid $200 to $300 daily, and other members of the security team got $15 an hour. The cost to satisfy du Pont's fears ran in the hundreds of thousands of dollars.

There was another toll. Many of the workers at Foxcatcher were very uncomfortable in the presence of Aegis security agents. It wasn't just the fact that they carried guns, or seemed to investigate every incident—noises in the house, a light in the laundry room—with their weapons drawn. The atmosphere at Foxcatcher, they said, changed when they were around. It was extraordinarily tense. Some employees, used to walking through the front door to talk to du Pont, now were told by Aegis agents to wait until they were announced, and then were escorted. Landscaper Terry McDonnell, who had known du Pont for nearly forty years, was once spread-eagled on the porch and frisked. Du Pont was walking out of the kitchen at the time, and said to the security man, "Leave that man alone. I have known him longer than I have known you."

Du Pont never went anywhere without being accompanied by an agent. And he never drove anywhere until security people would search the car, inside, outside, and underneath.

Du Pont's demeanor also was altered. To deal with du Pont's moodiness, one of his hunting partners and friend of thirty years, Sandy Deveney, had a kind of code with Dave Schultz to determine whether du Pont was approachable. He'd ask Schultz, "How's the weather?" If Schultz said, "It's sunny and clear," it was a good time to visit. If the answer was, "The weather is poor," it was a good time to stay away.

"When this agency was there it was chaotic and anxious," said Georgia Dusckas. "Time stopped, and we all endured until they left."

Dusckas recalled two incidents that convinced her Aegis personnel purposely fueled du Pont's fears. Once, she said, she was summoned to the trophy room because du Pont was hearing voices. She believed Aegis agents were in the tunnel under the house to spook du Pont.

On another occasion she was called into du Pont's bedroom. There du Pont and Mike Reeves, a senior agent for Aegis, were looking out the window to the front field. Reeves, Dusckas said, claimed a person was roaming outside. But, said Dusckas, the distance was so vast that there was no way to tell if it was "a weed, a stick, a fence post, or a person."

Nevertheless, said Dusckas, Reeves fired a laser-scope rifle out the window. "I don't even know what the heck he was shooting at," she said. She silently hoped that Reeves was firing high in the air because the area at which he aimed had running trails; athletes could have been out jogging.

"Then they all went off in a big to-do about searching the front field," Dusckas said.

Du Pont was always armed during the period Aegis was

on the property. Although, as D'Alessandro said, despite his reputation as an expert marksman, du Pont was a little awkward as a gunslinger.

"He carried it more like somebody would carry—well, he carried an iced tea, so it was pretty much the same," said D'Alessandro. "A gun and an iced tea, very relaxed and informal about it.

"I had asked him at one point, 'Wouldn't you be more comfortable with a holster?' And he said, 'No, I am much quicker with it this way.' "

D'Alessandro learned early on what a harsh—and frustrating—taskmaster du Pont could be. If du Pont disapproved of something, he would stand inches from D'Alessandro and let him know. More than once he expressed his dissatisfaction when he ordered D'Alessandro to redo work, starting from scratch. For instance, he didn't like a structure that had been erected, even though he had previously approved it. Down it came. At another job site, du Pont was incensed that long nails were used to fasten roof tiles because they made small punctures in the roof frame. He had it all done over with shorter nails.

D'Alessandro found it almost impossible at times to get du Pont to make a decision. He learned never to guess. When his men needed to move something out of the way during a project—usually a routine matter—it couldn't be done without a lengthy conversation. It made the work take longer, and the costs rise; during one eighteen-month period, J.S. Cornell billed $800,000. Du Pont was oblivious.

"He didn't talk in a normal, direct term," D'Alessandro said. "He could have a long conversation and then there may be two or three facts that you could hang your hat on, and say, 'Okay, I know what to do.' ... You had to extract from this menagerie of information, which could be mixed in with hundreds of different thought patterns."

To say the least, D'Alessandro never felt completely at ease.

That was only heightened during the occasions when du Pont's behavior entered the realm of the unreal. Like the time there was some confusion about billing. Du Pont warned D'Alessandro of the consequences if it wasn't resolved. "You better get this accounting straight," said du Pont, "because if you don't, then the United States won't have a national budget. They can't pass their budget if you and I can't come to terms."

One time, the two went into a barn where hay was stored; much of the wood bore teeth marks from the horses. D'Alessandro assured him that could be fixed.

"No," said du Pont. "I want you to know that's there for a reason. Those are messages. Those are messages from Mars."

Another time, du Pont was talking about the history of his property when he unrolled a flag—a Nazi flag. He told D'Alessandro he now possessed the power of the Third Reich; it had been personally handed over to him by Albert Speer, the architect for Adolph Hitler.

As with many things du Pont did or said, it had a kernel of truth. He had, in fact, met with Speer in Heidelberg, Germany, on the trip with his old Haverford School teacher.

He asked D'Alessandro, somewhat apologetically, not to carry a briefcase. "You could be carrying a bomb," he said. D'Alessandro took to toting a clipboard.

On a clear day, du Pont appeared at a job site wearing a red jogging suit and carrying a red umbrella.

Once, he almost jumped out of his skin when D'Alessandro touched him.

That took place in the wrestling center, where the two were discussing repair work. D'Alessandro had already been hollered at for not moving fast enough on carpet replacement, even though du Pont didn't give the okay on the color. Frustrated, D'Alessandro put his arm around du Pont's shoulder and said, "Mr. du Pont . . ."

He didn't get any more words out. Du Pont jumped back. He was in a rage. "Don't ever touch me!" he sputtered. "I'm the Dalai Lama." And he stuck his ring in D'Alessandro's face. That was proof of his lofty position.

That was eerily similar to an incident—without the rage—that took place with Beverly Collier, the secretary for the Foxcatcher wrestling club. At the gym one day, du Pont told her he could no longer be touched because he was the Dalai Lama, the Holy One. His servants, he added, wore gloves if they had physical contact with him.

Not long afterward, in a conversation with Collier, he added a litany of other titles. "He said he was the Christ Child, he was the devil, he was the president of Bulgaria, and he was the Dalai Lama, all in one breath," Collier recalled. "At that point I said, 'No, you are John du Pont. You are not those people.' He was very, very agitated and he pushed his ring up at me, and he said, 'You see this ring. I got this ring many years ago. This is the reason that I am who I am.' "

Collier told a few of the athletes what happened. They had some simple advice: Don't confront him. So not long afterward, when du Pont again claimed to be the Dalai Lama, she kept quiet.

Walter Fitzgerald also held his tongue when he got instructions from the Dalai Lama.

"He told me that this was holy land," said Fitzgerald, "[and] don't let the people in the neighborhood know that he's there because there would be hordes on the front yard wanting to see him."

Throughout the next three years, du Pont would periodically lapse into the Dalai Lama persona, adding layers onto the story. He had, he believed, been offered the title in 1977 by a group from the Buddhist Church. At that point he had undergone brainwashing to erase traces of his previous life. Everything in front of his house, he decreed, was holy, Buddhist land. That included the house where the Schultzes lived.

Du Pont acknowledged that there was another Dalai Lama; that one, he maintained, had the power only at night when du Pont removed his ring.

Fitzgerald tried to take the ramblings in stride. He had been introduced to du Pont's odd behavior as soon as he started working for him in April 1992. He had retired the previous June after forty years with the Philadelphia Electric Company; with his background, he was asked to come to Foxcatcher to remove some electrical conduits. That turned into a regular part-time position until he took over all maintenance in December 1995.

When he first arrived on the property, Fitzgerald was invited to join some others in the trophy room to watch videotapes du Pont had made.

Actually, it was a tape of a meadow on the property. The picture never changed. But Fitzgerald, wrestler Rob Calabrese, and another employee, Frank Strassacker, sat there for nearly ninety minutes watching the image with du Pont. Periodically, du Pont would make a comment.

"Do you see that moving in the right-hand corner?" he asked. "Did you see that on the left side? Did you see that moving?"

Nobody saw anything. But when they tried to say something, du Pont became upset. "I see it," he'd say. "I don't know why you cannot see it."

"So," said Fitzgerald, "thereafter we sort of went with the program and saw what John saw."

He also was taken to the second floor. There, a video camera on a tripod was pointed out the window, recording the pastoral scene.

Photographs also held secrets for du Pont. He showed one to Georgia Ducskas, pointed to a tree, and said, "Do you think that looks like Mark Schultz in that photo?"

Fitzgerald eventually learned, too, why he was asked to take out the conduits—which were rigid—and replace them with flexible material; du Pont thought the mansion moved of its own volition. In fact, he thought a lot of the buildings on the property moved, and that there were treadles located around the grounds that could control the movement. At one point he banned parking in one area because he felt the cars would set the treadles in motion. The phone company was called in to relocate a wire after du Pont complained that it could be pulled to make the buildings move. He ordered two buildings to be anchored down by cables.

Du Pont had spent his life getting what he wanted, having his whims and demands met without questions. And now, no matter how absurd his beliefs, no matter how outrageous his requests, his employees simply shook their heads and complied with his orders.

That, apparently, included kicking Goodale and Aegis off the property in November 1993. No one was quite sure why. Charlie Reed, one of du Pont's newer employees, simply told Goodale his services were no longer needed.

About a month later, though, du Pont called and asked Goodale to return. Back came Aegis; this second stint on the estate lasted until June 1994. At that point, Terry Wochok fired the agency. Again, Goodale said, no reason was given.

If du Pont seemed more relaxed when Aegis was gone—his appearance changed, he was more humorous, less anxious, and he was back to wearing pants and shirts—he wasn't completely free of demons. Fitzgerald remembers an incident in the fall of 1994 when he was in the library replacing fluorescent lightbulbs. Du Pont came in, got up on a ladder, and told Fitzgerald to cover his ears. He pointed a gun at the ceiling, and said, "My mother said, if you don't come out soon . . ." The rest of the words were drowned out by the gunshot.

Although du Pont no longer employed Aegis, he still kept his ties with Goodale. In September 1994, the two had lunch. Du Pont asked Goodale to help out from time to time, and after that they had intermittent contact. On one assignment in late 1994, Goodale accompanied du Pont to Bulgaria, where du Pont attended an awards ceremony and made arrangements to fund a wrestling meet. One of the men at the ceremony was the president of Bulgaria. Du Pont would later claim he himself was the president of Bulgaria.

Du Pont and Goodale had no contact for most of 1995. Then, in August, du Pont asked Goodale for a meeting. The purpose was twofold. Du Pont wanted Goodale to conduct some research into raising exotic animals; he talked about bison. They settled on llamas, and Goodale soon trucked in six llamas, which were let loose on the farm. The experiment obviously failed, because six weeks later, he rounded them up and took them away.

The second thing du Pont wanted to talk about was refurbishing his armored personnel carrier.

Du Pont and Goodale had discussed that project two years earlier when they first met. The APC, bought thirty years earlier in California, was sitting in a hangar on the property, unused for years. It had badly deteriorated. Du Pont thought he could donate it to a museum, but he first wanted it in tip-top shape. That meant finding an original .50-caliber machine gun to mount on top.

"I asked him would a replica be suitable because it's much easier to acquire and it's cheaper and doesn't require a tremendous paper trail," said Goodale. "He did not want that. He wanted a real, functioning machine gun."

Goodale went to Wochok to tell him his concerns about getting a real one. According to Goodale, Wochok's reply was, "Give the man what he wants."

Goodale made regular visits to Foxcatcher for the last four months of 1995 and into January 1996, almost all regarding the APC restoration.

During that time, du Pont's concerns about his safety went deeper and deeper—bolstered in October 1995 by two suspicious fires in two buildings on the property, not far from the mansion. One destroyed a small house, the other the powerhouse and greenhouse. The latter was the more serious because it knocked out phone and electrical service.

Fitzgerald was able to get the electricity up in about an hour. But the phone cables were another matter. Du Pont told him not to worry about it.

"Don't connect the phone lines because they're just a bother to me anyway," he said.

Besides, said du Pont, things were going to be changing anyway. The greenhouse would be the new site of Red Square. And the wrestling center nearby was going to become the post office. That would be convenient because in Russia the post office serves as the communications center. There one can get mail, hear the latest gossip, and use a phone if needed. It would soon be the same at Foxcatcher.

More and more du Pont became obsessed with Russia, with a war between the United States and Russia, with Russian agents coming onto the property and harming him.

He asked Fitzgerald to make sure his Lincoln was filled with gas at least twice a week. "In case the Russians would come after him," Fitzgerald said, "he wanted to be able to get out of there quickly."

So twice a week, whether it needed two gallons or twenty, Fitzgerald took the car to the Mobil station in town and filled it.

He put something else in the car, too, at du Pont's request.

"He asked me to make up a red square out of plywood, two-foot-square, paint it red, get a hammer and a sickle, paint that gold, and mount that on the two-foot square of plywood," Fitzgerald said. "And he asked me to put that in the trunk of his Lincoln."

Du Pont initially said it was a joke he wanted to play on the East European wrestlers who were coming to train at Foxcatcher. Later, though, it took on added significance. It became his protection against a Russian attack.

Du Pont, though, didn't spend all of his time worrying about the Russians. He saved a big chunk of his concern for Daniel Chaid.

Chaid had been one of the first wrestlers at Foxcatcher, and first coaches at Villanova, moving into a house on the estate in the summer of 1987. A native of California, he had known the Schultz brothers—David and Mark—on the West Coast. Later they all wrestled at the University of Oklahoma.

The birth of Chaid's son in April 1994, bothered du Pont; he considered it immoral that Chaid and his girlfriend, Theresa, weren't married. In October of that year, Chaid and his girlfriend got into a fight that quickly got out of control. Chaid took the baby and went to the Newtown police station. Theresa followed in her car and used a hammer to smash the passenger window in Chaid's van. The police told du Pont, and he got word to Chaid that he wanted to talk to him.

Chaid apologized, said he was embarrassed, and it would never happen again. Du Pont, according to Chaid, said he, too, was embarrassed, but didn't go beyond that. He seemed to accept the explanation. But it obviously gnawed at him.

That winter, pipes froze in Chaid's house, causing a lot of damage. Du Pont told Chaid the house was old and rather than fix it, he would tear it down and build a new house for Chaid on the grounds.

That never happened; in July 1995, Terry Wochok—
the "Axe Man"—told Chaid that du Pont wanted him to
leave. For wrestlers, that was usually a death sentence. Du
Pont had complete control over who was on the team.
Each year, wrestlers were culled from the twenty to thirty
who made up the Foxcatcher pack. Once kicked off, they
were never allowed to return.

Greg Strobel, the assistant coach from 1991–95—du
Pont, of course, kept the title "head coach"—said wrestlers could be fired simply because they weren't performing well in tournaments. Du Pont only wanted the best,
and he usually got them. In 1994, six of ten World Championship wrestlers were from Foxcatcher; the following
year, five Foxcatcher wrestlers won World Championships, which are held in non-Olympic years.

One of those stars, and clearly a du Pont favorite, was
Valentin Jordanov. While du Pont had his pets among the
athletes, there was always one wrestler elevated above the
others. Early on it had been Mark Schultz, Dave's brother.
For a while Rob Calabrese was "the fair-haired boy,"
according to Strobel.

In 1992, Jordanov became the anointed one.

Jordanov was one of the best wrestlers in the world. At
114 pounds, he had won seven World Championships but
never an Olympic title. He hoped 1996 could change that.
He had been living at Foxcatcher with his wife, Zdrava,
and their two children, first spending six months in the
Schultz house before moving into their own home on the
estate.

Du Pont became annoyed if he didn't see Jordanov
every day. He constantly inquired about his whereabouts.
If Jordanov didn't show up at the wrestling center, he'd
call Strobel.

"Has Valentin been in?" he'd ask. "Has Valentin been
in? Call me when he comes in."

Strobel was under instructions to call du Pont with reports on Jordanov's whereabouts. Once, Strobel forgot. Du Pont was furious.

Although Sunday was a day of rest for the wrestlers, it wasn't for Jordanov. Du Pont reserved the day for private workouts with him. Trevor Lewis once asked if he could use the gym on a Sunday.

"No," du Pont said, "that's my time to work out with Valentin. I prefer that we were just alone."

"About the only time he got off," Strobel said of Jordanov, "was when he left the country."

When he did go overseas, du Pont would instruct a wrestler to sit by the telephone in the mansion waiting for Jordanov to call. Lewis was often that wrestler.

"When Valentin was in Bulgaria, he would tell John, 'All right, I'm going to call on this date around this time.' So we would sit and wait for Val to call," Lewis said. "And if John had to go do something, he would ask me to sit and wait for Valentin's call. And if he called, he would want me to come over to the gym and tell him that Valentin was on the phone."

Du Pont's possessiveness of Jordanov led him to fire Dave Schultz after a New Year's Eve party at Jordanov's house in December 1994. Schultz had worn a Russian army uniform he had picked up on a trip overseas. Du Pont walked in the door, saw Schultz, and left. He was incensed. By wearing the outfit, he felt, Schultz was trying to undermine his special relationship with Jordanov.

After the party, Schultz was summoned to the mansion. Rob Calabrese and Rico Chiapparelli, another wrestler, were there, too. Stick around, du Pont told them.

They all went into the library. Du Pont pointed to a book with the words "Au Revoir" on the cover. "*Au revoir*, that means 'good-bye,' " he said to Schultz. "You're off the farm, Dave."

Schultz was stunned. Still, he thanked du Pont for all he had done. He offered his hand. Du Pont refused.

After he left, Calabrese told du Pont if he didn't change his mind, he was leaving. Jordanov did the same.

The next morning du Pont called Schultz.

"I'm sorry," he said. "I made a mistake. Please stay. I apologize for my behavior."

Though he changed his mind that time, he refused to a few months later, when he needed to replace Greg Strobel. Strobel was earning $80,000 a year and lived in a house du Pont bought for him off the estate; that would be hard to match. But with du Pont talking more and more about getting out of wrestling, Strobel didn't want to be left hanging. So he accepted an offer to become coach at Lehigh University.

Du Pont told Strobel he was going to elevate Jordanov to the assistant coach position. Strobel was concerned. Jordanov was not considered a great teacher; nor did he seem interested in the administrative parts of the job. Plus, his English was limited.

Schultz, recognized as one of the finest wrestling teachers in the world, was clearly better qualified.

But du Pont was emphatic. Schultz, he complained, interfered with his relationship with the Bulgarian.

So strong were his feelings for Jordanov, that even when the wrestler wasn't around, his presence was felt. During a February 1995 trip to a tournament in Bulgaria, the Foxcatcher entourage settled into a hotel in the mountains. Jordanov, though, left to spend the night in Sofia, the capital. Everyone knew he would not return. But at dinner du Pont would not allow anyone to sit in the chair next to him.

"Even though he wasn't coming back, and we all knew that he wasn't coming back, we weren't allowed to sit there because in case Valentin came back, he wanted to have a chair for him," Lewis said.

Lewis himself wound up making a mistake in Bulgaria that ended his career at Foxcatcher. He, Strobel and du

Pont were in Lewis's hotel room. Du Pont began talking about his Bulgarian heritage.

"I told him he was not a Bulgarian," Lewis said. "He was an American, a very famous American with documented heritage back to France."

A week later, back in the States, Wochok told Lewis to pack his things. Why? Lewis asked. Because, he was told, of the comments he made disparaging du Pont's belief that he was Bulgarian.

Kanamti Solomon was also fired in 1995 for what he says was an entirely different reason: he was black. Solomon, at the time one of the top three wrestlers in his weight class in the country, had trained at Foxcatcher for five years. Du Pont even helped him with his tuition at Delaware State University.

Then, one day, it ended. Strobel told Solomon that du Pont ordered him off the team. There was no reason given.

But Solomon needed a reason. A month later, at a tournament in Las Vegas, he confronted du Pont.

"He stopped and he looked at me and then he pointed to the Foxcatcher sweatshirt," said Solomon. "And he said that Foxcatcher was now part of the KKK and that was an organization that didn't accept blacks."

Two other black wrestlers, Olympic gold medalist Kevin Jackson and John Fisher, had also been released. (In 1997, the three wrestlers, plus another black wrestler, Robert Pritchett, all filed a group suit, charging discrimination.)

Jackson, thirty-one at the time, had known du Pont much longer than Solomon, who was twenty-two.

"I talked to him in the lobby, all the way up the elevator and all the way to his room," Jackson said. "I asked him to talk to me, man to man, to explain this thing. He had promised me a lot of things. He'd told me he would endorse me all the way through the Olympics.

"I just kept saying, 'Tell me why. Give me a reason,

and I'll drop the subject.' But he wouldn't answer the question.

"Finally, next time I saw him, he told me that some wrestlers had been released from the top and some from the bottom. I was one of the ones released from the top."

Jackson and Solomon did what they—and others—usually did when they had problems with du Pont. They appealed to Dave Schultz.

"Dave Schultz told me he would discuss the matter with John," Jackson said. "He'd say, 'KJ, I don't know what the deal is. He's tripping. I don't know what's going on.' And du Pont kept putting him off and putting him off.

"Dave kept trying, and then John told him the situation was resolved. I got a check at the end of that month, and I was officially off Team Foxcatcher."

Chaid, though, was more nettlesome. He just wouldn't leave. During the summer he repeatedly tried to talk to du Pont about the situation. Du Pont refused. Instead, Wochok told him that du Pont wanted him off the estate by Labor Day.

That, Chaid told Wochok, was impossible. "I told him there was no way that I could do that," he said. "I was planning on being out of town, and there was just no way that I could do that. He told me that if I wasn't moved out, that the house might be bulldozed with all my stuff in it when I got back."

When Chaid returned from his vacation, there was a notice on his door giving him thirty days to vacate the property.

Chaid talked to Dave Schultz. Schultz talked to du Pont; he was told to mind his own business.

Then, Chaid said, on September 23 he was at Calabrese's house when du Pont walked in unexpectedly.

"He asked me if I wanted to go up to the big house and look at some statues that he had recently purchased," said Chaid. "And so I said 'Yeah,' and we took a ride up.

"I said, 'John, I'd really like to talk to you about this housing situation. You know, I'm not sure what I'm going to do about moving.' And he stopped the car and pulled over, and we had a conversation. And he said, 'Well, what do you want to do?' And I said that I wanted to stay there and train on the farm and raise my family in the area. And he said he was going to get me a house."

The next morning Chaid told du Pont he had looked at some homes in the area and found one he thought would be perfect. "I don't want to talk about that now," du Pont said. "You talk to Terry about it."

Chaid did. Wochok tried to speak with du Pont, but du Pont was leaving for a wrestling tournament in Vladivostok, Russia, and didn't have time. Wochok told Chaid it would have to wait until he returned.

The evening of October 9, Chaid called du Pont to discuss the housing situation. Du Pont said he was too tired from his trip and slammed down the phone.

Two days later, in the early-morning hours, a house next to Chaid's burned down. Also burned was the greenhouse/powerhouse behind the mansion. Fire officials labeled both blazes as arson. They made a report and turned it over to the Newtown police.

State Trooper Nicholas Saites, who investigated, immediately came up with a number one suspect:

Dan Chaid.

Saites had interviewed Chaid and learned he was being forced to leave. Chaid also told him he had been staying with Calabrese and returned to his home sometime during the night to check on his dog. Saites thought Chaid had motive and access.

The same day Saites went to the mansion to talk to du Pont about the fires. Du Pont, though, had his own suspicions about who set them.

He thought it was the Russian Mafia.

Saites returned to Foxcatcher a few weeks later to talk to du Pont. He enjoyed listening to the stories about his travels, about wrestling, about his life. During the somewhat rambling conversation, which du Pont conducted as he paced the room, the name "David Schultz" was mentioned.

"So David Schultz could have started these fires?" Saites asked.

Du Pont stopped and spun around. "Oh, no," he said. "David Schultz is my best wrestler. He would never do anything like this."

He then launched into a minute's worth of praise for Schultz, pointing out all the pictures of Schultz throughout the room.

If he displayed fondness for Schultz, though, his distrust for Chaid only mounted. So much so that he talked to Pat Goodale about it.

"He indicated that he had to evict Chaid from the property, and . . . that he asked his attorney to do it," Goodale said. "He didn't get the job done, and he had to do it himself, and he was irritated about that. He considered Dan Chaid could be a problem for him."

One of du Pont's biggest concerns was his standing in international wrestling organizations. Because of his millions of dollars in contributions to the groups, he was on the Board of Directors of USA Wrestling, and an advisor to FILA, the international group. He had it in his mind that Chaid was bad-mouthing him to officials of both.

At the same time that he fretted about his image in wrestling, he apparently had already decided to get out of the sport. He'd had a great decade-long run with it, but as far back as 1994 he told Greg Strobel he was thinking of ending his support. In fact, du Pont had Strobel tell USA Wrestling that his financial backing would end after 1996.

In the meantime, though, Chaid had to be dealt with. And this time, frustrated by the inability of his underlings to get rid of Chaid, du Pont took matters into his own hands.

The day after the fires, Chaid was in the gym lifting weights. Du Pont came through the front door.

"Hi, John, how are you doing?" Chaid said.

Du Pont was carrying a gun. "Do you want to talk to me?" he asked.

"Yeah, John. I'd like to talk to you about this housing situation."

Du Pont lifted the gun and pointed it at Chaid's chest.

"Don't you fuck with me," he said. "I want you off this farm." Chaid thought he was going to be killed. He put his hands down by his side and stepped back.

"John," he said, "I don't know what this is all about. I've just tried to be your friend."

Chaid lowered his eyes. Du Pont lowered his gun. He turned and walked out.

That was all Chaid needed to convince him du Pont wasn't going to buy or build him another home. Five days later, the Schultzes helped him load his belongings into a U-Haul. He parked his van behind the Schultz house, planning to return for it in a few weeks. And he left for California.

Du Pont asked Goodale if he could locate him.

"I [asked] him, did he want me to try to locate Dan Chaid in the form of investigate his whereabouts, put people on the street to find him," said Goodale. "And he said, 'No, no, you don't have to go that far. Just keep an eye out on where he's at.' "

If Chaid was gone, his van wasn't, and that aggravated du Pont. He had it checked constantly. Once, Nancy Schultz used it to do some errands and left the van at a friend's house. The next day, du Pont sent someone to tell her the van was to be returned immediately; du Pont wanted it where he could see it.

On November 10, Chaid flew to Philadelphia, was picked up at the airport by a friend, and driven to Foxcatcher. There were people waiting for him in the Schultz driveway. One was Frank Strassacker, a Foxcatcher employee who was just a few weeks from retirement. He told Chaid that du Pont wanted to see him. "No," said Chaid. "I'm not going to do that."

The van needed a jump start; after revving the engine a few times, Chaid took off. He was on the property no more than fifteen minutes.

He did not return.

As always, du Pont got his wish.

But Chaid was trying to get the last word. Du Pont's fears that Chaid was spreading tales about him had come true. Chaid was complaining about du Pont to the wrestling community, to FILA, and USA Wrestling. He said du Pont was dangerous. He said du Pont had a cocaine habit. He said du Pont threatened him with a gun. He even called du Pont's brother, Henry, in Delaware.

On top of that, Kenny Monday, one of the black wrestlers who was fired, strongly suggested to USA Wrestling officials that their association with du Pont could prove to be an embarrassment at the 1996 Olympics should word get out that the organization was supported by a man whose odd and apparently dangerous acts were increasing.

On November 16 there was a conference call among wrestlers, including Schultz and Monday, and officials of USA Wrestling to discuss du Pont. The issue was removing du Pont from power.

Kanamti Solomon and Kevin Jackson also complained.

"What upsets me is that USA Wrestling did nothing about it," said Solomon. "USA Wrestling hurt me more than John du Pont, because they knew what they were doing."

Larry Sciacchetano, the president of USA Wrestling, conceded that du Pont's status made the issue particularly sensitive.

"We're talking about a benefactor who gave half a million dollars a year to the wrestling program," he said.

A steering committee looked at the situation and decided not to take action for two reasons. One, du Pont was not expected to support the organization anymore; he was, in effect, removing himself.

Secondly, the committee concluded that du Pont was not racist, just ill.

"What happened to us should have been the icing on the cake," said Solomon. "This was one of many things. They'd heard about him and guns. Alarms should have gone off in their heads. They ignored the alarms. Of course, it was the money."

Wrong, Sciacchetano said. USA Wrestling wasn't expecting any more money from du Pont.

"We did not prostitute ourselves for the money," he said. "But let's say we had refused further association with du Pont. Would any of those guys have left the farm? No. Especially not Dave Schultz. He was a thirty-six-year-old man, and he didn't think John was dangerous. Neither did any of us."

Solomon said he and Schultz talked about du Pont before Solomon was kicked off the team.

"Dave knew what it was," Solomon said. "We'd talk, and he'd say it was just one of those things with John. He didn't have to tell me how John was. I already knew that. It was upsetting, but it was not a shock. It was the risk you took with John."

What du Pont never knew was that during that conference call, there was one wrestler whose support for him was unwavering, one wrestler who said, "I will talk to him. I'll get him to straighten out his act. I'll handle this."

That wrestler was David Schultz.

Twelve

When du Pont heard that Chaid had been on the property, he got very upset. That was the night he also got very drunk, drove to the Schultz house, and smashed his forehead. The next day, the story that Chaid had hit him with a baseball bat began to take root.

Or maybe it was a Russian who had wielded the weapon.

Both versions flitted in and out of du Pont's head. Both were put together with his increasing fear that there was a conspiracy out to get him. Maybe it was the Russians. Maybe it was Chaid.

No matter, whoever hit him, he seemed to have a question: Why hadn't Schultz protected him? Could he trust Schultz anymore?

"He was more fearful of being down around there or being around in Schultz's company after the November incident," said Georgia Dusckas.

For five of the six years they lived on the farm, the Schultzes hosted du Pont at Thanksgiving. Again in 1995, Dave Schultz made the formal invitation.

This time, Du Pont refused.

Then two days before Christmas du Pont called the Schultzes and left a message: Don't come to Christmas dinner at the mansion. That had been another tradition at Foxcatcher, one that often ended with du Pont handing out checks to everyone present. In 1994, even Nancy Schultz's father and stepmother were recipients of du Pont's largesse.

When Dave Schultz heard the message, he drove to his children's elementary school, where Nancy was helping with a party, to tell her. Though they were no longer welcome, du Pont didn't halt his gifts. On December 23, he made out checks for $5,000 to Dave Schultz and $2,500 to each of the Schultz children, Alexander and Danielle.

Two snowstorms hit the area, one in late December, one the first weekend in January 1996. The second arrived in blizzard conditions, dumping two feet of snow around Philadelphia. The estate looked like a winter scene by Currier and Ives.

After the December storm, Foxcatcher workers set about to clear the roads. They did all but one; du Pont gave an order not to plow the interior road leading to the Schultz house. So Schultz asked Roy Hamilton, who had lived and worked on the estate's dairy farm for thirty-five years, if he could borrow the plow to do it himself. Hamilton had to say no; du Pont had decreed the road remain buried.

"He told me," said Hamilton, "that if we watched carefully, we could see footprints in the snow if anybody was walking around there at night."

When Walter Fitzgerald told du Pont part of the road had to be plowed to get to the horses, he acquiesced. But, he added, make sure you pile the snow seven or eight feet high on the road so no one can come up it.

When the January snowfall was over, Terry McDonnell, who had done landscaping and other work for the du Ponts for nearly four decades, was there to help with the plowing. He was told not to bother with the road that led to Schultz's house.

Du Pont also had another way to show his displeasure with Schultz. Schultz had already made arrangements to spend some time in Colorado Springs, the headquarters of USA Wrestling. In the amateur wrestling world, the Colorado training camp was considered a necessity for those aspiring to the national team. But just before he left, du Pont told Schultz to stay put. "I want you on the farm," he said.

In early January, du Pont purchased a red cape. It was, he said, his Dalai Lama cape. He also asked Dusckas to buy a map of the United States. When she brought it to him, he went into the billiard room and rolled it out on a pool table. He took two red billiard balls and placed them on California.

"That should take care of the two of them," he said. Dusckas believed he was referring to Schultz and Chaid.

On January 17, Dusckas drove du Pont to the airport, where he had chartered a private jet. She didn't know where he was going until she met the pilot. "Ready to leave for San Francisco?" he asked du Pont.

Du Pont turned to Dusckas. "Remember, this is top secret," he said. "Don't tell anybody."

Actually, he had gone to buy stamps. He was an avid collector, could speak articulately about stamps, and owned what had been considered the rarest stamp in the world: the 1856 British Guiana one-cent magenta. It cost him $850,000, plus an $85,000 commission to the auctioneer, in 1980.

He was in California about a day and a half. When he returned, he saw Walter Fitzgerald in the kitchen. Du Pont took him aside and leaned toward him.

"I know who on the estate is after me," he said, ominously. "You should carry a gun in case they come after you."

There had been a lot of violent wind the weekend of January 19 and 20, a Friday and Saturday. On Tuesday, January 23, McDonnell was on the estate to help with the cleanup of brush and tree limbs. He was talking with Fitzgerald near the greenhouse when du Pont pulled up in his Lincoln. McDonnell walked over and du Pont lowered the window. McDonnell saw two items on the car seat: a camera and a pistol.

McDonnell was surprised. He had not seen du Pont with a pistol for some time.

"John, what is that for?" he asked.

"I'm going to do a little hunting," du Pont answered.

"John," said McDonnell, "I don't think there's anything in season now. There is no reason for you to be hunting."

"Well, I'm going to take some pictures with my camera."

"I don't think you need the pistol."

Du Pont then decided to take McDonnell into his confidence.

"Terry, last week I flew out to California," he said. "I was only out there for a very short time and confirmed my suspicions."

"What was that, John?"

"The threat is on the farm."

"John, there is no one here working for you that is threatening."

"No," du Pont said. "The threat is on the farm, and I want to be ready for it."

For the next few minutes the conversation turned to storm damage. Du Pont then drove off.

The next day, Wednesday, there was a torrential rainstorm, adding to the extensive damage on the grounds, including felling several trees. McDonnell returned on Thursday to take care of them.

That same day du Pont had a slight accident with the car; he told Fitzgerald to bring it to the dealer on Friday and to pick up a loaner.

He also reminded him to transfer the homemade hammer and sickle from one car to the other. He apparently still felt he needed protection.

Thursday afternoon, du Pont went to the gym and had his first workout since the November 10 injury suffered in the fall at the Schultz house. His partner was one of the Bulgarian wrestlers who had been training at Foxcatcher for the week. John Giura, a Foxcatcher wrestler since August 1990, went over to give du Pont some encouragement.

"John, it's good to see you back on the mat," he said. "You look good."

Du Pont snapped. He pointed to the scar on his forehead. It was because of Schultz, he said, that he hadn't been able to train. He was very worried about an upcoming competition he had entered the next month in Macedonia.

Giura was taken aback. "Well," he said, "it's just good to have you back on the mat again."

Another young wrestler, Tony DeHaven, was in the locker room when du Pont finished. DeHaven, who had graduated the month before from Villanova—his tuition was paid by du Pont—was thinking about going for a master's degree and hoped du Pont would help again. He asked du Pont if he could talk to him on Friday about taking two education classes at West Chester University.

Du Pont said sure.

There was a pause. "Tony," du Pont finally said, "one of your friends is playing games with me."

"Look, John," said DeHaven. "Nobody's playing games with you. We all care about you. We would never harm you. You know, don't worry about this."

"No, Tony," du Pont said. "My life could be in jeopardy."

"Look, John, you're fine."

"Tony, I'm serious."

And he walked into the shower.

Part of du Pont's regimen included dinner each night at seven. He was in the mansion then when Dusckas was getting ready to leave. Du Pont, she knew, was scheduled the next day to take the drive with Jordanov and the Bulgarian wrestlers to Kennedy Airport in New York. But he suddenly expressed concern about that.

"I'm undecided whether I'm going to go tomorrow," he said to Dusckas. "I don't want it to become strike three."

Dusckas was a little puzzled. Du Pont explained that the first strike was the fire on the estate in October. The second was the accident—the "baseball bat" incident—at the Schultz house in November.

The trip to New York, du Pont said, "Would be the third strike, and three strikes and you're out." He said he had a bad feeling about going with the wrestlers. He thought he'd be safer if he remained at Foxcatcher. That's what he decided to do.

On Thursday night there was a party at Jordanov's house. David Schultz attended with his son, Alexander. Apparently, at some point they were on the deck with a bottle rocket, a piece of plastic pipe about three feet long.

The pipe was left over from a project Schultz and his boy had worked on, building a soccer goal for Jordanov's child for Christmas. Alexander had such fun that he asked his dad if there was anything else they could make. David and Nancy got to talking about shooting pop bottles out of pipe when they were kids, and Alexander wanted to do it, too. It wasn't sophisticated; an opening at one end, a disposable lighter at the other, and suddenly you had a crude launcher. Dave and Alexander used it a few times, both at their house and at Jordanov's. They may have shot it off again during the Thursday night party. It was just a toy.

Or was it? Not, some have maintained, to du Pont. He

had another name for it: a bazooka. A bazooka owned by David Schultz.

Was Schultz planning on using it?

January 26 was a cold, gray day, typical for Pennsylvania in late January. Early in the morning, du Pont met with Rudy D'Alessandro, the construction manager whose company was doing work at Foxcatcher. D'Alessandro was carting around a window in his van he planned to install. He wanted to show it to du Pont.

"I'll see it later," du Pont said. "I'll see you at the site."

There was nothing in his demeanor that was any cause for alarm. "He seemed sharp and attentive," D'Alessandro said. "He didn't seem to be going out into left field with me."

About nine-thirty in the morning Walter Fitzgerald walked into the mansion to tell du Pont he had returned with the loaner Lincoln Town Car.

"John," he said, "your Lincoln's back "

"Thank you," du Pont answered.

About the same time, du Pont saw Tony DeHaven out for a run. "John, is it still okay for me to come see you today?" he asked.

"Yes," said du Pont.

The day was shaping up as a busy one, with decisions to be made.

Du Pont then went to the wrestling center, where there was a party for the Bulgarians. He had decided he wasn't going to accompany them to New York, so he went to say good-bye.

Dave Schultz was there.

He was wearing his Russian outfit.

Du Pont remained just a short time. He had a planned meeting at 10 A.M. with Wochok to discuss the Larry Eastland case.

Eastland, of Boise, Idaho, had been involved in a lucrative deal with du Pont. He worked for du Pont from 1988 to 1995 on a month-to-month contract that, he said, paid $25,000 a month, plus expenses. He described his job as "devoting himself faithfully to du Pont." That devotion included such projects as ghostwriting books by du Pont, including *Off the Mat* and *Never Give Up*, the two volumes of thoughts and anecdotes about athletics and citizenship that du Pont published for himself and friends.

The job also encompassed tasks like hiring a scientist to analyze the air at du Pont's home in order to reassure du Pont that no biological irregularities were present. He tracked the pedigree of du Pont's animals. He researched du Pont's genealogy. He designed a computer system to catalog du Pont's antiques.

Eastland had been threatening to sue du Pont for months, claiming his agreement included a provision that promised a severance package of three years' salary, or $900,000, if he were dismissed after five years. (He eventually did file suit, two months after Schultz's death.)

Wochok arrived at Foxcatcher at ten and talked to Georgia Dusckas and Barbara Linton for about fifteen minutes. Du Pont came about ten-fifteen, and they spent an hour or so together. Wochok brought them up-to-date on the case, and explained that process servers might be bringing subpoenas that day.

Du Pont seemed to be in good spirits.

"He had a cigar and he made a gesture to me and he did like a Groucho Marx kind of thing with his cigar," said Dusckas. "He was in a great mood."

Around eleven-thirty, shortly after Wochok left, du Pont talked again to Fitzgerald at the greenhouse.

"Make sure there's wood under the front porch," he said. "And make sure you feed the ducks."

At one point he called Zdrava Jordanov, Valentin's wife, from the gym to say he might be over to take a language lesson. He got the machine and left a message, ending it with "Have a nice day."

Part of his routine was lunch at 1 P.M. On this day he ate extraordinarily fast. It was so fast, that Dusckas noticed the time he finished: 1:04 P.M.

"How could he eat so quickly?" she thought.

He walked out the kitchen door, and quickly passed her. "I remember looking and I was absolutely astonished that he walked by so quickly," she said.

He said he was expecting Pat Goodale. "Should Pat come, tell him I'll be right back," he said. "I'll be out of the house."

The meeting with Goodale had been arranged a week earlier. During the third week of January, when du Pont was in California, Goodale was at Foxcatcher, supervising the APC restoration. He returned to his Virginia home on January 19, but before he left he and du Pont set up a get-together the following Friday, January 26, at 2 P.M.

On his way out of the mansion, du Pont ran into McDonnell. The two walked toward the wrestling center for about five minutes; McDonnell needed to know where du Pont wanted the wood stacked from the fallen trees. Du Pont was lucid, McDonnell said, and in good spirits. When they got to the center, they parted.

"Have a nice weekend," du Pont said.

However, they ran into each other again about thirty minutes later. McDonnell had just gotten into his car when du Pont pulled up and rolled down the window. He pointed out a tree where a large limb, about a foot and a half in diameter, had been sawed off.

"Terry, would you please paint that cut?" he said, referring to the liquid material commonly used on cut tree limbs. "It looks like an eye looking at me."

McDonnell assured him it would be done.

Du Pont was on his way off the estate, heading to a stamp store in Ardmore, about twenty minutes away. On his way out he saw Walter Fitzgerald. They each waved.

He arrived at Main Line Coin and Stamp close to 2 P.M. When he walked in he was greeted by Steve Pendergast.

Du Pont had spent tens of thousands of dollars on stamps, coins, and supplies at the store in the past six months. Pendergast figured he had seen him fifteen or twenty times. One was in October, shortly after the fires; du Pont purchased a number of twenty-dollar gold coins.

"I'll give them to people around the farm and maybe we can get some information about how this thing started and get to the bottom of it," he explained to Pendergast.

In November, du Pont came in with his face swollen and head bandaged. Pendergast asked what had happened.

"Someone hit me with a baseball bat," du Pont said.

On January 26, du Pont and Pendergast looked at a number of stamp albums. Du Pont picked a few, but wasn't particularly happy with the covers. Pendergast said he'd try and make the covers more attractive.

He also told du Pont that one stamp album, which required some work by store employees, had been completed.

"Fine," du Pont said. "I'll come and pick it up on Monday."

They said their good-byes, and du Pont left for home and his meeting with Patrick Goodale.

Goodale had left Virginia that morning for the drive to Foxcatcher. He got to the estate about one-forty-five in the afternoon, parking his car in the staff lot. Georgia Dusckas let him in through the kitchen entrance, and he followed her up the stairs to a second-floor office.

Du Pont came in about a half hour later. They didn't talk that long before du Pont stood up.

He asked Goodale: "Do you want to go for a ride?"

About the same time, less than a mile away, Dave Schultz was finishing lunch and having his last conversation with his wife.

PART THREE

A Matter of Sanity

On January 26, 1996, John du Pont took the final step into the very depths of madness.

THOMAS BERGSTROM

He controlled everything in his life. And then he took a human life because of that.

JOSEPH McGETTIGAN

Thirteen

When Dave Schultz was killed, Delaware County District Attorney Patrick L. Meehan had been in office barely three weeks. Not only was Meehan brand-new, but his office was about to tackle the prosecution of the wealthiest murder defendant in the history of American justice.

Making matters worse from a prosecution standpoint, Meehan himself had never tried a criminal case. He had the physical presence of a D.A.—tall, good-looking, square-jawed, ruddy-complexioned, hair turning a dignified sandy gray. At one time, he had been a minor-league hockey referee. But his career was one driven by politics, his most recent stop being in the office of Pennsylvania's middle-of-the-road Republican senator Arlen Specter—the same man whose campaign for Philadelphia district attorney had been directed twenty years earlier by Terry Wochok.

Meehan had been Specter's top aide; his expertise was in running campaigns, not putting bad guys in jail. He was, however, the handpicked candidate of the county's powerful GOP political machine that, in years past, had simply been called the War Board. By the time Meehan was running for D.A., the old War Board label was gone, but the county Republican party could still put whoever it chose into office merely by putting its stamp of approval on a candidate.

Meehan was their man. Despite his lack of prosecutorial experience, Meehan won his 1995 election in a cakewalk.

Fortunately, Meehan also had a sense of putting the right pieces in the right places. He looked to Harrisburg, the state capital, for somebody to run the day-to-day operations of his office and picked a career prosecutor named Joe McGettigan, who had been working for the state attorney general's office.

McGettigan joined the D.A.'s office with Meehan just weeks before Schultz's murder. He brought with him a track record of having put scores of killers behind bars and on death row, and he had a style that was every defense lawyer's worst nightmare: rapid-fire, condescending, and abrasive.

McGettigan, forty-eight, grew up in Southwest Philadelphia and was, he admitted, a handful as a young man growing up in a tough neighborhood. He had taken a circuitous route to becoming a lawyer. He attended junior colleges in Philadelphia and Florida and earned his undergraduate degree at Temple University. He tended bar, taught college English, and operated a bookstore. He ran around Europe playing professional basketball in Sweden while dating a girlfriend in Spain. Eventually, a half dozen knee surgeries made him think about doing something more serious than shooting jump shots and he got his law diploma from the University of San Diego at age thirty-one.

He never married.

Prosecuting murderers was his passion.

From the very outset of the du Pont case, McGettigan was infuriated by the attention it attracted. He didn't like publicity himself, and he loathed the idea that a killer could be thought of as a celebrity.

"As far as I'm concerned," McGettigan said of the multimillionaire, "this guy is just another moke who took someone's life."

"Moke" is a Philadelphia street term, used mostly among the Irish. It describes someone with little talent and less ambition—a ne'er-do-well.

McGettigan had another moniker for du Pont: "Defendant." In court, he never referred to him by his name.

"When a person is arrested, they get a new name as far as I'm concerned," McGettigan said. "It's 'defendant.'"

With a mop of prematurely white hair and a pug nose, McGettigan was bulldoggishly combative in court. The more intense he became, the faster he talked. He spit out words like machine-gun bullets, sometimes so rapidly—particularly during cross-examinations—that court reporters had to ask him to slow down. When opposing lawyers were talking, McGettigan would appear to lose interest, and he'd fidget in his chair, finger his watch, and play with his tie, simply champing at the bit to rip apart whatever argument the defense was presenting.

Before getting the call to join Meehan, McGettigan had been in the Pennsylvania State Attorney General's Office, where he had prosecuted cases involving Philadelphia election fraud—a job that, given Philadelphia's reputation, kept him busy. But it was before that, when he was in the Philadelphia D.A.'s Office, that McGettigan earned his reputation as a legal street brawler and courtroom zealot.

Anyone—opposing lawyers, the judge, a witness—who McGettigan perceived as getting in the way of him achieving what he believed to be a just outcome became an enemy who, in his own words, he'd "condemn to the depths of hell."

Unlike Meehan, McGettigan was apolitical. He wasn't interested in elected office, and he served in Philadelphia under a string of district attorneys, both Republicans and Democrats, including Ed Rendell, who became mayor of Philadelphia.

"My sister tells me I'm self-righteous," McGettigan said wryly. "It's easier to be self-righteous this way."

McGettigan rose through the ranks of a crowded D.A.'s office by taking cases no one else wanted, particularly ones involving kids, either as victims or witnesses. Children made iffy witnesses, especially children from poor urban neighborhoods who were frightened and lost in the overwhelming complexity of the legal system, and whose testimony was, more often than not, being elicited to bring to justice a parent or guardian.

"It's easy for me to spend four hours goofing around with a kid for fifteen minutes of talking about bad things," said McGettigan, who has no children of his own.

In the city D.A.'s office he prosecuted a number of high-profile homicide cases, including Philadelphia's infamous "sneaker case," where a fifteen-year-old boy was killed for his Air Jordan basketball shoes. McGettigan won convictions of three men for the killing.

He also got a double-death penalty for a Philadelphia man who bludgeoned, scalded, and choked to death his wife, then killed his nine-year-old stepdaughter with a hammer.

McGettigan tore into defendants like those with a vengeance.

"I just decided that I wanted to prosecute the worst criminals committing the worst crimes," McGettigan said.

Soon after the Schultz homicide, Meehan brought in another lawyer to assist McGettigan. In style, Special Assistant District Attorney Dennis McAndrews was the antithesis of McGettigan. The forty-three-year-old McAndrews, whose looks reminded many of Richard Dreyfuss, was scholarly and tactful. He grew up in Moscow, Pennsylvania, near Scranton, in the state's northeast region. His father and older brothers had built a man-made lake to be used as a private swim club and when it came McAndrews's time to join the family business, he worked morning to night cleaning toilets, collecting trash, gathering rocks. "After that," he said, "nothing seemed like work."

McAndrews went to college and earned his law degree from Villanova University and spent fifteen years in the Delaware County District Attorney's Office. A few months before Schultz was killed, McAndrews went into private practice. He had a strong background in mental-health issues. In 1982, when the Commonwealth of Pennsylvania was looking into a notorious mental-health hospital called Pennhurst—which was eventually ordered closed—McAndrews visited 130 mental-health facilities gleaning information.

However, it was his background in another area—appeals work—that made him a key figure in the du Pont case. And it would be McAndrews who, almost single-handedly in the months ahead, would attack the mountains of legal paperwork that du Pont's squadron of lawyers generated through dozens of petitions and challenges in three different court jurisdictions.

In the end, though, McAndrews would prove much more influential than simply as the D.A.'s "appeals man."

Although McAndrews's demeanor was certainly milder than McGettigan's, his gut burned for as harsh a conviction as could be mustered for du Pont. Unlike his colleague, McAndrews was married and the father of four daughters. He empathized with the two children left fatherless by du Pont's bullets.

McGettigan—for all his fire and zeal—was a realist. Early on, he figured that third-degree murder was a likely outcome with a sentence approaching the maximum of twenty to forty years in jail for du Pont. He probably would have taken such a deal in a plea bargain, putting du Pont away perhaps until he turned eighty. McAndrews, however, wanted nothing less than first-degree.

"I was concerned that for the prosecution to agree to [third-degree murder] would be perceived to be giving du Pont a benefit that others would not get. Whether that was true or not, that would have been the perception," McAndrews said. "And we have a very real obligation to maintain public confidence in the justice system."

As the du Pont defense hurled petition after petition at the prosecution, McAndrews deftly handled each one. Routinely, the defense would deliver its motion at the end of the business day. By 9:30 the next morning, McAndrews would have already dictated a 15-to-20-page response.

"I'd say there were a half dozen lawyers who could have done what Dennis did," McGettigan said, "but there was only one who would have been willing to do it because of the commitment involved."

In fact, McAndrews turned down the first request that he join the prosecution team. In the end, McGettigan—who hadn't known him prior to the du Pont case—prevailed by appealing to McAndrews's sense of justice. McGettigan knew a fellow zealot when he saw one.

Meehan selected a third lawyer a week after Schultz's death, Joseph Grace. Grace, thirty-six, was a lawyer in a Philadelphia firm and former reporter for the *Philadelphia Daily News*. He had the title of Assistant District Attorney, and performed some of the day-to-day functions of the office. But he was brought on primarily to handle the media in the du Pont case. His job was to sate the press's thirst for information while protecting his employer's desire for discretion.

"We have to be professionally responsive to the press and prepare for the case," said Meehan.

Preparing on the other side were the two big-ticket lawyers brought into the case by Terry Wochok. Richard Sprague and William Lamb each signed retainers paying them an up-front fee of $100,000. Both came into the case backed by associates and investigators, and it wasn't unusual to see a dozen members of the team during du Pont's court appearances. Before they were through, their firms would bill du Pont nearly $3 million.

Asked if having so many high-profile lawyers could prove a problem, Lamb said, "We all have prosecutorial experience. We'll all add to the effort. This is a case of obviously large proportion. There'll be enough work for all of us to do. I can assure you we won't be stepping on each other."

One of the first things they did, on the day of du Pont's arrest, was hire psychiatrist Robert Sadoff, who charged $400 an hour.

The "Three Wise Men" of the defense and the prosecution's "Big Mac Attack" learned right away that they would be arguing the case before Common Pleas Court Judge Patricia H. Jenkins. Jenkins had been on the bench less than three years when the du Pont case landed in her lap. At forty-four, she was among the youngest major players in the case. Only McAndrews, at forty-three, was younger.

Jenkins found herself presiding over the blockbuster case purely by chance. Court assignments in Delaware County are made randomly by computer, and Jenkins's name popped up. However, her selection would become fortuitous. For a case that would turn on fine legal points involving complex psychological issues, Jenkins was a terrific choice. She was an expert on Pennsylvania's Mental Health Procedures Act, a body of law that would be referred to often during the case. And for sixteen years before becoming a judge in 1993, Jenkins had been a part-time solicitor for the county's Human Services Department, handling mental-health cases.

As a lawyer, she had frequently argued to have people involuntarily committed to mental institutions.

"When I took the job, I was afraid it would be depressing," Jenkins said of her solicitor's job. "And while there were depressing instances, I found it to be just the opposite. I had the opportunity to see so many people go into remission and function perfectly well. On occasion, I would pass people on the street who would remember me as the attorney who advocated their own commitment to the hospital and be very friendly, saying, 'I'm glad that happened, that was for the best.' "

Jenkins was born in Canada and moved to Delaware County as a child, growing up just a short drive from the courthouse where she would sit as a judge. The daughter of a newspaper executive, she went to Albright College in Reading, then to Dickinson Law School and Villanova University for a master's degree.

In 1984, while driving alone in New Jersey, she was in a head-on automobile accident when a car traveling toward Jenkins pulled left in front of hers. In piecing together the accident, authorities theorized that an unbelted child may have interfered with the driver. Two women and a two-and-a-half-year-old child in the other car were killed. Jenkins was the lone survivor, but ended up temporarily wheelchair-bound with severe leg injuries. She also needed plastic surgery on her face.

From that accident, Jenkins said, she developed a greater appreciation for people who grapple with disabilities. She continues to suffer from an occasionally achy ankle but said she was grateful to "become virtually whole again."

But she never overcame her self-consciousness about her face; she shied away from candid photos of herself, choosing instead to hand out her official court portrait to newspapers.

Jenkins's appointment to the bench had raised some eyebrows. An attractive, dark-complexioned woman with high cheekbones, hazel eyes and dark hair that she frequently wore pulled back severely, Jenkins was the wife of one of the most powerful politicians in Pennsylvania, Speaker of the State House Matthew J. Ryan.

The marriage had been the second for both Ryan and Jenkins. He was twenty years older; she had worked in his law firm. Ryan's district, the 168th, included Newtown Square, and John du Pont was one of Ryan's more prominent constituents.

In Pennsylvania, judgeships have frequently been associated with politics. Jenkins acknowledged that her marital circumstance made it ''not uncommon to wonder about'' her own appointment.

Interestingly, while Jenkins was married to an influential Republican politician, it was a Democratic governor, Bob Casey, who appointed her to the bench to fill the unexpired term of Judge Melvin G. Levy, who gave up his judicial robe to go into private practice. While her selection raised questions that politics was involved, she said that her husband's role was limited to his suggestion in November 1992 that she make known her interest in the opening.

''The [interview] committee,'' she said, ''was not comprised of my husband's fans or nearest and dearest friends.''

From a field of nearly twenty candidates, Jenkins made the short list of finalists, and she believes she became Casey's choice after the withdrawal of another lawyer who had previously filled temporary bench vacancies. After her appointment, Jenkins was elected to a ten-year term in November 1993.

At the outset, there were whispers that the Jenkins-

Ryan connection would work in du Pont's favor, since he had been a friend to Republicans. But from the start, Jenkins was resistant to the du Pont defense's early tactics, a strategy that often seemed designed to delay the proceedings through the filing of what would become thousands of pages of petitions. And nearly every time one of Jenkins's decisions went against du Pont—which was often in the months before trial—the defense response was appeal on top of appeal, at times all the way to the State Supreme Court. It crossed Jenkins's mind that the case might be dragged on for so long, in the glare of such bright publicity, that it would never get to trial.

The higher court, time and again, upheld her rulings. And it backed her when Richard Sprague complained to her face in court that she favored the prosecution and asked her to excuse herself from the case.

Jenkins said she learned to sympathize with Judge Lance Ito, the Los Angeles jurist whose every move in O.J. Simpson's criminal trial was scrutinized and dissected.

"You have to have an appreciation for the difficult position any judge is in who has a case in which there is an abnormal amount of interest," Jenkins said, "because all of us are accustomed to working with some degree of anonymity and privacy."

The challenges of handling any high-profile case, she added, was "balancing the right of the public to be aware and informed, and the right of the defendant to a fair trial.

"The other challenge is that the reason justice works is that people can look at it as the way in which society is going to right its wrongs. For that reason, we don't have anarchy, because people can rely on the justice system. Therefore, people have to know what's going on in it."

Unlike Ito, though, Jenkins did not have television cameras to deal with. In Pennsylvania, tape recorders and cameras are prohibited in courtrooms, something that was a relief for Jenkins.

Still, the du Pont case promised to be more help than hindrance to Jenkins's career. While the trial was in progress, local politicians talked up her possible candidacy to a higher court. And there would be other benefits, such as a speaking engagement in Bermuda a few months after the verdict, where she discussed the du Pont case.

Jenkins got her first glimpse of du Pont in her courtroom on February 21, 1996, nearly a month after the murder, when he appeared before her with a request to be released from jail to retrieve documents from his mansion library.

His case would dominate her life for the next year.

Fourteen

Patricia Jenkins was not the first judge du Pont faced after the murder. That had been Richard Burton, the district justice who conducted the brief hearing shortly after du Pont's arrest on January 28, 1996.

Another district justice, David Videon, was scheduled to see du Pont next, on February 1, at a preliminary hearing—often just a formality—dealing with the *prima facie* aspect of the case; that is, prosecutors had to establish that a crime was committed and present evidence that du Pont committed it.

Bail was not yet an issue. In Pennsylvania, district judges can't set bail for homicide cases; that matter must be dealt with on the Common Pleas, or criminal court, level. That was Jenkins's bailiwick.

All of that became temporarily moot, though, when Richard Sprague announced he was tied up with another case out of town.

"We're just not ready to proceed," second-in-command William Lamb explained. "This is a big case. We've got to give it the proper attention. Quite frankly, we just can't be rushed."

So the hearing was pushed back to February 9.

Before that date, though, the first of what would become a blizzard of petitions and motions was filed by du Pont's team.

This one sought permission for du Pont to be transported, under guard and at his own expense, to the University of Pennsylvania Medical Center for a neurological examination.

In effect, du Pont's lawyers wanted to have his head examined to determine if there was an organic basis for the abnormal behavior he'd been demonstrating in recent years. It was a small indication that they were thinking of a defense based on his physical or mental health.

"This kind of preliminary testing comes first, before planning any defense," Lamb said.

Doctors have long categorized brain disorders as either organic or psychiatric. Organic disorders are caused by physical damage to the brain—a blow to the head, for example, a tumor, a stroke. Psychiatric disorders, of course, are problems of the mind.

But in recent years, brain research has muddied the line between the two. Scientists now believe that behavior, structure, and chemistry are all interrelated.

And at least one of du Pont's destructive behaviors—alcoholism—could have affected him beyond the normal problems associated with the disease. Heavy drinking of the type du Pont did could have caused lesions on the brain, and that, in turn, could lead to aggressiveness.

More commonly, though, the result of excessive drinking is actual shrinkage of the brain. In that case, behavior changes are more likely on the order of memory loss.

But even if a brain disorder or brain damage were discovered in du Pont, it would be almost impossible conclusively to link it to his actions. Still, his lawyers were leaving nothing overlooked.

The request to leave prison for the day had to be decided by Jenkins, and she quickly gave her okay. On February 7, du Pont was put into a van and driven to the medical center in West Philadelphia. He arrived at 7:45 A.M. and underwent magnetic-resonance imaging of his brain, an electroencephalogram, which traces changes in electric activity in the brain, a blood test, a physical history evaluation and a physical examination. He returned to prison about three o'clock.

If the excursion proved anything, it was never revealed. Du Pont's day at the hospital never came up again.

That was on the medical front. On the legal front, du Pont's team sent a letter to the district attorney's office that included these two odd sentences:

"We are led to believe there may have been a weapon or weapons in the car of Dave Schultz, the victim in this matter. Would you kindly provide us with that information if, in fact, we are correct?"

There was no elaboration, but that passage was likely based on a statement Nancy Schultz had given to police shortly after Dave was killed. She said that when she heard the first shot, she thought it might have been her husband taking target practice. The defense, with very little else at this point, was sniffing around for a possible motive of self-defense.

Dave Schultz, in fact, was known occasionally to carry a gun. He owned a rifle and was a hunter. And a rifle had been recovered from his Toyota Tercel. But like the trip to the hospital, this was never a factor in the case.

Meanwhile, the prosecution made its first complaint about du Pont: that at least six times he refused to take the physical examination routinely given to new prisoners, preventing him from being moved from his solitary-confinement cell in the medical wing of the prison. That was just the first shot fired in what was to become an eight-month battle; du Pont never did take the prison exam.

He did, however, sign a prison questionnaire regarding his health. One question asked whether he had "medical, dental or mental health needs or complaints at present time?" The "yes" box was marked.

Next to it, in a column marked "comments," there was a single word written in:

"Head."

Du Pont's heavily anticipated, first public appearance since the day of his arrest finally came shortly after 10 A.M. on Friday, February 9 in the beautifully restored Delaware County Courthouse in Media, the county seat. Normally, Videon's hearings were conducted in his small courtroom in Newtown Square, but the expected crush of onlookers and journalists—more than eighty media outlets had requested credentials—prodded officials to move it to the biggest courtroom in the county with room for about 180 people.

On du Pont's side of the aisle sat his brother Henry. No other family member was present. The section reserved for family and friends of the Schultzes was packed.

An expressionless du Pont, wearing a dark, blue-hooded sweatshirt zipped to the neck, dark baggy pants, and sneakers, was led into the courtroom. His handcuffs were unlocked, and he took a seat next to Lamb, Sprague, and Wochok.

Videon asked du Pont to stand, then read the list of charges: murder in the first degree, murder in the third degree, voluntary manslaughter, involuntary manslaughter, recklessly endangering another person, simple assault, and possessing instruments of crime.

"You have the right to remain silent," Videon said. "Anything you say now can and will be used against you in this court or in any other court of law in Pennsylvania. Are there any questions?"

"May I speak to my client, Your Honor?" Sprague asked.

"Yes."

Sprague leaned toward du Pont.

"Your Honor," he said, looking back toward Videon, "my client has advised me that he does not understand what you have said and that he is not answering anything."

"Mr. Sprague, have you or cocounsel had an opportunity to discuss with Mr. du Pont the purpose of this preliminary hearing today?"

"Yes, we have."

"Thank you. You may be seated."

Joe McGettigan declined to make an opening statement. He really didn't have to. Not with the testimony of the one witness he called to the stand.

"Your Honor," he said, "the commonwealth would call Mrs. Nancy Schultz."

Nancy, dressed in widow's black, was sworn in, took the chair, and moved forward to be close to the microphone. McGettigan led her through the events surrounding the death of her husband.

"I heard a shot," she said. "I heard a loud scream from David—long. I began running to the front door. Before I reached it, about halfway there, I heard a second shot. I approached the door and picked up the phone and as I came into view, the glass in front of the door—I could see outside and I could see David's body facedown in the snow and I could see the front of John's car.

"I pushed the door open. I could see John sitting in the car with his hand out the window with a gun in his hand, and I started yelling, 'John, stop.' He raised the gun at me. I pulled back inside the house and I saw him drop his hand and shoot David in the back."

"Mrs. Schultz, I'm going to interrupt a second," said McGettigan. "When you say 'John,' to whom are you referring?"

"John du Pont."

She told how she tried to turn David onto his back. How she noticed Pat Goodale running up the porch steps. How she saw David's eyes go fixed and heard gurgling sounds just before the paramedics arrived.

"I believe he passed away at that moment," she said, fighting to maintain her composure.

She said she called her father, then her friend, who rushed over and accompanied her to the hospital.

And then, in one long sentence, she described her final seconds with her husband:

"When I arrived I asked if my husband was there and they said 'yes' and I asked if he was alive and they made me wait for a little while until somebody could speak to me and they told me he had been dead when he arrived and I was allowed to go in and view his body and I gave him a kiss and said good-bye."

"I have nothing further of this witness at this time, Your Honor," said McGettigan.

Sprague stood up and immediately launched into a question:

"Mrs. Schultz, just prior to hearing that first shot, how much time had elapsed between hearing that first shot and when you had seen or talked to David?"

"Maybe ten minutes."

He asked if she had heard any shouting or yelling before the fatal bullets were fired. She said no. He asked how long she'd known du Pont. She said they'd met shortly after the 1984 Olympics. "For several years," she added about the relationship, "it was mainly by phone, that he would call and contact Dave about different wrestling events."

He asked if there were any fights or animosity between Dave and du Pont from the time she and her family moved onto the estate in July 1989 up to the murder. McGettigan objection to the question. "Sustained," said the judge.

Sprague then spent a few minutes exploring Pat Goodale's actions on the day of the killing. He turned to another subject, asking if Dave collected weapons, or had any guns in the Toyota. Again, the objections were sustained.

Sprague honed in on the time between the first and second shots. Nancy said five seconds. And another six or seven seconds before the third shot.

"Now," he said, "when you saw John du Pont, you saw him fire this third shot, can you describe what sort of expression, if anything, you saw on his face? I mean, was it just, you know, a flat face? Was it a face that was showing anger? What was the face showing, if anything, to you?"

"I don't recall examining his face close enough to notice whether he had a specific facial expression," Nancy replied.

Sprague asked if Nancy knew of any reason why du Pont would want her husband dead. She said no.

He then gave the first hint of what was to come a year later at du Pont's trial.

"Have you been aware that the property that you and your husband was living on was at least considered by John du Pont to be holy land of the Dalai Lama's?"

"Objection."

"Sustained."

"Were you aware of your husband building what's called a bazooka?"

"Objection."

"Sustained."

It is unlikely that Sprague—an experienced criminal lawyer whom District Attorney Pat Meehan called "aggressive and crafty" and "pretty good at theatrics"—intended to get answers to either question.

But it was obvious what impression he wanted to leave about his client: that du Pont might have been so delusional he didn't know what he was doing.

That was the strongest clue yet that the defense was laying the groundwork for an insanity defense. Despite the perception that the insanity defense allows people to get away with murder, however, statistics show that it rarely works; it's used in less than 1 percent of felony cases, and successful in only one-quarter of those.

So Sprague could have been setting the stage for another claim: that du Pont was guilty not of first-degree murder, which had the specter of the death penalty hovering over it, but of voluntary manslaughter.

Voluntary manslaughter is a finding that the homicide was committed, but the killer was impaired by an irrational fear that his life was threatened. Could du Pont have believed that Schultz posed a threat to him with a bazooka? Or that Schultz was desecrating holy ground?

Insanity is a legal term that asks the question: Was a person so crazy that he didn't know what he was doing? In other words, was du Pont so out of touch with reality that he had no ability to understand that shooting Schultz could result in his death—or that shooting him was wrong?

Suppose, though, that he did know what he was doing, but his evaluation of the situation was so distorted by mental illness that he thought he was going to be attacked by Schultz. Suppose he truly believed—delusionally or not—that his life was in danger? Hadn't he told people at Foxcatcher that the threat was on the farm? Didn't he say to wrestler Tony DeHaven, the night before the murder, that he felt his life was in jeopardy?

Maybe in his warped mind, killing Schultz was justified. If a jury believed that, then his crime would no longer be called murder, but manslaughter.

And that typically carried a penalty of four to seven and a half years.

Since there was no hope for a straight "not guilty" verdict—there were, after all, two eyewitnesses to the crime—the best scenario for du Pont would be not guilty by reason of insanity. In that case, du Pont would have been sent to a mental-health facility for treatment and re-examined periodically. When the doctors pronounced him fit, he would walk away—although there was no guarantee that pronouncement would ever come.

Second best seemed to be voluntary manslaughter. In that scenario, du Pont, fifty-seven when he shot Schultz, could return home before his sixty-fifth birthday.

All of that, of course, was pure speculation, because Sprague and his mates refused to discuss any aspect of their strategy. That might have been because they weren't sure themselves. Du Pont wasn't helping matters much. Initially, he denied any knowledge that Schultz was dead. Then he refused to believe it. Never did he acknowledge his involvement.

Not once in their daily conversations or visits with him, his lawyers said, could they get him to focus on the case.

To learn just what du Pont did or did not understand, one of the first things Jenkins did was order a competency exam to determine if du Pont could stand trial. Commonly called the "understand and assist" test, the competency exam was designed to determine if du Pont could (1) understand the charges against him, and (2) help his lawyers prepare his defense.

The issue of competency—which addressed du Pont's present state of mind—could get confusing. He could have, for instance, been judged competent to stand trial, but found insane at the trial. That's because insanity looked backward to the time of the crime, while competency was a question for the present.

Du Pont's lawyers felt strongly he was incompetent to stand trial. But Sprague didn't want him to be formally evaluated until there was a private hearing regarding his mental condition. He kept throwing legal roadblocks in front of Jenkins, and until those were dealt with the exam couldn't take place. In fact, it wouldn't be until September—when Sprague and Lamb were no longer in the case—that the competency question was addressed.

By then, the whole process became stranger because of

the entrance of du Pont's family. Du Pont's sister, Jean Shehan, led a number of relatives who went to court trying to have du Pont declared incompetent to manage his affairs. That put his lawyers in the position of maintaining he was incompetent to stand trial, but competent to run the estate and manage his assets.

In the meantime, they made another attempt to get du Pont out of prison. On February 14 they asked Jenkins to allow him to be escorted to his mansion. The purpose, they said, was to retrieve materials from his library that could be important for the defense.

There was also another part of the request. Du Pont wanted the items returned that had been taken from him at his arrest—including the laminated pass to the World Wrestling Championships that had been around his neck.

And all his guns and ammunition.

Sprague really wasn't sure what he'd find in du Pont's inner sanctum, the room with the vaulted doors. He simply wanted to see what papers were there, if there were any writings from du Pont that could help explain some of the delusions he'd been hearing about since he first visited him in prison. Du Pont, though, refused to give up the combination. Sprague told du Pont he didn't need to know the combination; let someone he trusted open it, someone who could watch Sprague and guide him. Du Pont's response was that no one could get in the room except for him because there were secret compartments, and only he could tell what was hidden there.

The documents, du Pont insisted, could prove he had nothing to do with the killing of Schultz.

They also proved he was the Dalai Lama, a citizen of Bulgaria, and a government official for the United States and other countries.

The request led to another court hearing on February 21, du Pont's first appearance before Jenkins. He was gaunt and pale, and his clothes were almost identical to what he had worn in court for his preliminary hearing twelve days earlier.

Sprague called three witnesses. Two were Lamb and Wochok. Both testified to the necessity of du Pont accompanying them to his library. Only he, they said, could sift through the hundreds of thousands of pieces of paper to locate appropriate items.

Of course, they said, du Pont would foot the bill, just as he had for his trip to the hospital.

The third witness was Georgia Dusckas, called primarily to emphasize that only du Pont would know where things were in that private room.

McGettigan attempted to find out more about the material, but Sprague objected every time, citing lawyer-client privilege, so it never was clear how the documents could help the defense.

McGettigan scoffed at the whole thing, calling the request nothing more than an attempt to have a "little road trip" to get du Pont some time out of prison. He questioned how the defense could call the papers "absolutely necessary" at the same time they couldn't be specific on what they were looking for.

"I can see next week there will be an attic in Havertown. The following week it will be a basement in Clifton Heights," he said, naming two nearby towns.

Plus, he emphasized, don't overlook the squadron of legal help du Pont was able to buy.

"He has a platoon of lawyers who could not only go through these documents," he argued, "but they could alphabetize, categorize, and scan them for him."

Sprague acknowledged du Pont's wealth, but put a different spin on it. It worked against him, he said.

"If it weren't Mr. du Pont, we wouldn't be in here fighting tooth and nail over every little thing," Sprague said.

Jenkins only need a few hours after the hearing to issue

arently comfortable, du Pont talked for seventy-five
s. Rather, he rambled for seventy-five minutes. He
about the Soviet Union and about how he was ap-
ed by a group from the Buddhist Church to become
lai Lama. He told how he caused anger in America
ching both the American and Bulgarian wrestling
in the 1992 Olympics. He said he was Bulgarian
h. He talked about the Church of Satan. He said
rs shouted "du Pont, you murderer" at night. He
ed how he and Dave Schultz set aviation history
w he came into possession of the Shroud of Turin.
e you familiar with history books and history les-
du Pont said. "Then you must know that the East
st have always had war between the Soviet Union
Western world, whether it be with armies and with
it be with sports, one or the other.

he Olympics, it's been the medal count as to who
e most. And in the wars with guns, it's the body
s to who wins the most, or the real-estate count,
ame of capture the flag or destroy cities, one thing
other. It's always been this way throughout his-
d it goes on today, but on a much lesser basis."

have you had a particular role in this of recent?"
asked.

ve found myself dragged into that position by ac-
es."

you explain that more?"

I'm a coach and a wrestling coach, and I coach
des of the Iron Curtain. And it has brought some
ngs among several groups of people."

have you antagonized by coaching on both

nternational Olympic Committee, the United
mpic Committee, and USA Wrestling."

Pont said, one man came to his rescue and
ings out.

her ruling: "The defendant has failed to demonstrate that
the relief requested is necessary to afford him his right to
effective assistance of counsel."

Two days later, Sprague appealed to Pennsylvania Superior Court. He was turned down there, too.

Six days later he tried to get du Pont out again, this
time to be taken to the office of Robert Sadoff in the next
county for a psychiatric exam.

Sadoff had met with du Pont in prison on January 30,
but didn't get very far. Phillip Resnick, another psychiatrist added to du Pont's team, was also unsuccessful when
he tried on February 14. Du Pont, they said, simply
wouldn't talk.

He wouldn't talk because he believed his cell was
bugged.

Sadoff, earning $400 an hour, and Phillip Resnick, a
five-hundred-dollar-an-hour doctor from Ohio, told the
court that du Pont refused to speak with them in any
meaningful way in prison. He feared his conversations
were recorded, and he believed he was being spied on.

Sadoff and Resnick were nationally known forensic
psychiatrists. Resnick, director of forensic psychiatry at
Case Western Reserve University School of Medicine in
Cleveland, had been a consultant for the prosecution in
the Jeffrey Dahmer case. At the same time he joined du
Pont's team he was working for the defense in the trial
of John C. Salvi III, charged with killing two abortion-
clinic workers in December 1994 in Brookline, Massachusetts. Salvi's lawyers were trying to prove that he was
insane at the time of the killings.

Sadoff had been involved in a number of high-profile
cases in the Philadelphia area, including those of Sylvia
Seegrist, a Delaware County woman who went on a
deadly shooting spree at a local shopping mall, and Har-
rison "Marty" Graham, who strangled several women
and left their remains in his Philadelphia apartment. Sa-

doff was a defense witness for Seegrist and worked for the prosecution in the Graham case.

Jenkins scheduled another hearing to deal with the issue of transporting him out of jail. But she couldn't hold it until March 15. That was too late, du Pont's lawyers felt.

So they sought relief in the Supreme Court of Pennsylvania. That didn't work. They went back to Common Pleas Court and got another judge, Joseph Battle, to hear their request on an emergency basis.

That took place on March 4. This time Sprague only called one witness.

Himself.

First, he made an opening statement. Then he was sworn in, and was questioned by Lamb. Then he made a closing statement.

It was urgent, he said, for psychiatrists to talk with du Pont, and to have that talk videotaped. Since du Pont wouldn't do it in prison, what was the harm of having him taken out for the day?

Because of the unusual circumstance of Sprague moving from lawyer to witness, McGettigan had an opportunity to cross-examine him. From the tone they took with each other, it was obvious there was no love lost. McGettigan, for instance, pointed out that Sprague had visited du Pont more than a dozen times.

"You were actually able to conduct interviews with him on some of those occasions and some of these were satisfactory, were they not?" he asked.

"Mr. McGettigan," Sprague said, "why don't you learn to ask one question at a time, instead of three. Which question do you want me to answer?"

McGettigan turned to Battle. "Your Honor, would you ask the witness to refrain from the gratuitous comments as much as possible?"

"All right," said Battle. "Let's slow down. Ask him one question at a time and get an answer."

"If the witness can't understand to make it clearer," McGettigan sai

"Mr. McGettigan, I can understa asked. Ask them one at a time."

"Give evidence of that, sir, and ness. And a better lawyer."

When Sprague stepped off the v his closing argument, he urged Battl

"The man needs a further examir have our people who need to do it is now, not down the pike. It does entist to understand that delay caus ination process."

McGettigan would have none o trying to, I guess, do what apparen time he was in custody," he said. he pleased and say . . . 'I'm not go

The hearing lasted almost two only a half minute to turn down day ended Sprague went back to tl with his latest appeal.

The high court didn't have a c The next day, March 5, du Pont c Resnick. Special arrangements w use the warden's conference roo sion was videotaped. Before Sprague made some reassuranc

"John, you remember Dr. I And as I said to you yesterda They're just as much working Wochok is, as Bill Lamb is.

"I've had this room debug day, 'Well, debugging today they can listen in to stuff ou outside check. . . . he is outst for bugging and all that."

That was David Schultz.

"For many years," he said, "he has been my guardian."

"You were close to Dave Schultz?"

"Yes, yes. He lived on the farm in Newtown Square at that time."

Resnick steered the conversation to the topic of the fires on the property. Du Pont put the time as August 1995, not October.

"Now a couple of weeks after that I went down to see a young man that was suspected of setting the fires, and I was hit on the head in the middle of the night," he said. "And when I woke up the next morning, I was all sewn up. And Dave Schultz had found me and he brought me back home and again looked after me all that night in my home."

"Who was suspected of hitting you?"

"I'm not going to say at this time because I'm not going to put the shadow of doubt on somebody else. I'm too important a person to put fingers on somebody like that because what I often say becomes law.

"The thing is," du Pont continued, "after that incident I did some further investigations and things were going along fairly smoothly, and then Dave was shot on the farm."

"Do you know when that happened?"

"I no have the exact . . . I don't recall the date, no. Now there is a little more to it than that."

Du Pont then went off on a speech with such convoluted passages—but all connected in du Pont's mind—that Resnick and Sadoff simply let him go on and on.

He didn't stop until he explained why Schultz died.

"As the Dalai Lama," he began, "I picked up a few very interesting artifacts or positions of power along the way that I regret having picked up. And one of them was the Shroud of Turin, that Hitler had during World War II, that the Americans captured. And I got that. And Albert Speer, in 1981, signed the Reich over to me.

"If you believe that history repeats itself . . . I will tell you what happened. I found out about this too late and I put it together.

"I recognized Dave Schultz as one of my protectors. Because, you see, Dave Schultz married Nancy Stoffel. And the Schutzstaffein was the name of the SS in the Reich. And he is the one who used to run around and help guard me, Dave did. And from time to time I let him carry the Shroud because he liked it. And it went to South America, it went all over Europe, and around about with us.

"The other interesting thing is that in my greenhouse there's a man named Speer and he would draw lines on the benches for the greenhouse in squares for the plants to go through, very much like Albert Speer did for the engineering for Hitler in World War II.

"I have a recording of Albert Speer telling me how he tried to put Hitler—how he tried to put poisonous fumes through a tunnel in the bunker to get Hitler. And the greenhouse was connected to the big house with a tunnel, and fumes came through the big house and it carried the pesticide fumes from the greenhouse, and poisonous gas, into the big house.

"And if you'd note, if you remember, Hitler had a man named Mengele who was in the prison camps. And the fact is that I have a Polish doctor in my kitchen who cuts things up and puts them in the oven.

"If you believe that history repeats itself, you'd say this is all a big coincidence. It is not a coincidence, because I showed some of my Russian pictures to a man who saw the Shroud in Russia and he was very much upset.

"I carried the Bulgarian colors; Dave Schultz carried the other colors in southern Russia with him. We did this and showed it to some of our friends once in a while as a lark, if you want to put it this way.

"Well, the whole thing backfired because somebody got wind of this in Washington, D.C., didn't like the whole idea of what I was doing, decided to come up and do away with both of us at one time. They killed Dave, and they tried to pin the murder on me by having a double that was made up to look like me.

"Now I was on movie sets in California with Mr. Randolph Scott, who married Mr. William du Pont Jr.'s sister, Marion du Pont and whatnot. He was a cowboy actor. And I was on movie sets with him . . . And the stunt people looked almost identical to the real people who were doing the acting in dangerous positions.

"And it's my position that somebody was dressed up to look like me that killed Dave Schultz. And they pinned it on me."

He went on to outline his belief that the United States government was behind the plot to kill him and Schultz.

"Is there any possibility in your mind," Resnick asked, "that you pulled the trigger?"

"No."

"You're positive of that?"

"That's right."

"And do you recall where you were at the time that Dave Schultz was shot?"

"I don't know when he was shot."

Resnick tried to refresh du Pont's memory with some details of the crime. He mentioned Pat Goodale.

"He's somebody that I trusted for a while," du Pont said. "But he's been off and on the payroll and off and on the property for some time. And the thing is no one really liked him. And I didn't find out until later that, you know, he was not trusted by other people as well."

Resnick mentioned Nancy Schultz's role as an eyewitness. Could she have been mistaken? he asked.

"I have no opinion at this time."

The tape left little doubt that du Pont had severe mental illness. However, was he disabled enough to escape a murder conviction?

Fifteen

On March 12, six weeks after du Pont's arrest, District Attorney Patrick Meehan made an announcement.

"We investigated the matter and took the facts as presented through the investigation, and applied them to the precedents in this county and across Pennsylvania," he said.

"It was my conclusion that the facts did not support asking for the death penalty."

No matter what happened, du Pont would not be executed for murdering David Schultz.

To be successful in a death-penalty case in Pennsylvania, the prosecution has to prove beyond a reasonable doubt that at least one of sixteen specified aggravating circumstances existed at the time of the murder—a killing committed while the victim is a hostage, for instance, or a murder as a result of torture.

Meehan said there was one circumstance that seemed to fit the du Pont case: creating "a grave risk of death to another person" other than the victim. That was based on the testimony of Nancy Schultz, who said du Pont pointed a gun at her before putting the third and last bullet into her husband.

But prosecutors ultimately decided du Pont's actions didn't qualify.

"We all did a great amount of evaluation of the kinds

of situations that have been found in the past to be sufficient evidence of grave risk, and applied it to this case, and it really was not a close call,'' said Meehan.

In addition, there were mitigating factors—those the defense could use to avoid a death sentence—that seemed to carry more weight. Du Pont had no criminal history. He had ties to the community. And his precarious mental state would actually work in his favor.

Meehan's decision did two things. It left du Pont facing an automatic sentence of life in prison without parole if convicted of first-degree murder. That sentence could only be changed by the governor.

More important for his defense team, though, was that it opened the door for his lawyers to seek bail.

Normally, bail was granted in noncapital cases; that is, where the death penalty has been discounted. But judges have wide discretion to turn down a bail request, especially if they feel the defendant poses a danger to himself or the community, or is a risk to flee.

Before getting their paperwork together to deal with bail, though, du Pont's lawyers had another appearance before Judge Jenkins, one more attempt to get du Pont released for a trip to the psychiatrist. That took place on March 15, and this time two of du Pont's siblings sat a few rows behind him: his brother, Henry, and sister, Jean Shehan. Du Pont, though, didn't even make eye contact with them.

Once again, Sprague put one of his sidekicks on the stand, calling on Terry Wochok to answer a few questions about the need to take du Pont out of prison. That was a risky move, and soon made for some fireworks.

Joe McGettigan warned Jenkins that if he felt Sprague and Wochok entered an area of questions and answers that seemed to waive their attorney-client privilege, he intended to exploit it on cross-examination.

He wasted no time.

"In what fashion," he asked Wochok, "do you contemplate the need for psychiatric evidence that you would obtain from your psychiatrist?"

Sprague objected. Jenkins overruled it.

"To understand a variety of issues that will involve the defense of the defendant," Wochok said.

"Name one," said McGettigan.

"Your Honor," Sprague said, "I am going to object to any inquiry into what the areas of the defense are."

Jenkins stared at him. "Sir," she said, "you opened the door."

"No, I did not open the door," said Sprague.

"You said it is necessary for the defense, and Mr. McGettigan is simply saying in what way."

"Well, then, I do not think it opens up the areas of the defense. And I am going to tell Mr. Wochok not to answer."

Jenkins was taken aback. "Sir," she said, "you are not the one who instructs witnesses in this courtroom whether or not to answer."

"Your Honor, Mr. Wochok has a duty as an attorney to Mr. du Pont."

"Sir, as do you. You called this witness to the stand, and you started asking him questions about what was important to his defense."

She overruled the objection. The question was read back. Sprague wouldn't give up.

"I would ask leave to instruct him as counsel for the defense not to answer that question."

"Your request is denied."

"At this time, Your Honor, I move you to disqualify yourself because you are not acting fairly."

"Sir, I didn't ask the questions. Your motion is denied."

She turned to Wochok. "Please answer the question, Mr. Wochok."

Wochok said, "State of mind."

It didn't seem like such a crucial answer to have caused Sprague such angst. But he did continue to object to just about every question McGettigan posed—usually to no avail. In the end, nothing really changed. Jenkins wasn't convinced du Pont needed to leave jail, and she denied the request.

Then, at almost the same time, word came from the Superior Court backing up Jenkins on her decision not to allow du Pont to return to his home to gather whatever he could find for his defense.

Sprague and his mates were on a losing streak.

While they continued to pursue those lines, they branched out into another area: on April 8, a formal petition was filed to get du Pont released on bail.

Bail is designed to assure that a defendant appears for trial. The money is forfeited if the defendant fails to show. But that posed a problem for prosecutors in this case: How much bail would be enough to keep a man worth perhaps hundreds of millions of dollars from fleeing.

"We don't believe that any amount of bail for this defendant certainly can ensure his presence at trial," said Dennis McAndrews.

His lawyers claimed du Pont's health had deteriorated since he was locked up in prison. He was subsisting on tea and crackers and had lost weight, they said.

One clue to life in prison for du Pont came from his own mouth. During the March 5 interview with Robert Sadoff and Phillip Resnick, he was asked what he ate.

"Tea and whatever else that just might happen to come my way," he said. "But I eat no lunch, no breakfast, no dinner."

"Well, what might come your way?" Sadoff asked.

"Well, sometimes if I'm given a few crackers, because the medicine upsets my stomach. But other than that, there's not much."

"But if you hadn't eaten anything in the last thirty-some days since I had seen you, I would think you might be wasting away."

"The thing is, I came in here with some fat on me, some excess weight, and that's probably what I've been living off of."

"Are you able to work out while you're here?"

"No."

"Exercise at all?"

"No."

"Keep in shape, run up and down in your cell, or anything?"

"No."

"You sleep most of the time?"

"I'm in a hospital cell."

"How about reading? Are you able to read?"

"I am not allowed any books. I have requested a couple, but that's not gone through yet."

"They don't allow you books? How about newspapers? You don't want to read the newspaper?"

"I no allowed to have that." Du Pont had lapsed into the broken English he sometimes used.

"No TV?"

"No, I do not have that."

"Is there anybody you can talk to in here?"

"No."

"Nobody? Really?"

"Just the guards and the nurses, when they come by. Remember, I'm in the hospital. I'm the patient here."

It was crucial, his lawyers contended, to du Pont's health that he be removed from prison. But they didn't want him to simply be put out on the street to walk around free.

"We are asking for bail, and the condition of that bail is that he be admitted to the Pennsylvania Institute," said William Lamb.

The Institute of Pennsylvania Hospital was a 137-year-old psychiatric facility on a serene twenty-eight-acre oasis in the middle of a graffiti-scarred section of West Philadelphia.

There, on one of the institute's secured floors, du Pont would have a definite upgrade in creature comforts: a private room with its own lavatory, meals available in a day room, and television.

The average daily charge for the accommodation was $1,195, although the hospital rarely collected that much; it accepted whatever insurance paid.

From time to time, the Institute took prisoners ordered there by the court, so it had some experience.

To the prosecution, however, it made no difference. Security was the real issue.

"Our position is enormous wealth can activate enormous resources for the purposes of flight," said Joseph Grace, the chief spokesman for Pat Meehan. "We believe that this defendant would be a significant risk to flee."

The D.A.'s office laid out this possible scenario: Du Pont hires armed thugs to help him break out of the building, rushes to a helicopter that has landed on the hospital grounds, and flies out of the country.

Far-fetched? Not at all, prosecutors said. Look at what had happened in another du Pont family case a couple of years before. Millionaire Newbold Smith was accused— and eventually acquitted—of conspiring to kidnap his adult son, Lewis du Pont Smith, who was affiliated with a controversial political organization. According to federal prosecutors, the father wanted to have him "deprogrammed" and engaged a deprogrammer and a former police officer to help. There was talk of hiring mercenaries for the kidnapping. All of that would have been facilitated by the du Pont money.

John du Pont was a guy who had piloted a helicopter, traveled under an alias, was a marksman, and had made frequent trips out of the country—including eleven to Bulgaria in the previous eighteen months.

Who's to say, asked McAndrews, that he couldn't break out if he wanted, land in some foreign country, and live the rest of his days off his fortune?

In fact, during a bail hearing on April 15, McAndrews—filling in for McGettigan, who was at a funeral—asked this question of Carl Ausfahl, the institute's assistant director for quality management:

"If Mr. du Pont was a patient on the fourth floor and I had a master key to get in and had a weapon, had another individual with a weapon to assist me, would there be anything to stop me from removing Mr. du Pont from the fourth floor, putting him in a car or a helicopter, and leaving?"

"I would suspect that that's possible," said Ausfahl.

McAndrews asked another question along those lines, but Ausfahl said he didn't understand it. So McAndrews rephrased the query:

"I come in with a key card. I open the door. I walk in. I put a gun to people's head. I say, 'John, you're coming with me. Let's go.' Anything to stop me from going out the door, down to a car, and driving away?"

"No, sir, other than the staff. I can't comment on their heroic behavior."

McAndrews got into the same territory with Sadoff. Sadoff said the security setup would prevent du Pont from getting past the door on the fourth-floor unit.

"If he had assistance by people with arms to try to assist him in leaving the hospital, you're saying that could not happen?" McAndrews asked.

"Oh, you mean if somebody came into the hospital armed with weapons?"

"Yes."

"I hope everybody ducks."

It was Sprague's job to convince Jenkins that the hospital was as secure as a prison. That, in fact, was what the law mandated.

He also had to prove that du Pont's health risk could only be alleviated at the hospital.

He called a number of hospital employees who testified on both points. But McAndrews had his own witnesses, who did their best to shoot holes in that testimony. One, police investigator John McKenna, described how he visited the institute the previous week and walked throughout the place, up and down the stairs, without ever being challenged.

"Did anybody ask who you were?" McAndrews asked.

"No, sir."

"Did anybody ask you what you were doing?"

"No."

"Did anybody tell you that you couldn't go in a particular spot?"

"No, we were unchallenged in the parking lot or the building."

"How long were you in the building?"

"Forty-five minutes."

"At any time did anybody ask for your identification?"

"No."

McAndrews asked about the grounds.

"Is there adequate room for you to land a helicopter in that area?"

"Definitely."

"If an individual wished to escape, do you believe that would be possible?" McAndrews asked.

"Sure," McKenna answered.

"If an individual wished to get assistance from people on the outside, would the individual be able to remove himself from the building?"

"It would be extremely easy."

McAndrews then took McKenna back two and a half months to the weekend of the shooting. McKenna had been one of the officers conducting a search of the mansion at Foxcatcher after du Pont was taken into custody. He listed all the weapons that had been recovered.

"Did you also find a note?" asked McAndrews.

"Yes."

"Where did you find that note?"

"This note was on the nightstand in the master bedroom."

"And what does it say?"

" 'Tell Taras Wochok that his family is going to be killed first, and he will go last.' "

Lamb handled the cross-examination of McKenna. McKenna had said that at one point he stood next to a door on the fourth floor when someone came up, rang the bell, and the door opened. McKenna said he could have easily walked through the door; it was, he said, an ominous breach of security.

"You never got inside, did you?" said Lamb.

"No, I didn't attempt to."

"Okay, so you don't know what kind of other security facilities were inside that ward, do you?"

"No, I do not."

"You don't know that there's a glass cage there or a glass enclosure where there are staff on duty twenty-four hours a day that have a complete panorama of that floor, do you?"

"No."

"You don't know that the windows are Plexiglas windows which are secure windows, do you?"

"No."

"You don't know that the only way that those windows can be opened to the small area is with a key, do you?

"And you don't know that the door that you approached and looked at was the only way in and out of that facility, do you?"

"No."

The defense scored some points.

After McKenna had stepped down, McAndrews called a detective to draw out a single piece of information: that du Pont knew how to fly a helicopter. But before he took the witness stand, Sprague indicated he would stipulate— or agree—to that fact, negating the need for the detective's testimony.

"How many years ago are we talking about?" he asked McAndrews.

"Eighteen, twenty years ago."

"Eighteen or twenty years ago, I'll stipulate," said Sprague. "I'll stipulate he flew with Lindbergh if you'd like."

Du Pont hadn't done that, but he did have a pilot's license that had expired in 1983.

McAndrews's last witness was Cynthia Ward, a nurse at the prison. Her primary purpose was to counteract earlier testimony from defense witnesses that du Pont had lost weight. In fact, her charts showed that from January 29 to March 6 his weight had increased from 150 pounds to 163 pounds.

That would be hard to do on tea and crackers. As it was later learned, du Pont's diet was supplemented by food brought into the prison by Wochok.

Wochok was the final witness called during the six-hour hearing that lasted until 9 P.M. Sprague had two purposes in mind. The first was to have Wochok describe the layout of the institute and contradict McKenna's statements that it would be easy to enter the secured unit.

"From the testimony offered by Chief McKenna, it did not appear to me that he had gone far enough into the facility to be at the place where the secure portion of the fourth and fifth floor is located," Wochok said.

Sprague asked, "Where are you when you come in through that first door that gets open when you ring the bell?"

"You come down a hallway, which leads to other rooms," Wochok said. "And I'm not sure exactly what all of those rooms are used for, but you reach another area that has another locked door that requires a person coming from the outside to have a key to enter that first door. You then enter through the first door and come to a second door that is also locked. And after entering the second door, you come into the unit that we have described."

McAndrews repeatedly challenged Wochok on his description. Wochok repeatedly stuck to his description.

Until the next day, that is. After Wochok left the courtroom he realized he was wrong. Wochok wrote a letter to Jenkins explaining his testimony had been incorrect.

"I apologize to the court for the error and I point out that there is, in fact, presently only one locked door to the entrance to the fourth- and fifth-floor units," he wrote. "I wanted to correct this error at the earliest possible moment."

Wochok said later that he had been at the facility more than once and had come through different doors. That got him mixed up. "I made a mistake and I corrected it," he said. "It's just simply a mistake."

The D.A.'s office could have gloated, but didn't—at least, not publicly.

"We're glad that Mr. Wochok has brought those inaccuracies to the attention of the court," said Joe Grace.

Sprague's second purpose for calling Wochok was more important: he had to dispel any wild ideas about the strange death-threat note found in the mansion. Wochok remembered it as coming at a time when he was representing du Pont in a suit involving a former employee in California.

"A telephone call was placed to my home, saying, 'Tell Taras Wochok that his family is going to be killed first and he will go last,'" he testified. "My wife received that telephone call. She called Mr. du Pont's house. And

Mr. du Pont took this message from my wife and showed it to me when I arrived.''

The note was not, he said, in any way a threat written by du Pont to him or his family.

But he also said the call had been received twelve years ago.

Why had du Pont saved it that long?

That was never answered by Wochok, or anyone else.

Though the hearing had concluded with Wochok's testimony, the paperwork on the bail question went on and on, with both sides filing dueling documents. The defense made fun of the prosecution, accusing it of engaging in fantasy.

''The Commonwealth has concocted a wild scenario that assault weapon–wielding mercenaries (perhaps including James Bond, Rambo and/or the KGB) will swoop out of the skies in attack helicopters . . . and secure du Pont's freedom by whisking him away to some foreign land,'' defense lawyers wrote.

If the court accepted such an argument, they said, no wealthy person could ever be released on bail because of the fear that he would have the ability to escape through such a plan.

The defense also emphasized that du Pont had to be moved for his physical well-being. It said nothing about his mental condition as a reason. In fact, just the opposite.

''Nowhere is there any allegation, testimony, or evidence that du Pont is in need of commitment to a mental-health facility.''

No evidence? What about the interview with Sadoff and Resnick in which he claimed to be the Dalai Lama and said he had mystical powers from the Shroud of Turin? What about his wild ramblings during the weekend stand-off? What about his fear that his cell was being bugged? What about the barrage of tales of his paranoid-schizophrenic behavior?

What about shooting Dave Schultz?

Sprague, Lamb, and Wochok were trying hard to keep questions about his mental state out of the legal arena, partly to bolster their plan to push back the competency hearing as long as possible. They also were successful twice in postponing the date of his arraignment, when du Pont would be required to enter a plea. The arraignment was a key date in the case because if, as expected, du Pont pleaded not guilty, his lawyers would have thirty days from that point to alert the court if it planned to mount an insanity defense. And that would require it to turn over all kinds of material in support of that defense to the prosecution.

For their part, prosecutors hammered away a number of points in their fight to keep du Pont in jail: his refusal to cooperate with prison authorities, his refusal to surrender after the shooting, the contention that he was not deteriorating in jail and had, in fact, gained weight.

On April 30, Jenkins sided with prosecutors. Du Pont would stay right where he was, she ruled. No bail.

She found no compelling evidence that his health was worsening in jail. She was troubled by his request after his arrest that his passport be returned, and his contention at his preliminary hearing in early February that he did not understand the charges against him. She said his behavior after the shooting was "inconsistent with a willingness to stand trial and to submit to sentence if found guilty." Instead, she determined, he demonstrated he would "take significant risks in the service of avoiding the justice system."

She also pointed to a remark du Pont allegedly uttered after his capture: that his diplomatic immunity prevented him from being arrested.

"Such a remark, if made, is inconsistent with an appreciation by the defendant of the circumstances in which he finds himself or the need for his continued participation in the process of adjudicating the charges against him.''

All that, plus a worry that the institute could provide adequate security, made bail out of the question.

Sprague, et. al. immediately appealed to Superior Court, but that would ultimately prove unsuccessful. So would their attempt in State Supreme Court. Du Pont's hopes of getting out of jail to see the psychiatrist, to live at the hospital, or to return to Foxcatcher seemed remote at best.

And what was happening at his beloved Foxcatcher estate during his imprisonment?

There were some physical changes taking place. Du Pont was visited in jail fairly regularly by his loyal employees, like Georgia Dusckas and Walter Fitzgerald, the maintenance manager. Fitzgerald would go once or twice a week, for up to an hour each time. Much of the conversation, Fitzgerald would later say, was "out in space." But there was some coherent chat.

"The first five minutes we talked about the farm and what happened on the farm, what he would like me to do on the farm."

Some of the requests were bizarre, to say the least.

"He told me that he was going to have the four-hole posts removed from his property because that would allow the Russian soldiers to get out and come and rescue him from the prison," Fitzgerald said. "The three-hole posts were for American horses and they were smaller than the Russian horses."

Du Pont also asked Fitzgerald to take out the post in the meadow in front of the mansion, and the posts and wood around the trees on the property.

"He told us to remove them so the spirits out there in that pasture could go back to heaven, because at that time that was the Holy Land," said Fitzgerald.

One of the projects Fitzgerald carried out was the erection of a sign at the main entrance of the estate. It was about five feet tall, with three wooden slats. On the slats were these words:

FOXCATCHER
PRISON
FARM

The sign appeared on the property during the first week in May. Township officials were checking into the legality of erecting such a sign without a permit.

Before long they would have other billboards to fight over; du Pont ordered two large ones put up on the side of the road, one painted red, the other white. They were ten feet by ten feet, standing on twenty-foot poles. No words, no graphics. No one but du Pont knew what their significance was. And even though it was an unusual request, and du Pont wouldn't be able to see them, it didn't occur to Fitzgerald to refuse an order.

He didn't refuse when du Pont told him to paint the buildings on the farm yellow. They had been a pristine white.

He didn't refuse when du Pont to him to paint a gigantic black cross on a barn that was painted red.

He didn't refuse when du Pont told him to paint the Schultz house black.

He simply didn't want to get fired for disobeying. After all, as maintenance manager he had been able to hire his brother and son to do work, paying out tens of thousands of dollars of du Pont's money to them.

"If I leave, someone else is going to come in and do the same job I do," Fitzgerald said.

Meanwhile, a few wrestlers continued to work out at Foxcatcher, including Valentin Jordanov, who was still the coach. But Foxcatcher had ceased to exist, as far as USA Wrestling, the sport's governing body, was concerned. Team Foxcatcher was no longer recognized as an official wrestling club; those still affiliated with it had to compete in matches unattached.

After Schultz's death, the Foxcatcher wrestlers were divided over whether to continue accepting du Pont's largesse. The meetings among the athletes were fractious. The majority left the team.

"This has been a very emotional time for all the wrestlers," said Wochok. "The wrestlers have certainly had difficulty as a group in determining where their loyalties lie and where their loyalties should lie. The unfortunate thing is there's a facility available for wrestlers to use, and many have been convinced to leave because to continue to stay would be an act of disloyalty to Dave Schultz."

Where'd they go? To a new club.

The Dave Schultz Wrestling Club.

Backed by money from USA Wrestling, donations from a sporting-goods manufacturer and the U.S. Olympic Committee, and private gifts, Nancy Schultz—who had moved to California with her two children—organized a new squad as a tribute to her husband.

"A lot of the wrestlers turned to me for a little leadership," Nancy said. "They had questions, not only about how to continue to compete but how they could honor Dave. They needed financing and asked me for ideas."

On the final weekend in April, the Dave Schultz Wrestling Club made its debut in Las Vegas at the U.S. National Wrestling Championships, a stepping-stone to the Olympics. A handful of Schultz team members, who had been Foxcatcher athletes, earned spots for the final Olympics trial in June.

Overall, about thirty-five wrestlers were affiliated with the club.

"I want to ensure that Dave's friends, teammates, and competitors have the same opportunities and financial backing that Dave did," said Nancy. "Following in his footsteps, I would like to continue to educate the world about amateur wrestling. It is a sport for everyone and can help young athletes learn about dedication, discipline, and self-respect."

While Nancy was working to move the club forward quickly, du Pont gained a new ally in keeping the progress of his murder case slowed. And it was someone he didn't know.

Byron Keith Cooper was a career criminal who, in 1989, murdered an eighty-six-year-old man during a burglary in Oklahoma. He exhibited such bizarre behavior during early court proceedings that he was sent to a psychiatric institution for more than three months. Still, he was convicted and sentenced to death.

In April 1996 the U.S. Supreme Court overturned the conviction. Its reason was that Oklahoma's standard for determining a defendant's competency to stand trial placed too heavy a burden on the defense. Oklahoma forced the defendant to prove by "clear and convincing evidence" that he was incompetent. That was too hard, and the court suggested the standard should be lowered to "a preponderance of the evidence," meaning just slightly more than 50 percent.

Pennsylvania was one of the few states that also set the bar at "clear and convincing."

Du Pont's lawyers grabbed the high court's decision and ran with it. They went to the State Supreme Court and asked that it order a halt to du Pont's competency hearing until it reviewed Pennsylvania's competency standards. The state court agreed.

There was little doubt what the outcome would be; the State Supreme Court would simply follow the lead of the U.S. Supreme Court. But the exercise would buy some more time for the defense.

D.A. Pat Meehan complained the tactic had the same purpose as all the other petitions and motions: delay, delay, and delay the case some more. And he said it was almost to be expected.

"I can understand, if I were a wealthy person and charged with a serious crime, I would use all my resources to try to defend myself," said Meehan. "I can't fault an attorney who, armed with those resources, challenges every single matter, whether or not one might question the appropriateness of the challenge."

All he could do, he said, was meet each matter head-on and try to keep the case on track.

"We have to make sure the case is not subverted by the tremendous resources of the defendant," he added.

Because Pennsylvania had no law that forced a case to be kept to a schedule, du Pont's lawyers repeatedly were able to delay proceedings, keeping motions and petitions flying through three state court jurisdictions—trial, Superior, and Supreme—at the same time.

In California, there was a law called the speedy trial initiative—prompted by victims' groups—enacted in June 1990. It not only mandated that the prosecution keep to a schedule, but made the defense do the same.

Compared with the du Pont case, the O.J. Simpson matter in California, which featured a defendant with a smaller fortune but a higher profile, moved at a lightning pace. Simpson was charged with murder on June 17, 1994. His probable-cause hearing was June 20. He pleaded not guilty at his arraignment in court July 22. On September 26, jury selection began, slightly more than three months after his arrest.

By the end of May, du Pont had been in jail four months and hadn't even had his arraignment.

Of course, du Pont's lawyers argued that they had good causes all along, from bail issues to the competency debate.

The State Supreme Court was involved in that competency fight now, raised by the case of the thirty-three-year-old Cooper.

Cooper, a drifter, continued to show odd behavior after he was released from a psychiatric institution. He refused to change out of prison clothes, saying other shirts and pants burned him, and complained that his lawyer was trying to kill him.

On four occasions during the trial phase, his competency—his ability to understand the charges and help his lawyers—was called into question.

But Cooper's trial judge consistently ruled that Cooper had not proved incompetency by "clear and convincing evidence."

After a two-week trial in 1992, during which Cooper often crouched in a fetal position and talked to himself, he was convicted and sentenced to death; the Oklahoma Court of Criminal Appeals affirmed the finding.

That's when the U.S. Supreme Court weighed in with its opinion.

As both sides in the du Pont case were busy filing briefs on that issue, the third date for his arraignment, May 30, arrived. Du Pont appeared in court with long hair and a full, gray beard; his disheveled, bewildered look would only get worse as the year moved ahead.

Sprague expected a short session. Among the first words out of his mouth was a request to postpone the arraignment until after the State Supreme Court reviewed the competency question.

Maybe du Pont was competent, maybe he wasn't; Sprague felt he didn't have to say anything about that until the state high court ruled. Until then, he suggested, there should be no arraignment.

"It certainly seems to me when there is a question of competency . . . that must be determined first before you proceed with legal proceedings such as an arraignment," he told Jenkins.

McGettigan argued to move forward. Because no one said otherwise, competency had to be presumed, allowing the arraignment to take place.

"If counsel is willing to state that the defendant is not competent based upon his contact with him or that he believes a substantial issue exists as to the defendant's competency and ability to assist in his own defense and to move forward, then he should so state," he said. "The commonwealth will readily reexamine its position without continuing this arraignment.

"All he has to do is stand up here and say, 'Based upon my contact with my client, I believe a substantial issue exists, and he's incompetent at this time to go forward.'"

But neither Sprague nor Lamb felt they could do that. Du Pont didn't feel there was anything wrong with him. And for his lawyers to bring up incompetency in front of him, they felt, would have deepened du Pont's distrust— or gotten them fired.

McGettigan didn't see that as his problem.

"There is nothing that should prevent this court from arraigning the defendant today," he said. "The presumption of competency exists. The commonwealth is ready to move forward. We seek to move forward without further delay."

Jenkins did just that. She had already put off the arraignment twice. There was nothing about the Supreme Court's involvement that indicated to her it had to be put off a third time.

Sprague seemed surprised by her decision.

He asked Jenkins to stay—or set aside temporarily— her decision, so Sprague could file an immediate appeal with the Supreme Court. She denied that.

Then he said he thought she was violating an order of the higher court.

"I ask Your Honor to disqualify yourself," he said.

She refused, and asked Sprague a question: "Are you

prepared at this time to proceed with the arraignment, sir?''

No, Sprague was not.

McAndrews popped up. ''Could Mr. Sprague state why he's not ready to proceed?'' he asked. ''Are you claiming your client is incompetent? Why are you not ready to proceed with an arraignment some four months after the commission of this offense?''

Jenkins looked at Sprague. There was some back-and-forth dialogue before she asked, ''Are you requesting a competency examination?''

Sprague, who often had a rambling style of speaking in court, answered this way:

''Your Honor, I find that that question by Your Honor after the prosecution said what they said to be suggestive of Your Honor and the prosecution being of the same mind and the same purpose, and I have thought that throughout much of these proceedings. . . . and I will not respond to the Court. And again I move for your disqualification even for that question.''

''Your Honor,'' McGettigan fairly shouted. ''That's outrageous. It's outrageous and ridiculous.''

Sprague and McGettigan tried to speak over each other. When they quieted down, Jenkins simply said she refused to step off the case.

''Would you please bring the defendant forward? At this time I would ask our clerk to arraign the defendant,'' she finally said.

At 11:55 A.M., du Pont stood before the bench and heard the litany of charges against him read.

Sprague turned to him. ''Do you understand what was just read to you?'' he asked.

''I didn't understand,'' du Pont said, speaking for the first time in public since being arrested. ''I didn't understand.''

''And who are you?''

"Dalai Lama."

"How does the defendant plead, Mr. Sprague?" said Jenkins.

"Since we object to this arraignment and you have heard what you've just heard," he said, "there is no response."

Automatically, a plea of not guilty was entered.

"And Mr. du Pont," said Jenkins, "you are represented here by counsel today. You do have the right to continue to be represented by counsel. If you cannot afford an attorney, one will be appointed for you."

That brought some smiles in the courtroom; du Pont didn't ask for a court-appointed attorney.

After Jenkins informed du Pont of his legal rights, Sprague asked him, "Did you understand any of that?"

"No."

Jenkins said, "Did you understand it, Mr. Sprague?"

"Do I?"

"Yes."

"Yes. I happen not to be a defendant here."

McGettigan and McAndrews both asked Jenkins for permission to colloquy—or question—du Pont about his understanding of the charges. Jenkins approved.

"I object," said Sprague, "and I am going to advise my client not to answer . . . I believe the court may conduct its own questions. I do not believe that the prosecution has that right."

"Do you have some authority?" Jenkins asked.

"My authority, Your Honor, is my own view of the matter."

That wasn't good enough. McAndrews looked at du Pont, and said, "Mr. du Pont, good morning. Would you look over this way, please?"

Du Pont didn't respond. Jenkins tried to help. "Mr. du Pont," she said, "would you please look in the direction of Mr. McAndrews, the man with the glasses, who is speaking to you?"

"Good morning again, Mr. du Pont," McAndrews said. "You were brought in today from the prison, correct?"

"Yes."

"And you have been there for a few months, correct?"

"Yes."

"And this is a courtroom, correct?"

"Yes."

"You're charged with murder, correct?"

"I don't understand."

"You don't understand that you're charged with murder?"

"I don't understand."

"Do you understand that's Mr. Sprague next to you?"

"Yes."

"Do you understand that's Mr. Lamb to his side?"

"Yes."

"Do you understand that this is a courtroom where legal proceedings occur?"

"Yes."

"You understand that you have signed a Rule 1100 waiver"—waiving the right to a speedy trial—"that was discussed here today?"

"Yes."

"And you understand that that's part of this murder prosecution, correct?"

"No."

"What is it you don't understand, Mr. du Pont?"

"I don't understand procedure of court in the United States of America."

"It can be confusing at times, can't it, Mr. du Pont?"

"Yes."

"How old are you, Mr. du Pont?"

"I don't know."

Du Pont then started to respond by saying he didn't

understand or he had to confer with his attorney.

"What do you not understand?" Jenkins asked. "Are there any questions you would like to ask me about the matters that you do not understand, so that I can help you understand?"

"I confer with attorney again," du Pont said.

Jenkins tried a few more times, then realized she wasn't getting anywhere. McAndrews didn't have any better luck.

"Are you comfortable that you're here in the Delaware County Court house? Are you comfortable with that information?"

"No."

"You're not?"

"I don't understand."

"Okay, you don't understand again. Those people on either side are your lawyers, right?"

"Yes."

"They've explained to you what's going on here, haven't they?"

"I don't understand everything."

McAndrews turned to Jenkins.

"Thank you, Your Honor," he said.

Court was adjourned.

The next day, Sprague went back to the State Supreme Court.

He asked that it void the arraignment.

And remove Jenkins from the case.

Sixteen

The summer months were busy and eventful for John du Pont.

On June 10 the State Supreme Court refused to void the arraignment or force Jenkins off the case. Terry Wochok said the defense would look into the possibility of an appeal to the U.S. Supreme Court.

That never happened.

On the twelfth, the Superior Court upheld Jenkins's decision to deny bail.

"Given the accused's apparent resources, associations, and familiarity with international travel," the court concluded, "the lower court's consideration of the potential for elopement was not fanciful."

On July 1, Jenkins said, "I want to get this matter to trial," and informed both sides that it would start September 30.

With the weighty matter of competency still up in the air, that was wishful thinking. But putting it on the court calendar had the psychological effect of at least appearing to move everything forward.

By the time a trial date finally was set, du Pont had been in an eighty-square-foot isolated cell for five full months. He was paying as many as a dozen lawyers who had various hands in filing more than two dozen petitions and motions in three court jurisdictions, many designed to get him his freedom.

None was successful.

On July 8, another lawyer was added to the defense team: Joseph T. Labrum Jr.

Labrum, sixty-eight, had been a Delaware County Common Pleas Court judge for twenty years until retiring in May 1995. In fact, he had often sat where Jenkins now did, looking out over Courtroom 1. He declined to say what his role would be. Some observers suggested he was hired for his thorough knowledge of county court proceedings; others thought his job was solely to sit in the courtroom and intimidate Jenkins. He had handled arbitrations and some court-appointed matters since stepping down from the bench, but did not do a great deal of criminal defense work. As time went on, he didn't appear to have much impact on the defense, although he lasted on the team until the end.

His first task was to make a couple of visits to prison to see du Pont. After that, he helped file a document with the court in which he contended that du Pont "exhibited delusional and disjointed thinking." Maybe he was hired just to add another voice to the chorus that du Pont wasn't ready for trial.

But du Pont was still clearly giving orders to his Foxcatcher employees because new decorations went up in mid-July. Two rusty bear traps now adorned the columns flanking the driveway of the estate's entrance, and two black trash cans sat on stone pedestals nearby.

No one could even guess at their significance.

On July 15, du Pont was back in court. His lawyers were supposed to finally tip their hand about the insanity defense. Actually, they were supposed to have done that on June 30, but got a two-week extension. They asked for another extension.

Du Pont, said Labrum, "is incompetent to stand trial,

delusional and incompetent of cooperating with his defense.''

That made Joe McGettigan wonder what his lawyers had been doing in their nearly four hundred visits to du Pont in jail.

"What are they discussing, the menu?" he asked.

But Lamb said the hundreds of visits didn't prove anything.

"It's misleading to suggest that the number of visits by counsel indicate anything about competence," he said. "It is our job to establish as much of a rapport as possible with our client. People who are incompetent in some ways can be very competent in other ways."

Competent enough to run his estate from prison? McGettigan thought so. He pointed to du Pont's purchase—while in jail—of a truck, and to numerous changes at his Foxcatcher estate, including the installation of a guardhouse, barbed-wire fencing, billboards, and painting, all done at his behest.

Wochok had all but confirmed who ran things during another hearing in July, one of eleven du Pont had attended since his arrest.

"Whatever happens at the property is ultimately his responsibility," Wochok said. "Whether he directed that certain things be done, or that certain other things be done by other individuals and he subsequently ratified them, those are his responsibilities."

Privately, Wochok was frustrated by all the goings-on at Foxcatcher. In some cases he didn't learn of the bizarre changes at the farm, such as the huge black cross painted on a red barn, until a reporter called to ask about them. Du Pont not only seemed to be giving orders but segmenting duties among employees.

So the question remained: Was du Pont delusional and befuddled by the murder charge he faced?

Or was he, as prosecutors believed, helping to direct

his defense in the same firm-handed manner that he used to order employees around on the estate?

Jenkins refused to grant another extension; was it an insanity defense or not? she wanted to know.

Sprague wouldn't say; he was trying to dance around the state statute that required his disclosure. As he was making a point to Jenkins, though, the animus between Sprague and McGettigan spilled over. Sprague noticed McGettigan wearing a smirk—not an uncommon look for the lead prosecutor. He cut his speech short.

"I see this stupid smile over here," he said.

"Your Honor," said McGettigan, rising to the bait, "I'm going to have to object."

Sprague continued: "And it has been there time and time again."

"Excuse me, Your Honor," McGettigan said. "If counsel wants to be insulting, I mean his appearance should not be the subject of discussion here . . ."

Jenkins knew where this was going, and tried to cut him off. McGettigan, though, plowed on.

"I mean," he said, "his appearance should not be the subject of discussion here where . . ."

"Mr. McGettigan," Jenkins said.

". . . Mr. Sprague is going to come out the loser."

That was clearly a reference to the fact that Sprague, who had undergone surgery on his scalp, appeared in court with the top of his head wrapped in bandages. Jenkins wanted to get McGettigan calmed down.

"I don't find that descriptions of facial expressions of others in the courtroom assist me in resolving the important issues that are here to be resolved," she said. "I would prefer that not to be addressed."

But it was too late.

"That's the most unprofessional behavior I can contemplate," said McGettigan, "on the part of someone who wore a turban for half the proceedings."

"Your Honor . . ." said Sprague.

"You're even," said Jenkins to McGettigan.

"Thank you," McGettigan said.

But Sprague wasn't finished. "If reference to a turban makes up for a stupid smile," he said, "I'm glad to be even in that case."

"Once again," McGettigan said, "professional behavior is not Mr. Sprague's benchmark."

On July 23 the ghost of ghostwriter Larry Eastland reappeared. Eastland was the Idaho man, a former employee of du Pont's, who was suing for $900,000 in severance pay. Du Pont's lawyers sought to dismiss the suit, but a federal judge refused to throw it out. So that became one more thorn in du Pont's side.

Perhaps most significant in July, though, was an act by the state legislature that amended the competency standard. The law, signed July 2, established the less-stringent "preponderance of the evidence" standard rather than "clear and convincing evidence." When the state legislature did that, it brought Pennsylvania in line with the U.S. Supreme Court's decision in the Cooper case.

The defense had been able to stall a competency exam until the State Supreme Court weighed in. But now the legislature seemed to have settled the matter. So the prosecution went to the high court to say that its deliberations on the matter were no longer necessary.

"The need for this court to exercise its extraordinary jurisdiction has been eliminated," Dennis McAndrews wrote in his brief.

The Supreme Court didn't drop the issue, but on August 19, when it did make a decision, it bowed to the new state law. The lesser standard would now be the rule.

With that settled, Jenkins set a new date—September 13—for a competency hearing. It looked like a September 30 trial date was possible.

Meanwhile, as the murder case made its way through

the justice system, the Summer Olympics in Atlanta, where Dave Schultz had hoped to make his comeback, opened with the customary fanfare. There were sad, nationally televised tributes to Schultz. Nancy attended the Games to watch Schultz's wrestling buddies compete. Valentin Jordanov, representing Bulgaria, finally won a gold medal on August 2, beating Azerbaijan's Namik Abdullayev 4–3 in overtime at 114 pounds.

Kurt Angle, representing the Dave Schultz Wrestling Club, won the 220-pound weight class in a close judges' decision over Abbas Jadidi of Iran.

"I still love being around wrestling," said Nancy Schultz, who watched from the stands. "All of these people are such good friends. It's a high. Then I think that Dave should be here and I get low. But I'm going to miss Dave anyway. I don't miss him any more at wrestling than I do every second of every day."

In court later that month, on August 23, everybody got a glimpse of what the defense would claim at the competency hearing. Richard Sprague put psychiatrist Phillip Resnick on the stand to summarize what he learned during five meetings with du Pont.

Resnick concluded that du Pont was a paranoid schizophrenic, suffering both persecutory and grandiose delusions.

"He believes he is the subject of a conspiracy, and fearful of being killed by the CIA, the U.S. government, the International Olympic Committee," Resnick said. He added that du Pont believed he was in danger of being poisoned and that bugging devices that could pick up his conversations had been placed in the prison and other sites.

"He has a belief that he is the Dalai Lama for America," Resnick said. "He acknowledges there is another Dalai Lama for some Asian countries."

Resnick said du Pont had told him that he was the president of the Soviet Union and the last of the Russian czars.

"It is my opinion that Mr. du Pont is not able to rationally participate or cooperate in his defense at this time," said Resnick.

It wasn't his opinion, though, that would ultimately decide du Pont's immediate fate. It was Jenkins's. The first step was for du Pont to be examined by two court-appointed psychiatrists, Theodore Barry and Thomas Gutheil. That took place on September 9, seven months after Jenkins first ordered it.

The two tried to conduct their exam in a conference room at the prison. Du Pont, though, was totally uncooperative and almost completely uncommunicative. He spoke only three words: "Me no understand." Despite cajoling by Wochok to be responsive, du Pont remained mute. "Catatonic" is how Gutheil described him. After about forty-five minutes, Barry and Gutheil gave up, turning their attention to interviews with the others present: lawyers Sprague and Lamb, defense psychiatrists Resnick and Robert Sadoff, and Park Dietz, one of the most renowned forensic psychiatrists in the country, who had been hired by the prosecution.

For Lamb and Sprague, it turned out to be their swan song. The day after the exam they were fired.

During a break, the doctors and lawyers walked out together. Du Pont had seen Sprague and Lamb with Dietz. He was unhappy about that. The next day, when Sprague returned to prison, he made a comment about du Pont not answering any questions during the exam. Du Pont then had his own complaint. He saw Lamb and Sprague interact with Dietz—the "state's doctor," is how he put it. To du Pont, that meant one thing: his own lawyers were part of a conspiracy against him that included the judge, the district attorney—and the CIA.

"You're dismissed," du Pont said. Sprague got up. "I wish you well," he said, and walked out.

His dissatisfaction with Sprague and Lamb was not the first time he had complained about his defense team. He had told Resnick he was upset over Sprague's inability to get him out on bail. That, at least, had some basis in reality.

So Sprague and Lamb exited, if not any wiser, certainly a lot richer. Sprague's firm billed du Pont more than $1.5 million for the seven and a half months' work, and Lamb collected at least $1 million for himself and his associates.

That was really pocket change for du Pont. But with the dream team dismantled, Wochok did have an immediate concern; the competency hearing was less than two weeks away—rescheduled for September 20—and he couldn't handle that himself. He needed to get a new lawyer to lead the defense team, and he needed to do that quickly.

And there was another big headache. Two days after Sprague and Lamb got the boot, du Pont's relatives went to court to try to take over du Pont's life.

The family, led by du Pont's sister Jean Shehan, seventy-three, and her son, James H.T. McConnell Jr., forty-three—du Pont's nephew—filed a petition seeking control over all aspects of his life, including medical and financial matters. Joining them were sister Evelyn Donaldson, brother Henry, and a half brother, William III. Perhaps ironically, their position was bolstered by Sprague himself, who had finally asserted that du Pont was incompetent.

The family action had not been completely unexpected; relatives had talked about it earlier, but agreed to put it off for a bit. In anticipation, though, in late August still another attorney, Mark Klugheit, was brought into the case, at least the twelfth lawyer who landed on du Pont's payroll.

Klugheit, a former general counsel to Pennsylvania's Senator Arlen Specter who now worked for a large Philadelphia firm, would have minimal involvement in the criminal case. His Herculean task was to defend du Pont against his family, and against the parade of civil suits, both those already filed—like Larry Eastland's—and those that were on the horizon, including a wrongful death suit by Nancy Schultz that was sure to come, and sure to generate a multimillion-dollar settlement.

Klugheit was also entrusted with finding a replacement for Sprague. He did that quickly, bringing in Thomas Bergstrom, fifty-four, a tall, almost courtly ex-Marine with a thespian style in the courtroom.

Bergstrom had a solo practice; his one employee was a longtime secretary who wore jeans and a fanny pack and worked alongside him on the second floor of a barn-turned-office situated in the backyard of Bergstrom's handsome piece of property in Pennsylvania horse country.

His presence reminded some, even in the prosecutor's office, of his hero, John Wayne. Portraits of Wayne hung near his desk. A magazine cover of the Duke was nearby, close to a miniature statue. At night, Bergstrom and his wife would pop in videocassettes of John Wayne movies. Bergstrom's favorite was *The Searchers*, the Western yarn about a Texan on a dogged, obsessive, years-long search for a young girl who was captured by Indians as a child.

However, unlike John Wayne—who was never in the service—Bergstrom had spent time in a combat zone, serving in Vietnam as a Marine legal officer. A native of Chicago who went to the University of Iowa, Bergstrom joined the Marine Corps after getting his law degree from Iowa in 1966. He went through Marine Corps Officer Candidate School in Quantico, Virginia, and by 1967 was assigned to the First Marine Division, traveling the Vietnamese countryside as a defense counsel in court-martial proceedings usually held in field tents.

"I handled murders, rapes, you name it," he said.

Bergstrom spent four years in the Marines, teaching military law and serving as a military judge. Back at Quantico as a captain, he met his future wife, a Marine lieutenant.

"She didn't outrank me then," he said. "She does now."

After the service, Bergstrom was a prosecutor with a federal organized-crime strike force, and he worked in the U.S. Attorney's office in Philadelphia. By 1977, he was in private practice, representing organized crime figures, drug kingpins, and crooked cops. Bergstrom's job, usually, was damage control, getting his client the best deal possible under the worst possible circumstances. He was a natural for the du Pont case.

Du Pont, however, was a special challenge for Bergstrom. While there was no doubt that du Pont pulled the trigger, there was the obvious presence of mental illness and, just possibly, a chance for a verdict of not guilty by reason of insanity. That required massive resources, and few had as massive resources as du Pont. For Bergstrom, who truly loved his work, this was the opportunity of a lifetime.

"I find something fascinating about all my cases," he said. "But I guess this case is the most fascinating—and most substantive. In most cases, the deck is pretty well stacked against you. We have something to work with here."

But Bergstrom also had a unique problem in the du Pont case that he had never faced: cocounsel Terry Wochok. It was Bergstrom's plan to portray du Pont as a victim of his illness, and a victim of the people around him who watched du Pont spiraling out of control for years and did nothing about it.

Such an approach, of course, would beg this question: Why didn't Wochok—the longtime lawyer, the man who was admittedly in contact with du Pont on a daily basis, the self-described gatekeeper to the millionaire's wallet—step in and get his client help?

It was a question the prosecution wanted hanging there, like a black cloud, over the defense table. That's why McGettigan had made the tactical decision of not challenging Wochok's role as defense counsel. And it's why Bergstrom filed a motion barring Wochok from being called as a witness.

To divert attention from Wochok, he had to find a lightning rod for the blame. He decided early on who would be the subject of his most withering examination: Patrick Goodale, du Pont's onetime security expert.

Bergstrom's style, in and out of the court room, contrasted greatly with Sprague. Sprague was feisty and combative. At times, he seemed to lecture Jenkins—decades his junior—on points of law. And he was never reluctant to tangle with McGettigan, ever the eager brawler.

Sprague also shunned the media. Not once in his time on the case did he make a substantive comment to reporters. That was left to Lamb and Wochok. Bergstrom didn't seek out the media, but he didn't avoid the newshounds either. He willingly stepped up to face the thicket of tape recorders and banks of cameras in front of the Delaware County Courthouse to give the obligatory quotes and sound bites.

After dealing with Sprague, Jenkins found Bergstrom's approach a bit of a relief. From the beginning, his goal was to get the case to trial as expeditiously as possible—provided, that is, that du Pont was competent.

But it took just one meeting with his new client to convince Bergstrom how far from competent du Pont was. Bergstrom couldn't, he recalled later, have a conversation with him that produced even an iota of helpful information.

In the months du Pont had sat around in his tiny cubicle in Delaware County Prison, he had gotten little, if any, meaningful mental-health treatment. Physically, he was evolving into a Howard Hughes–type figure: long, greasy hair, unkempt beard, his teeth literally rotting in his mouth. Frequently, he did not shower.

"By the time I saw him in late September, he was a raving lunatic," Bergstrom said. "He was flat-out nuts."

Du Pont was so far removed from reality that the decision to fight to have Jenkins declare him incompetent to stand trial was a no-brainer.

"The defense has to establish by a preponderance of the evidence that the defendant is incompetent," Bergstrom said. "And with the preponderance of evidence, believe me, that's more likely than not."

Still, he asked Jenkins if she could push back the September 20 date for the competency hearing to give him more time to prepare, but she refused. Bergstrom bit the bullet.

"I'm working very hard to get up to speed," he said, "and I think I can get ready."

But getting du Pont judged incompetent was not going to be easy. Only two of every ten defendants who went that route were successful.

The reality was that everybody could agree a person was as mad as a hatter—but still capable of understanding the charges against him, and able to work with his lawyer on the defense.

It was Bergstrom's task to prove du Pont couldn't do at least one or the other. Ultimately, he would aim to prove the latter, that du Pont could not assist in his defense. And to bolster that argument when the competency hearing finally did open on Friday morning, September 20, Bergstrom called two familiar faces as witnesses: Richard Sprague and William Lamb.

Two weeks earlier the pair expected to be standing where Bergstrom now stood; instead, they had become two important voices for a new lawyer.

They said essentially the same thing: every discussion they had with du Pont during their more than seven months representing him contained delusional ramblings, making it impossible to address even once the charges that he murdered Schultz.

"When I first commenced the representation," Sprague said, "I wanted to get some idea of his background because until this happened, I not only did not know Mr. du Pont, I never even heard of him. What I wanted to know, who he was. He told me that he was the Dalai Lama. He told me that he was the Christ Child.

"In the course of that same conversation he told me that he was the head of the Communist Party. He related to me that when he wore his Bulgarian uniform, he was president of Bulgaria.

"When I wanted to get some information concerning what he believed happened on the day of this shooting, he told me that there were bugs here in the prison and anything that was being said would be listened to and heard and he would not talk about that."

Sprague said du Pont initially denied knowing Schultz was dead, then said he did not believe it.

Another time, Sprague said, du Pont claimed that Schultz had been killed by Republicans because du Pont had not made a contribution to the GOP. He also said the CIA had committed the crime because Schultz "went into southern Russia and didn't give them the videotapes he was hired to obtain."

Du Pont took the name of Sprague's firm—Sprague and Sprague—and gave it his own interpretation: the SS meant Sprague was connected to Nazi storm troopers.

"And on the other hand," Sprague said, "I was an agent for Simon Wiesenthal and was a Nazi hunter. And Mr. du Pont really was the Fuhrer because he had obtained the property of the Third Reich from Albert Speer one time, from Mr. Goebbels another time. He owned all of that property, and I was really a double agent in a sense, and he was wary of me.''

Du Pont insisted to his lawyers that disasters occurring around the world—the crash of TWA Flight 800, fires raging in California, hurricanes—had been caused by supporters who were protesting his incarceration. He said he believed he was the only one who could prevent a religious war between the East and the West. He said if he remained imprisoned the 1996 elections would be called off, the Olympics would be canceled.

"I would try to say, well, let's deal with the day of the shooting because I have to know about that," said Sprague. "And the response then would be that Mr. du Pont, his father, really built the Church of Satan . . . and started it out in San Francisco."

Du Pont attributed his parents' divorce to the fact that he was the Christ Child; his father left his mother because of the conflict between the good of the Christ Child and the evil of Satan.

In an early meeting, Sprague said, du Pont told him he had been brainwashed by the Buddhists in 1977. "That was in a sense to cleanse him and to wipe away all his past memories . . . so that he could be the Dalai Lama," according to Sprague.

Only when bail came up did du Pont seem to focus on an issue of the case, but even that was filled with delusions, the lawyers said.

Du Pont complained constantly that his defense team had failed to get him released and urged Sprague to contact Pennsylvania Gov. Tom Ridge and President Bill Clinton, who he insisted could get him out on bail. If the president failed to come through, du Pont told Sprague, he would have a plane fly to Washington to drop eggs on the White House.

"When I heard that—at some times it is my nature to quip—I said, 'Oh, do you mean scrambled eggs?' And

Mr. du Pont said, 'You do not trifle with the Christ Child or Dalai Lama, and you don't make jokes like that,' " Sprague testified.

Du Pont complained, Sprague said, that the judge and D.A. wanted him to die in jail. "They tried to beat me down," du Pont told Sprague, "but I was specifically trained by the CIA, FBI, and MI5"—British intelligence—"for these kind of situations. They won't be able to trick me."

Bergstrom asked Sprague, "On the basis of your representation of him and your observations and your vast experience, are you able to render an opinion as to whether John E. du Pont is capable of assisting counsel with his defense?"

"I believe I am able to render such an opinion."

"And what is your opinion?"

"He is absolutely incapable of doing that."

Lamb said that du Pont once had Wochok bring to prison a painting of Jesus Christ in a long robe, with a beard and long hair.

"Who is that?" du Pont asked.

"A likeness of Christ," a lawyer answered.

"Well," said du Pont, "don't I look like that?"

"Yes."

"Well, now, do you know who I am?"

Du Pont, Lamb said, believed he was competent. He wanted to be found competent. And he told Lamb there was a surefire way to do that: hold his competency hearing on an even day of the month. He believed only on even days would that finding be possible.

"He said that was easy, and I could arrange it," Lamb said.

The testimony of Lamb and Sprague was bolstered by Resnick. Nine times out of ten, he told the court, he finds defendants he evaluates competent to stand trial. But du Pont, he believed strongly—"with a reasonable degree of certainty,'' is the legal term—was incompetent, a paranoid schizophrenic suffering from persecutory delusions, grandiose delusions, and disorganized thinking.

Resnick also offered an explanation of the large red and white billboards du Pont had ordered erected at Foxcatcher.

''He perceives the opposite of red as blue, the opposite of white as black,'' Resnick said. ''And that is a message to the world that he is feeling black-and-blue and beat up by the conspiracy and justice system.''

Resnick also discounted the idea—pushed hard by the prosecution—that du Pont was malingering, or faking his illness.

''People who fake mental illness often enjoy thrusting forward their illness,'' he said. ''In other words, they are glad to put forth their delusion, kind of in your face. The fact that Mr. du Pont was reluctant to see psychiatrists and was indeed silent when the court-appointed psychiatrist wanted to see him is consistent with his fear of a conspiracy and his buttoning up and remaining silent, rather than just blabbering forth delusional material, which you would expect if someone was faking an illness.''

McGettigan knew that he and McAndrews had no chance of showing du Pont was ready for trial. But, like a basketball player arguing over a call with a referee, he wanted to put up a good argument this time so that he would get the call he wanted from Jenkins the next time around.

The two prosecutors argued strenuously that du Pont was fit. McAndrews referred to what he called a ''chronology of competence,'' including statements made in court by lawyers and witnesses that du Pont continued to run affairs at Foxcatcher from prison. They noted that on the day Sprague and Lamb were hired du Pont was apparently coherent enough to sign a fee agreement.

That led to testimony from Sprague and Lamb about their fees. In addition to their $100,000 retainers, Sprague said each lawyer in his office who worked on the case— including himself—earned $300 an hour. He estimated that his firm had made $1.5 million, and all the bills weren't in yet.

Lamb said his firm's hourly rate was the same. While he would not guess as to the total bill, he said it was less than Sprague's. Each visit he made to prison counted as a two-hour bill, he said.

There were one hundred ten of those—$66,000 worth.

In fact, in arguing that du Pont had been involved in his defense, prosecutors pointed out that du Pont's lawyers had made 571 visits to the jail, including Lamb's 110, 88 by Sprague, and 373 by Wochok.

Sprague and Lamb responded in the same way: They felt that, despite du Pont's incoherence, it was important to continue to try to bond with him in the hope that he would trust them enough to direct his attention to the case.

"In almost every visit, our hope was to try to focus at some point to deal with the seriousness of Mr. du Pont's problems," Lamb said.

Jenkins adjourned court at 8 P.M. following ten hours of testimony, and ordered the hearing to continue the next day, a Saturday. That would be even longer, taken up largely by psychiatric testimony.

Resnick, who was cross-examined by McGettigan, and Sadoff reiterated that du Pont was psychotic, delusional, and did not meet the twofold test of competence: understanding the nature and consequence of the charges and being able to assist in his defense.

Sadoff, though, said that could change with treatment and medication.

"Based on my experience and treating patients with this kind of illness and what's in the literature about people with paranoid schizophrenia, the type of medication we have had over the past several years, the results have been very good for the vast majority of such people,'' he said.

To counteract the tandem of Sadoff and Resnick, the D.A.'s office hired John O'Brien, a Philadelphian who was both a forensic psychiatrist and a lawyer, and Park Dietz of California, whose reputation in the field of forensic psychiatry was unsurpassed. His four-hundred-dollar an hour fee was also near the top of the field. O'Brien charged $300 an hour.

Both O'Brien and Dietz—who had been a prime figure in the John Hinckley trial, arguing against the prevailing opinion that he was insane—sat in on the competency hearing, but only O'Brien was called by prosecutors.

O'Brien's entry into the case had a twist. He was originally asked by Jenkins to conduct the independent evaluation for the court. But Wochok objected; O'Brien was, it turned out, one of the doctors called into consultation in 1992 when Wochok looked into involuntary commitment for du Pont.

O'Brien had told Jenkins he didn't remember that consultation; he hadn't met du Pont, he said, but was simply contacted and asked to review some information and give an opinion. O'Brien said he didn't believe he even billed for his time, although Wochok said he did.

Jenkins agreed she shouldn't use him, so he became available to the prosecution. Wochok tried to have him disqualified from working with the D.A. But Jenkins was satisfied that because he had never actually communicated with du Pont, he could be unbiased.

O'Brien concurred with others that du Pont was delusional and mentally ill. He said he was also certain du Pont clearly understood that he faced murder charges and had shown an ability to follow his lawyers' instructions.

Typical of the differing medical opinions was how the doctors viewed du Pont's decision to fire Sprague and

Lamb. Defense psychiatrists said the move showed du Pont's incompetence because he saw his own lawyers as part of an elaborate conspiracy against him. O'Brien, though, thought the decision displayed competence because it showed a rational dissatisfaction with his attorneys for failing to get him released on bail. Firing just his two lead counsels, O'Brien said, illustrated that he was able to "weed out members of his defense team based on satisfaction with their performance."

O'Brien also put a lot of weight on the absolute neatness he found in du Pont's prison cell. Psychotic individuals, he said, often live in states of total disarray.

"They can't take care of themselves. They can't take care of their personal space," he said. But du Pont's cell, he said, was "tidy to a military degree.

"His bed was so neatly made that you might be concerned about brushing up against it for fear of creating wrinkles," he said. "And with the blanket draped down to the floor and then tucked underneath with military corners, it almost looked like he was lying on a box."

His cups and packages of crackers were arranged and lined up on the windowsill; there was no trash anywhere, O'Brien said.

"Well," said Bergstrom with undisguised sarcasm, "you didn't expect to see pizza and soda cans lying around, did you?"

"Not based on his dietary habits as I understood them to be," O'Brien replied.

The prosecution also called to the witness stand several members of the prison staff, who described du Pont's behavior in jail as unremarkable and mostly cooperative. McAndrews was very intent on bringing out the fact that du Pont—who claimed he was on a hunger strike, surviving on just tea and crackers—had actually gained weight. He asked many witnesses if they had seen him eating.

That led to a humorous exchange with prison nurse Sharon Sue Coffman.

"Did you ever see him eating?"

"Did I ever see John actually put food in his mouth? No. Have I ever seen him chewing and appear to have something in his mouth with his little cheeks bulging? Yes."

"How many times have you seen him chewing with his cheeks bulging?"

Coffman said on several occasions when du Pont and Wochok met she would see "John go down, come back up, and his cheeks would be a little fat and he would chew."

Bergstrom objected to the relevancy. McAndrews said it was an indication of malingering and feigning.

"He said he wasn't going to eat in prison," said McAndrews.

Coffman cut in unexpectedly. "Well, he eats crackers all the time," she said. "Maybe twenty, thirty packs of crackers a day."

"Okay," McAndrews said as laughter rippled through the courtroom. "You're going to have to hold off."

"I withdraw the objection," said Bergstrom.

One witness, Dominic Spigarelli, the assistant prison superintendent, dropped this tidbit: just before du Pont was to meet with Gutheil and Barry, the court-appointed psychiatrists, Wochok grabbed du Pont by the arm, and said, "You don't know your name." That, prosecutors intimated, was why du Pont refused to answer questions. They were again hammering away that du Pont was coached by his lawyers to feign mental illness.

Two sheriff's deputies, for instance, were called to testify that during the May 30 arraignment—the only time du Pont ever spoke in court—they heard Sprague direct du Pont to answer questions by saying "I don't understand."

Resnick, though, scoffed at that. "The idea they coached him to act more delusional, I think, is outlandish," he said in response to questions from McGettigan.

Sadoff and Resnick both characterized du Pont as paranoid schizophrenic. O'Brien, however, called du Pont capricious, willful, and manipulative. He said he believed he suffered from mixed-personality disorder and borderline narcissism.

Gutheil was the last to testify, and it was his finding, perhaps, that had the most influence over Jenkins. He, too, called du Pont paranoid schizophrenic. However, because he had gotten so little from his September 9 interview with du Pont, he initially thought there was "a significant probability" that du Pont was incompetent. That, in legal terms, was pretty low.

But after he watched the videotape of the March session with Resnick and Sadoff, Gutheil raised his opinion to "a reasonable degree of medical certainty." While he was unsuccessful in examining du Pont, he said, the tape represented a vicarious examination. He still couldn't come to a strong opinion on whether du Pont understood the charges against him. But he had concluded that du Pont could not assist his lawyers in conducting his defense.

"The totality of evidence and, particularly, the tape indicates to me that he was not malingering, that it's a genuine illness," he said.

Gutheil stepped down at 9:30 P.M., ending a thirteen-hour day. Over two days, about twenty-three hours of testimony exploring du Pont's mental state was heard. Jenkins gave everyone off Sunday and Monday, telling lawyers to come back on Tuesday, September 24, to offer closing arguments.

Bergstrom went first. He reiterated the testimony of the psychiatrists, but gave as much weight to the views of Sprague and Lamb.

"Notwithstanding the fact that these lawyers were retained by John du Pont and earned substantial fees as a result of their retention and work on his behalf, I suggest to Your Honor that their testimony is . . . unbiased and objective in terms of their relationship with their client. I suggest to you that they're credible. I suggest to you that they're believable. I suggest to you that perhaps they, among all of the other witnesses that you've heard in this courtroom, were the best people to evaluate, to see first-hand, over a period of weeks and months, the lack of ability of John du Pont to participate and assist in the preparation of his defense.

"We all know that he is mentally ill," Bergstrom continued. "We all know that he is paranoid schizophrenic. We all know that he is delusional. We all know that he is psychotic. We all know that his delusions and his psychosis permeate his thought process. And we all know that this delusional, psychotic thought process was in existence before the arrest in this case."

He suggested that O'Brien's testimony didn't address du Pont's psychosis, but simply took a few specific behaviors—his neat cell, his cooperation with prison nurses, his politeness with deputies—and made a gigantic, unfounded leap to finding him competent.

"The fact that this man just sits here and doesn't climb up onto the walls, I suppose, is a sign of competence. That's just not the issue," Bergstrom said. "The fact that he has a neat bed in his prison cell is simply not the issue. The fact that he marches back and forth with the sheriff's deputies is simply not the issue."

Then he asked the court to put aside the fact that it was John du Pont—the fabulously wealthy man with an internationally known name—before her. Lady Justice, Bergstrom said, is not supposed to see the color of one's skin, or one's standing in the community, or the size of one's wallet.

"She sees the evidence. She sees the law. And she acts

on it. And that's what I'm asking you to do here. I'm asking you to find him incompetent and to commit him.

"Commit him, along with the Dalai Lama and the Crown Prince, and the Christ Child and the presidents of the Soviet Union and Bulgaria. Commit them all, so that these good doctors, given time, can drive the demons from his mind, so that he can properly defend himself. That's all we ask for."

McGettigan handled the closing for the prosecution, and reminded Jenkins of all the times the defense seemed to indicate du Pont was competent.

"The defendant was more than competent to return to Foxcatcher to examine voluminous documents to assist— out of Mr. Lamb's mouth—to assist in his defense," he said. "He was competent to ask for the return of his passport and his weapons. He was competent to do that. But yet, when it served their purpose, he was incompetent. He was competent for bail. He was competent for all of those purposes, but incompetent for the purpose of proceeding with the object of what this court is about: resolving the charges against Mr. du Pont, the murder of David Schultz."

McGettigan was insistent that du Pont was rational when he wanted to be, irrational when it fit his purpose. Look at how he's run his estate from prison, he said. Look at how he approves expenses. And what was so irrational about firing Sprague and Lamb? He wanted to get out of prison on bail, and they were unable to do it, despite receiving millions of dollars in fees.

The audiotapes made during the two-day standoff with police, when du Pont called himself the president of the Soviet Union and complained that police were on holy property, might have been evidence of mental illness, McGettigan conceded. But the tapes also showed how he repeatedly refused to discuss the Schultz killing, instead asking for his lawyer. That, he said, was completely rational.

He accused du Pont of employing a strategy he had used his entire life: avoid issues that are unpleasant.

"When the situation becomes intolerable he elects to employ these figures he's conjured up," McGettigan said. "And he's been able to do that because the people who live off his money and who live on his estate, that's fine for them. Except for David Schultz. I think the choice that he has made, that he has been making, and that he makes here today is 'I'm going to be the Dalai Lama today because I don't want to deal with the situation. And I'm going to be the Dalai Lama as long as it takes for this situation to disappear.'"

Don't be fooled, he told Jenkins.

"The court should not permit the defendant to use a strategy that he's found successful in life because of his position and his wealth," he said.

"The commonwealth overwhelmingly demonstrated that the defendant has the absolute capacity to understand and to cooperate. He does understand, and he can cooperate. He won't. It's a strategy. The court should find him competent. We should proceed to trial."

Jenkins thanked both sides, said she'd review her notes, go over the arguments she'd just heard, and return to court in the afternoon to give her decision.

It was just after 2 P.M. when court was called back into session. All eyes were on Jenkins as she read from a piece of paper in front of her. And it was clear, from the first few words, who she blamed for the situation getting so far out of hand.

"The question is now regrettably ripe for determination," she said. "It is at best unfortunate that the issue of Mr. du Pont's competence has not yet been rendered moot by some form of mental-health treatment that could have been rendered to him either during the past eight months or even before in consideration of the universal agreement of the several professionals who have seen him that Mr. du Pont is actively psychotic and has been for a prolonged period.

"For a variety of reasons, some of which have been suggested in court, and some which may only be speculated upon, all of those in a position to step forward and timely address the situation by responsibly seeking either voluntary or involuntary mental-health treatment, have failed or refused to do so. And in their neglect have failed also the victim in this case, Mr. du Pont, and the people of the commonwealth."

She regretted, she said, that none of the examinations of du Pont were designed to help him; they were done purely for purposes of litigation.

"Accordingly, despite two full days of testimony, the information available upon which to base the requisite determination is limited," she said. "Nevertheless, I have concluded that the scales tip ever so slightly in favor of a finding that Mr. du Pont is not presently competent to assist counsel in his defense. And I make this finding mindful and hopeful that if it is erroneous that the consequences will be limited to a delay in the commencement of trial while the defendant is hospitalized in a secure mental-health facility."

She just couldn't take the chance of sending him to trial.

"The beauty of our system is that every individual who walks through the doors of this courtroom must be treated equally once inside," she said. "No civilized society has an interest in, or derives any benefit from, the trial of an incompetent person on any charge, let alone a charge of first-degree murder, whether he is John Doe or John du Pont."

After eight months, John du Pont was finally going to

leave prison, sent to Norristown State Hospital in the next county.

Bergstrom would not disclose du Pont's reaction to the news, except to say, "I don't really think he appreciated the nature of all that went on."

D.A. Pat Meehan said he wasn't really surprised. Besides, the prosecution figured they'd lose this battle, and there was nothing to be gained by second-guessing Jenkins. They were looking ahead to the next round.

"Is this justice delayed?" Meehan said at the time. "Not really. Clearly the issue is that justice will not be denied, because once this issue is resolved we can begin again to pursue this prosecution diligently."

Wochok, though not named by Jenkins in her rebuke, was clearly a target of her admonition. Surrounded outside the courtroom by reporters, he was asked if he felt responsible for failing to get du Pont treatment.

"No more responsible than the prison, than other officials who saw the same thing that we saw," he said.

Du Pont's new home was decidedly nicer than solitary confinement in prison.

Norristown State Hospital, opened in 1880, was on hundreds of acres of lush grounds, with exercise facilities including an indoor pool, spacious rooms full of antiques, and deer roaming around. There he would be assigned to the forensic unit, reserved for patients being treated for mental illness who had also been charged with, or found guilty of, a crime. About a hundred people resided there, some for years. Unlike the Spartan existence of his prison cell, du Pont would have some amenities, like a nightstand, a chair and closet, and be able to hang a poster on the wall. He also was able to wear his own clothes. And he'd have three roommates.

Jenkins ordered that du Pont's treatment team report back to her within sixty days; she wanted to hear its opinion on his progress and whether he would be ready for trial.

Though he was found incompetent by one court, his lawyers were preparing to argue quite the opposite in another month when du Pont was scheduled to appear in another court to fight his family. Wasn't that trying to have it both ways?

"I realize there may be a public perception that incompetent is incompetent," said Mark Klugheit, the attorney hired to run the show in civil court. "But I think any judge that has to deal with it will understand that the issues are quite distinct."

They were. In his criminal case, the question hinged on du Pont's comprehension of the charges. The civil case was built around his ability to manage his financial affairs and take care of his personal needs. True, he may have been judged delusional and schizophrenic in one court, but that didn't mean he wasn't a brilliant investor, or could run the farm.

But before du Pont and his family clashed, an old issue resurfaced. On October 16, Bergstrom and McAndrews stood before the State Supreme Court and argued over bail. It had been six months since Sprague and Lamb first put the request before Jenkins. It had been four months since the Superior Court turned it down.

In fact, so much had gone on since it was brought up, that the arguments for bail made by Sprague were no longer valid, McAndrews said.

"There's been a lot of water under the bridge since then," he told the court. "In fact, almost a flood has gone under the bridge."

As McAndrews finished his argument, Chief Justice John Flaherty called for a brief recess and all six justices filed out of the room. Minutes later Flaherty returned

"I say think it," Caplan answered. "I'm not saying it. I think."

"You think that Lenko . . ."

"I think he got Mr. du Pont sufficiently upset that Mr. du Pont called him a filthy Communist because he was badgering Mr. du Pont to an excessive degree. And Mr. du Pont responded. I don't know."

Bergstrom wanted to know if Caplan thought du Pont would improve on continued treatment by antipsychotic drugs.

"I don't know."

"You don't know?"

"I don't know. I'm not a fortune-teller just like Dr. Resnick said he's not a fortune-teller."

"You know there's been improvement over the last month, right?"

"So, what's that mean?"

"I don't know. You tell me. You're the doctor."

"I said I don't know what it will be in the next month. I know what happened last month, that's easy to tell, what happened in the past. I don't know what's going to happen in the future."

Later, Bergstrom noted that Caplan had ordered du Pont's medication increased after a meeting with him. Caplan got defensive.

"Is there something wrong with that?" he asked.

"No, of course not."

"I'm sorry. I don't mean to be jittery up here. It's fun being up here."

Jenkins finally broke in. "It would be sufficient if you would just listen to the questions and provide an answer," she said.

In his closing statement, Bergstrom tried as best he could to discount the testimony of Bauman and Caplan. Their idea that du Pont was ready for trial was based on superficial observations, he claimed.

"They observe he is happy when his lawyer shows up. They observe that he eats on a regular schedule. They observe that he gets up on a regular schedule. They observe that he participates in the regimen of the institution on somewhat of a regimented schedule.

"But what they don't appreciate and what they haven't even attempted to appreciate is the fact that the visits by counsel have been void of any substantive discussions about not only the events of January 26, but about the events that led up to it.

"Of course he gets up in the morning. Of course he's happy when people come to visit him. Of course he eats his food. Of course he ties his shoes. Of course he talks to people on the ward. But that's not the issue. The issue is whether he is capable, whether he has the capacity to interact on a meaningful basis with counsel."

That's absolutely right, said McGettigan in his closing. And two people—Bauman and Caplan—who had observed him and talked to him on and off for two months both agreed he had that capacity.

He noted that Resnick had spent a total of thirty minutes with du Pont in the last two months—including ten minutes just before the hearing—compared to the almost daily contact hospital staff had with him for more than sixty days.

"What did he do?" McGettigan asked rhetorically of Resnick's meeting that day with du Pont. "Just say, 'Well, how are you feeling today? Do you have any delusions?' "

He said not one statement elicited from Caplan indicated that du Pont "had in the past month or so offered any delusional material whatsoever. None. Zero.

"He just said, I'm competent. I can assist my attorneys. I know who my lawyers are. I trust them. I can cooperate with them, and I can testify in my own defense. That's the essence of competency here.

''The court should find that the defendant is competent, ready to go to trial, and we should pick a trial date.''

On December 9, Jenkins did.

Basing her decision ''upon the observations and conclusions of health-care professionals at Norristown State Hospital; the defendant's record of treatment and progress there; and in small part, upon the court's own observations of Mr. du Pont's demeanor and interaction with counsel,'' Jenkins ruled du Pont was ready to go to trial.

Pat Meehan was obviously happy. The prosecution got the call it wanted the second time around.

''We are particularly pleased for Nancy Schultz and her family,'' he said. ''It's been three hundred eighteen days since David Schultz was murdered.''

Nancy Schultz was obviously relieved.

''It has been difficult for Alexander and Danielle to deal with both the loss of their father and my continued absence due to the legal proceedings,'' she said. ''However, I will be attending all of the upcoming legal proceedings, because it is important to me that David is represented and remembered during this process.''

Thomas Bergstrom was obviously disappointed.

''In my heart, I believe John du Pont is not really there yet,'' he said. ''I believe that as a lawyer. I also believe it based on what has been some of the finest medical assistance I've had. I believe he's not ready, but I'm prepared to go and do what I have to.''

And what he had to do, he said, was file a notice of an insanity defense.

But as had happened throughout the case, there was a monkey wrench: Bergstrom filed a motion to reopen the competency question—based on what the defense claimed was untruthful testimony from Murray Caplan.

Right after the hearing, Caplan talked with Resnick. According to Resnick, here's what Caplan said: ''I think you are right and I am wrong.''

Resnick also said Caplan told him, "I've passed the point of no return. There are forces that will not permit me to change my opinion."

"At one point when I commented about Mr. du Pont being too fearful to talk about the crime, Dr. Caplan volunteered that he was 'more fearful than Mr. du Pont,' " Resnick said.

What did that mean?

To find out, Bergstrom, Labrum, and Wochok met with McGettigan and McAndrews on Saturday. Bergstrom made it clear he had no confidence in Caplan and wanted another evaluation done.

But Caplan denied he had been pressured by anyone. And what he really said to Resnick, he claimed, was "the decision was in the hands of the judge, who could find that I could be right, or you could be right." Caplan said Resnick misunderstood, or mischaracterized, their conversation.

Bergstrom said he would explore a possible appeal of Jenkins's ruling based on what he saw as contradictions in Caplan's statements. But he soon realized the futility of that, and turned his attention to preparing for trial.

Jenkins said that would begin January 21.

For one of the few times in the long case, it was a date written in stone.

Before the year ended, though, Jenkins made two other rulings.

On December 30, she decided the trial would take place in Delaware County. There was no need that she saw for a change of venue.

On the same day, in a three-line order, she denied bail.

John du Pont would not be going home soon.

And if he were going to be going home at all, he was going to need assistance from a man who had been dead for 131 years.

Eighteen

Daniel M'Naghten was a Scottish woodworker who died in an English hospital for the criminally insane in 1865. Now he represented du Pont's best hope of avoiding a life sentence for murder.

Du Pont's case was not going to be built around what happened: two eyewitnesses—Nancy Schultz and Pat Goodale—saw him shoot David Schultz at point-blank range. So the question for the jury was going to be why he did it.

Bergstrom thought he had an answer: Du Pont was insane.

Two days after Jenkins ruled du Pont competent, Bergstrom filed notice of an insanity defense. By doing so, he tied du Pont's fate to M'Naghten.

In 1843 M'Naghten was beset by delusions of being persecuted by the Tories. He set out to slay Tory Prime Minister Robert Peel, but instead shot and killed Peel's private secretary, Edward Drummond. His lawyer invoked the insanity defense, a legal concept that was still somewhat unclear; the House of Lords was asked to come up with a specific test for legal insanity.

Its decision: ''The party accused was laboring under such a defective reason from disease of the mind, as not to know the nature and quality of the act he was doing;

or, if he did know it, that he did not know he was doing what was wrong.''

That definition, known as the M'Naghten Rule, served as the basis for the insanity defense in Pennsylvania and a dozen or so other states.

Still, Bergstrom knew it was a risky tactic and tough to sell to a jury. First of all, there was skepticism about psychiatry, psychology, and excuses when dreadful deeds—like murder—were done.

Secondly, just because a person suffered from a mental disorder did not mean he automatically met the test for legal insanity. While everyone agreed du Pont suffered from mental disorders, in the legal world that was far from the equivalent of a get-out-of-jail-free card. Juries have consistently come back with guilty verdicts for people who were clearly mentally ill.

Jeffrey Dahmer ate his victims, but couldn't get an insanity verdict.

There was one well-known defendant, though, who did escape jail on a not-guilty-by-reason-of-insanity verdict. And that caused further problems for Bergstrom.

In 1981 John W. Hinckley Jr. was sent to a mental hospital instead of a prison when he was found legally insane after shooting President Ronald Reagan and press secretary James Brady.

As a backlash, a number of states passed legislation to give a jury an alternative verdict that enabled it to acknowledge the presence of a mental disorder but still dish out punishment. Pennsylvania was one that put the new verdict—guilty, but mentally ill—on the books.

Such a finding didn't relieve criminal responsibility or shorten a sentence. It simply meant the convicted defendant would be held in a mental institution until some measure of sanity was restored. Then he would be transferred to a corrections facility to serve his sentence.

The law passed in Pennsylvania in 1983. State Senator

Jeffrey Piccola—who helped lead the fight for its passage—said while the verdict affected a relatively small number of cases, the du Pont case seemed to be one for which it was tailor-made.

"This is a high-profile case where there's obviously some mental illness at issue and where a wealthy defendant could bring in a number of expert witnesses and overwhelm the prosecution," he said.

But the law was not without its critics. One of the most vocal was Stephen J. Morse, a professor of law and psychiatry at the University of Pennsylvania. Morse complained the law muddied the jury's fundamental task of determining guilt or innocence by requiring it to make decisions about the extent of a defendant's mental illness.

"It allows juries to say a defendant is not responsible for his actions but convict him anyway," he said.

Plus, he argued, defendants found not guilty by reason of insanity for serious offenses typically remained hospitalized for as long as they would have been imprisoned if they had been convicted and sent to jail for the same crime. The law needed to be repealed, he said.

At this point, Bergstrom likely felt the same way. By serving notice of the insanity defense, he elevated greatly the importance of testimony from Sadoff and Resnick, O'Brien and Dietz, and other psychiatrists who would be part of the case. He knew du Pont's future could hinge on their explanations of his actions.

But before he even got to that, an old, familiar issue came around again: bail.

The defense had never given up on that question, and this time brought in a set of lawyers from Pittsburgh— experts in Supreme Court appeals—to file an emergency petition for bail with the Pennsylvania high court. It was the fifth time the request for bail was filed, twice before Jenkins, once in Superior Court, and twice in the Supreme Court.

It was the fifth time it failed.

On another front, du Pont settled a minor dispute with his hometown when he agreed to dismantle the red and white billboards on his property and remove the word "Prison" from the "Foxcatcher Prison Farm" sign. The guardhouse he built, though, remained, as did the bear traps and garbage cans at the entrance to the estate.

Du Pont did receive a small victory in federal court; the Larry Eastland suit was put on hold. Eastland's lawyers wanted to get a deposition from du Pont at Norristown, but a federal judge blocked it.

That meant all resources could be concentrated on the murder trial, which rapidly approached. Both sides spent long, long nights in final preparations, going over details, fine-tuning questions, adding and subtracting names from witness lists.

Neither the defense nor the prosecution would talk about the case publicly.

Privately, though, du Pont's lawyers had already made a decision: shift the focus away from David Schultz's death and paint a picture for the jury of du Pont as a pitiable, lonely, friendless, familyless victim—a victim goaded by Pat Goodale and his security-team minions.

That wasn't a tactic pulled out of their hats. Du Pont's money had allowed his lawyers to hire Forensic Technologies Inc., a national trial consulting firm, and a Southern California research lab was brought on board to survey people in the Philadelphia suburbs to gauge public impressions of the case. A jury consultant, Lee Meihls, was preparing to sit with the defense team throughout jury selection.

The lawyers also conducted focus groups to prepare for the trial. And each time they did, Goodale's role raised questions: What did he say in the car on the drive to Schultz's house? Why couldn't he have stopped the shooting? Did he really think it was necessary to put razor wire in the walls of the house?

Prosecutors knew Goodale was going to take a beating. It was their job to soften the blow, to remind the jury that du Pont had pointed a gun at Goodale's face and, for a reason known only to him, didn't pull the trigger.

While that was going on, Jenkins was worried about getting eighteen people—twelve regulars, six alternates—for a jury. She knew she was going to find out quickly if the publicity of the case made it impossible to get an impartial panel, forcing her to bring in citizens from another part of the state.

On January 21, 1996, seventy-five randomly picked residents of Delaware County filed into Courtroom 1.

"Good morning, ladies and gentlemen," Jenkins said, hoping she could find a dozen to decide du Pont's fate.

She addressed the group, asking questions that might reveal any areas of bias they might have—for or against du Pont—that would interfere with their ability to be fair.

"Everybody who comes through those doors," she said, indicating the back of the courtroom, "is asking only one thing: fairness."

She explained that the trial was expected to take about four weeks, and that jurors would be sequestered only during deliberations. She acknowledged that some of those picked would be inconvenienced.

"But if convenience were the standard," she said, "we wouldn't have juries."

She asked who might have close relatives in law enforcement; if anyone had witnessed a violent crime or death; if they knew anyone who had been arrested.

The potential jurors were then led to a side room and called back individually to be questioned first by Jenkins and then the lawyers.

Jenkins, by necessity, was like a broken record. She told each person that it appeared there might not be a

dispute on the question of whether or not du Pont killed
Schultz. She explained that a large part of the case would
be taken up with the issue of legal insanity. She asked if
anyone was inclined to believe or disbelieve the testimony
of psychiatrists and psychologists.

And she learned quickly that not everybody was up on
the events of the day.

Two of the first eleven candidates said they had neither
read nor seen any news accounts of the case. Another said
he had never even heard of du Pont.

"I don't bother with the news," said one. "It's the
same thing over and over again."

"It may be hard to believe," Jenkins said. "But,
frankly, people have different lifestyles, and some lifestyles don't bring them in touch with the media."

The lawyers asked potential jurors if they'd ever been
on a jury before, if they'd ever been a witness in a trial,
and how they felt about deciding a murder case.

Do you understand, Joe McGettigan asked, that the
commonwealth has the burden to prove the crime beyond
a shadow of a doubt, but the defense has the burden of
proving insanity?

Bergstrom wanted to know if du Pont's famous name
or unlimited wealth would be a factor.

"I think everybody knows the du Ponts," said a
nursing-home maintenance man. "But he's a human being, just like me. He's no different than I am. God bless
him. I'm glad he's wealthy."

One man said he prayed before making any big decisions. McGettigan used one of his challenges to get rid
of him. Another said, "I like to think of all law-
enforcement officials as friends." Bergstrom disposed of
him. One didn't believe in the insanity defense. Another
said she couldn't get over her belief that du Pont was
guilty, guilty, guilty.

Still, after the first day, four jurors were picked, an encouraging sign.

"From this moment forward," Jenkins told them, "you don't get any information about this case from anywhere at all, except inside this courtroom."

You may be tempted more than ever to read about the case, or watch it on the news, she told the new jurors. Don't do it. If it comes on television, walk away. If it's in front of you in the paper, cover it up. It was imperative that they see or hear nothing that could color their opinions.

Four more jurors were seated the next day, including one elderly woman whose brother had been hospitalized for schizophrenia. Bergstrom was surprised that prosecutors allowed her to make the final cut.

Another four were picked on Day 3, completing the first twelve. One who didn't make the panel, however, was a man who offered this assessment of his ability: "You don't want some deadbeat up here. There are a lot of jurors back there who could do a better job for you."

"I'm going to defer to your opinion," said Jenkins, excusing him.

On Friday, six alternates were picked; the last chosen was Number 75 in the jury pool. That was fortunate; it avoided the need for another pool of seventy-five.

The average age of the jury was fifty, just what du Pont's jury consultants wanted. Most held middle-class jobs. There was a train conductor and a bank manager. A legal secretary, a medical secretary, and a receptionist. A retired waitress and a computer technician. A self-employed contractor and part-time bank worker. One man was unemployed, another worked in computers, another handled switch equipment for the phone company. All were in place by Friday evening. Opening arguments were scheduled to begin on Monday morning, January 27.

That was exactly a year and a day from the date of the murder of David Schultz.

Except Monday morning came and went before the jury was led into the courtroom to be greeted by Jenkins with a smile—and an apology. A number of pretrial matters had come up over the weekend, and she had to deal with them outside the presence of jurors. Bergstrom had filed a motion to ban any explicit mention of du Pont's net worth, estimated to be at least $250 million. Jenkins granted that.

He also was concerned that the prosecution would, in its case-in-chief—the first, fact-laying part of its case— bring up du Pont's alleged drug use. McGettigan assured him that it wouldn't come until the rebuttal phase.

That settled, the six men and six women of the jury, plus a half dozen alternates, filed in, put their hands on the Bibles placed in front of them, and listened as the clerk swore them in using the stilted language of the courtroom.

"Do you and each of you solemnly swear by Almighty God, and those of you who affirm, do declare and affirm that you will well and truly try the issues joined between the Commonwealth of Pennsylvania and the defendant John E. du Pont and a true verdict render and put into the evidence, so help you God?"

"I do," they answered in unison.

Du Pont sat stoically, his left leg propped up on a chair. He had fallen and injured it the Friday before at the hospital and was brought in and out of the courtroom in a wheelchair.

He looked like a hermit. His long, straggly, gray hair had gotten longer; it had not been cut since his arrest. He came to court in a blue sweat suit, the words "Foxcatcher Wrestling" emblazoned in gold lettering. He would wear a similar outfit every day in court for the next month.

His own lawyers said it was hard to be near him at the

defense table. "You don't want to be downwind from him," said one. "His uniform could walk away by itself," said another.

His sister, Jean Shehan, and nephew sat behind him. Schultz's parents and in-laws helped pack the rows behind the prosecution.

Jenkins introduced the court personnel, explaining their roles. She talked about the insanity defense and what it meant. She told jurors that the State Supreme Court had barred juries from taking notes. She was careful to explain what was evidence and what wasn't.

"For instance," she said, "if there's a witness on the stand and an attorney asks if the witness saw the cows in the field this morning, and the witness says, 'No, I didn't see any cows in the field,' the only thing that is in evidence then is that the witness didn't see any cows. There is still no evidence that there were cows in the field, and you cannot assume that there were cows and this witness failed to see them."

She alluded to the impressive surroundings in the courtroom, comparing it to a churchlike setting.

"Please remember that lives are in your hands, ladies and gentlemen," she said. "Be fair and be impartial. No one is asking you for anything more, but no one is asking you for anything less.

"We have a common bond in this room. Everyone who is here is seeking justice, nothing more and nothing less. Remember that, ladies and gentlemen, and honor your oaths."

She turned to the prosecution table and with one word—"Commonwealth"—brought McGettigan to his feet to begin the trial.

It was 12:28 P.M.

"Thank you, Your Honor," he said.

"Ladies and gentlemen of the jury, it is a terrible thing to get up and discuss the events of a murder of a human being, David Schultz, before his wife and family. But it is my duty.''

He outlined the witnesses who would be called, and offered a narrative of the day of the shooting. He briefly took the jury on the ride from the mansion to the Schultz house where, he said, David Schultz, ''with a smile, his last smile, and a wave, his last wave, said 'Hi, coach.' . . . Hi, coach. David Schultz. Sweat suit. Dirt on his hands from the radio. Hi, coach, and a wave.''

He talked about the weekend standoff, how du Pont repeatedly asked for his lawyer. ''A hundred times in the course of, oh, maybe a twenty-four-hour period,'' Mc-Gettigan said.

''You will hear a person in control. You will hear a person who doesn't want to discuss the issue of the day, the murder of David Schultz.''

McGettigan also tried to undercut the medical experts for the defense. ''The defendant will offer through his expert testimony an interesting version of the death of David Schultz, a very interesting version of the death of David Schultz. And it can be encapsulated in two words: I forget. That's what you'll hear. . . . And I would ask you, during the course of the testimony, to focus on the events of that day which give clear evidence of responsibility.''

He ended by pointing out one last thing.

''A few years or so before the murder of David Schultz the defendant said something which seemed to be a statement of intention: 'I could get away with murder if I wanted to.'

''This defense is an effort to make that statement true. It's for you to determine whether the evidence supports his attempt to escape responsibility.''

McGettigan was like a grasshopper, flitting from one fact to another without notes, trying to weave them together for the jury; Bergstrom was more measured in his opening as he referred to a number of yellow, legal pages in front of him. If McGettigan offered a portrait of a calculating killer, Bergstrom presented the picture of a man lost in a maze of madness.

"Ladies and gentlemen of the jury," he began, "this case is about a killing for no reason whatsoever at the hand of a man who suffered from a mental disease that took away his ability to know that what he did was wrong."

He chose his words carefully, and his voice went up and down as he spoke.

"On January 26, 1996, on a day that was as cold and gray as death itself, John du Pont drove his Lincoln Town Car out of the front gates of his estate and into the abyss of insanity.

"But he was not alone on that trip. There was another man in the car with him, a man by the name of Patrick Goodale."

His tactic, of course, was to soil Goodale from the beginning, and throughout his opening statement he continuously mentioned his name and that of Aegis Security, Goodale's employer. "When Aegis Security was on the property, John du Pont's paranoia went right through the roof," he said.

He spent five or six minutes going through the myriad delusions in du Pont's mind, from the mechanical trees to the Dalai Lama to the threat of a Russian army. He gave a preview of what the jury would hear about paranoia and schizophrenia and delusions. And he ended with Nancy Schultz's own words.

"On January 26, 1996, John du Pont took the final step into the very depths of madness. And I return only for a moment to that day.

"David Schultz is lying on his driveway, and he is mortally wounded. And Mrs. Schultz is holding him in her arms. And in the midst of this unspeakable tragedy, she speaks to 911 because she had called them for aid.

And she told 911 that John du Pont had shot her husband. And the 911 operator asks her why would he do that.

"And her response was, 'He's insane.'"

Nancy Schultz got a chance to talk about that 911 call after lunch; she was the first witness called by the prosecution. For McGettigan, it was déjà vu: he was in this same courtroom nearly a year earlier, leading Nancy through her testimony during the preliminary hearing. But that was just to convince a judge to keep du Pont behind bars, not a difficult task. This was to convince twelve men and women that du Pont deserved to be put behind those bars forever, something decidely harder. So his questions probed for far more background as he tried to show the jury that du Pont was angry at Schultz and had a motive for killing him.

He had Nancy recount the "baseball bat" incident, the times David tried to intercede on behalf of Dan Chaid and Valentin Jordanov, the refusal to attend Thanksgiving dinner and the message that the Schultzes were not welcome for Christmas at the mansion. Nancy said the Schultzes planned to leave after the Olympics for Stanford, where Dave had accepted a coaching position.

Then McGettigan came to January 26, 1996. There were no surprises there; pausing two or three times to keep her composure, Nancy re-created the few minutes around David's death.

"I just remember holding him and looking at him and telling him I love him," she said. "And right then I could hear the ambulance just coming up the street. And I remember looking down at David and he took a couple more breaths, but he was choking and at that moment as the ambulance was pulling up is the moment he died. His face went gray and his eyes went fixed and he didn't breathe anymore."

On cross-examination, Bergstrom tried to subvert the contention that du Pont was angry. He pointed out that despite not spending the holidays with the Schultzes, du Pont nevertheless wrote $10,000 worth of checks to Dave and the two children on December 23.

He then presented Nancy with a transcript of both her 911 call, and had a blowup of one page placed before the jury. Highlighted were the words "He's insane."

He also handed her the police statement she made a few hours after the killing. And he asked her to read a piece of it. McGettigan stood up.

"Asking the witness to read the words she said at that time, at that moment, I think, is objectionable," he said.

"Well," Jenkins responded, "unfortunately while I recognize that it may be difficult, I don't believe there is any legal basis for an objection to that, Mrs. Schultz. So if you wish, take your time. I'm going to ask you to go over that answer, if you would."

Nancy didn't hesitate. The question from the police asked her to describe du Pont. Her answer: "John du Pont is about 55 years old, silver hair, cut short, very thin. He's mentally insane. He hallucinates. He talks about things that he hears and sees. He thinks he's the Dalai Lama. But the last year he's been constantly under the impression that he is the Dalai Lama and usually dresses all in red. I don't know whether he was dressed in red, all in red today. I don't, I didn't notice. It seems to me that I saw gray on his arm with the gun, but I'm not 100 percent sure. It seems like that."

"Thank you," said Bergstrom. "I have nothing further."

McGettigan knew he had to use his re-direct examination to explain for the jury the words "he's insane." So he got right to it.

"Mrs. Schultz, how long after the defendant murdered your husband did you give the statement?"

"An hour, maybe a little more."

"How long had your husband been lying in the ground

of the driveway when you made the 911 call?''

"He was dying at the time that I was speaking to 911."

"At that point were you thinking about offering a legal and medical opinion as to the defendant's state of mind then or at any other time?"

"No," said Nancy. "I was holding David. And I believe that murder is horrible and crazy."

Court adjourned after her testimony.

Back in McGettigan's office, a key phrase from Bergstrom's opening statement was scrawled on a blackboard—"abyss of insanity." Someone took a magic marker and added the prosecution's counterpoint: "No, the height of arrogance."

On Day 2, the first witness was Newtown Officer Steven Shallis, who recalled his arrival at the murder scene and his brief conversation with Nancy Schultz and Pat Goodale. Goodale, Shallis testified, said du Pont made no comments about Dave Schultz before pulling the trigger. That was important, Bergstrom felt, to begin to undermine Goodale's credibility; he was, after all, the one who later put these words in du Pont's mouth: "You got a problem with me?"

Bergstrom didn't have to wait long to get at Goodale; he followed Shallis to the witness stand. McGettigan, though, went first. He knew what was to come, so he put Goodale in a position to deflect criticism. Sure, Goodale said, he had some reservations about some of du Pont's more bizarre security concerns. Like his fear that wrestlers were sneaking into the house and moving around the walls. But he couldn't ignore them completely.

"I viewed it as not a very likely occurrence," Goodale said, "but it was certainly possible . . . Myself and another member of my staff went in the walls and moved around and, yes, in fact, it could be done. . . .

"And there was always a kernel of truth in what he was telling us. So, therefore, there was nothing ever completely off the wall. Frequently there would be issues that had some basis in fact."

McGettigan asked Goodale if any of his security people expressed concerns about du Pont's behavior, and if they attributed it to anything. But Bergstrom objected, then asked Jenkins for a sidebar—a private conversation among the lawyers and judge, held off to the side of the judge's bench. That's where questions of law and testimony get solved before they are introduced in open court.

Bergstrom wanted to know what Goodale was going to say. McGettigan told him Goodale would likely refer to du Pont's drug and alcohol use, and the steps he took to address the problem. Bergstrom said he suspected as much, and reminded Jenkins that the prosecution promised not to introduce such testimony during its case-in-chief. Jenkins agreed. Despite itching to get that information out early in the trial, McGettigan backed off. He moved into other areas.

"Did he make reference to his family, and how did he describe them?" McGettigan asked.

"He described them as the lesser du Ponts."

"Excuse me?"

"The lesser du Ponts."

Goodale said du Pont believed the house, which had been built by his father, had some features that he had yet to figure out. For instance, there were supposed to be mechanical devices placed around the estate that could change the way the property looked.

"He felt that the controls for these devices were located on the property, but that his family had neglected to advise him of where they were," he said. "And he requested our assistance in trying to locate those controls. The way he articulated the issue to us it sounded reasonable given the vast wealth and unlimited resources of that family . . . And so we embarked on efforts to try to help him, try to find these controls."

McGettigan asked about the armored personnel carrier, which du Pont had purchased in California in the late 1960s. Du Pont decided he wanted it restored, and gave Goodale the task—including finding a .50-caliber machine gun to be mounted atop it.

"I asked him would a replica be suitable because it's much easier to acquire and it's cheaper and doesn't require a tremendous paper trail . . . And he did not want that. He wanted a real functioning machine gun." Goodale said he informed Wochok about du Pont's desire.

"And Mr. Wochok advised me to . . ."

Bergstrom shouted out an objection. That led to a sidebar, and Jenkins sustained the objection. But it didn't do any good. Because on the next series of questions Goodale blurted out, "I contacted the defendant's attorney and I was advised to give the man what he wants."

Jenkins told the jury to disregard it. But McGettigan got what he wanted to imply: that even du Pont's attorney didn't want to upset a cash cow.

Nineteen

On Day 4, firearms expert Howard Montgomery gingerly lifted Commonwealth Exhibit Number 20 so the jury could take a good look.

It was a Smith & Wesson .44-caliber gun.

Nancy Schultz flinched when she saw the weapon used to kill her husband. It was the first time she had been that close to it since it was pointed at her more than a year earlier.

Montgomery was the last of ten witnesses during the prosecution's case-in-chief. It had taken three and a half days for prosecutors to lay out their case for the jury. Now, the defense was coming to bat with several purposes: to give a short course in paranoid schizophrenia, to detail for jurors the depths of du Pont's mental illness, and to connect his mental state to the shooting.

The first defense witness was Lee Hunter—promoted to Newtown police chief six months after the shooting—who went over the "baseball bat" incident and the confidential report he had filed after interviewing du Pont. As he spoke, Tom Bergstrom placed a blowup of Hunter's report on an easel so jurors could read about du Pont's fears of the Russian army invading Newtown, his belief that he was the Dalai Lama, and his conviction that there was a conspiracy to kill the Holy Child.

Following Hunter, Foxcatcher employees Beverly Collier and Walter Fitzgerald recounted their stories of du Pont's extraordinarily odd behavior on the farm. They were also used to reinforce the defense contention that the presence of Aegis Security guards heightened the tension on the estate.

"During the period of time that Aegis was providing security services at Foxcatcher, what was Mr. du Pont's demeanor when he was in the presence of the Aegis employees?" Collier was asked by Terry Wochok, who was handling the questioning to give Bergstrom a respite.

"He was very agitated," Collier said, "much more upset than he normally was, and he carried a gun at those times."

"When they left, did you notice any change in Mr. du Pont's demeanor?"

"Oh, yes. There was a great change. He started wearing normal clothes. He went out and bought a new wardrobe. He was like a different person."

"Did there come a time when Aegis came back on the property?"

"Mr. Goodale came from time to time."

"And when Mr. Goodale came back on the property, what was Mr. du Pont's demeanor?"

"He always seemed very agitated when Mr. Goodale was around."

Joe McGettigan and Dennis McAndrews were particularly harsh during their cross-examination of Collier, the wrestling-club manager, and Fitzgerald, the maintenance manager. They wanted the jury to think that both witnesses would have done anything to keep the paychecks coming from du Pont. They depicted Fitzgerald as a lackey who brought his son and brother to work on the estate and who, months after the killing, accepted a $16,000 gift from du Pont to buy a truck.

McGettigan also got Fitzgerald to admit that he followed du Pont's orders to paint the farm buildings black—including the Schultz house.

In fact, during the lunch break on the day Fitzgerald testified, Nancy Schultz confronted him in the hallway outside the courtroom.

"She asked me why I painted those buildings black," Fitzgerald said. "I said, 'If I leave, someone else is going to come in and do the same job I do.' "

"And because if you didn't," McGettigan said, "someone else would take your job and make that money?"

"That's correct."

Collier had arrived on the estate in 1988; one of her first jobs was to refurbish and redecorate the mansion after the death that year of Jean du Pont. She then worked overseeing the maintenance of the wrestling facility and performing secretarial duties.

McAndrews focused on her personal relationship with du Pont.

"You'd like to help this defendant, correct?" he asked.

"I would like to tell the truth about this defendant."

"And you would like to help him out, wouldn't you?"

"I am loyal to this defendant. He is my employer."

"He is also someone that you have expressed on any number of occasions a desire to marry. Isn't that correct?"

"No, that is not correct."

"So you are saying that if anyone was to have heard Beverly Collier express a desire to marry John du Pont, they would be lying?"

"They would be."

Later, both Nancy Schultz and former coach Greg Strobel would be called by prosecutors to suggest that it was Collier who was lying. Strobel was asked by McAndrews if she ever made any remarks about her feelings for du Pont.

"One in particular that I recall," Strobel said. "She had a Victoria's Secret catalogue out and was looking at it and said 'Do you think Mr. du Pont would like me in one of these?' ''

''Was she serious?''

''Oh, yes, very much.''

Nancy Schultz testified that Collier spoke to her of her desire to share a future with du Pont, including marriage and adopting children.

While their testimony added some spice to the trial, jurors also sat through what amounted to a brief lesson in schizophrenia, offered by William Carpenter, a University of Maryland psychiatrist and expert in the field. Tall, bearded, with a thick fringe of white hair that hung over his ears, and a voice tinged with a drawl, he was the first of six psychiatrists who would testify about what they believed was du Pont's mental condition during the time of the murder and at present.

Carpenter's primary purpose was to educate the jury, as simply as possible, about schizophrenia.

''Schizophrenia is a disease,'' he said. ''It's a disease of the brain.''

Fairly common, he said, it appears in all cultures, seems to have been around since man began recording history, and affects about 1 percent of the population around the world. It is caused, he said, by ''something having gone wrong in the early development of the brain. The strongest evidence is around genetics . . . But we still do not have precise knowledge about exactly what genes are involved and what these genes are doing to contribute to the cause of schizophrenia.''

While results vary in people with the disease, Carpenter said, there are three major components usually found. One is a distortion, or split, from reality.

''People develop beliefs that are false, that are not shared by others who are in similar circumstances,'' he said. ''They're strongly held beliefs. Technically, they're called delusions.''

The second area he labeled "a disorganization of the thought processes." And the third he described as "a split between the thinking life and the emotional life.

"This is where you would see people who have silly giggling when they receive bad news, or are extremely sad suddenly when there is no context for any sadness. And some patients simply are not able to experience and manifest as much emotion and don't get as much gratification out of engaging in relationships, out of love, out of shared work, out of doing things with friends . . . because they have had some damage to the emotion systems that help us have these experiences."

While treatable, schizophrenia has no cure, and is a lifelong disease. He explained the difference between persecutory delusions ("people are out to get me") and grandiose delusions ("the belief that one has assumed some elevated status, like Napoleon or Jesus Christ").

"These people often will show anger or aloofness, anxiety, argumentativeness," he said. "They can come across with a superior air or in a patronizing fashion. There is often kind of a formal quality to their demeanor that other people would experience as cold and aloof, or withdrawn and condescending."

His definition seemed to fit du Pont like a bodysuit.

"Dr. Carpenter," Bergstrom asked, "can you explain to us whether or not a person suffering from paranoid schizophrenia can also carry on life functions?"

"Yes. This is something that is often difficult for people to understand, how in some ways a person's brain and their mind can be so disordered and at the same time other functions can take place in what would appear to be an ordinary fashion."

Carpenter was the first expert to tell the jury he believed du Pont suffered from paranoid schizophrenia. Just as importantly for the defense, he said he ruled out substance abuse as a cause. And he said he saw no evidence to suggest that du Pont was faking or exaggerating his illness.

Carpenter was the last witness on Friday, wrapping up the first week of trial. Bergstrom would have to wait until Monday to finish with him, and McAndrews had another weekend to plan his cross-examination. But D.A. Pat Meehan summed up the prosecution's feelings.

"There are plenty of people who are mentally ill who are not in our jails," he said, "simply because they know right from wrong and don't commit crimes."

When Carpenter returned on Monday, he offered two words that became a theme for the defense: "sudden clarification." What he meant was this: Sometimes schizophrenics can see or hear something completely innocent that triggers a delusion. A person who has a vague suspicion about someone else, for instance, may one day see the other person sitting in a red car and suddenly believe that he's a Communist plotting a conspiracy. Carpenter told the story of one of his patients who saw a word in a dictionary, became convinced that the dictionary had been purposely turned to that page, and went into a rage directed at his employer, making wild accusations.

Before shooting Schultz, Carpenter suggested, du Pont "may have noticed something that gave him this sudden clarification" that convinced him Schultz posed a threat that was so real, defensive action had to be taken.

In other words, there was no planning, no premeditation.

Why, Bergstrom asked, didn't du Pont shoot Nancy Schultz or Pat Goodale?

"I believe that he shot the person that he perceived to be a threat to him," Carpenter said. "He did not perceive the others to be a threat to him. So there would have been no reason for him to have shot them."

McAndrews tried to blunt Carpenter's testimony with a series of general questions.

"Most people with schizophrenia understand right from wrong. Isn't that correct?"

"Yes."

"You would agree, doctor, that schizophrenics can take steps to conceal or excuse their criminal conduct?"

"Yes."

"They can knowingly and intentionally lie or misrepresent the truth?"

"Yes."

"They can, if they choose, be cunning, conniving, and manipulative?"

"Yes."

McAndrews then queried him about substance abuse. It was, of course, the prosecution's intent throughout to hammer away at du Pont's alleged cocaine habit. Although there would be only one eyewitness—wrestler Rob Calabrese—to testify that he saw du Pont using the drug, McAndrews and McGettigan were able to consistently keep the issue floating in front of the jury. Even Carpenter said that he thought du Pont had used cocaine, and he pointed to a number of incidents that he felt could have been induced by drug use.

For instance, he said, du Pont had gone through a period where he felt he had bugs crawling under or over his skin. Du Pont also searched for bugs in the carpets, and thought things moved around in the wood paneling. Carpenter also referred to reports that du Pont had cut his fingers, trying to drain out poison.

His testimony was reminiscent of one of the most horrific tales about du Pont that had surfaced shortly after the murder. A businessman recalled a visit he made some years earlier to Foxcatcher to complete a transaction. When he arrived, he found du Pont sitting in a Chippendale chair, holding a penknife, and methodically slicing at his leg. "I've got one," exclaimed du Pont, blood running down his legs, as he put the pieces of skin in a jar;

he was convinced he was capturing bugs from outer space.

The businessman quickly made out a check and fled.

Just how far prosecutors could go with du Pont's drug use was a constant source of contention during trial. Bergstrom tried to parry some of the attempts to bring it up. He jumped up and objected when McAndrews, during his questioning of Carpenter, tried to introduce a letter from psychiatrists dated December 1992, when Wochok inquired if du Pont could be involuntarily committed. Part of that letter read: ". . . there has been some evidence over the past few years of probable cocaine snorting; it is possible other drugs used as well." Judge Jenkins banned the introduction of that letter.

Bergstrom also objected when McAndrews asked Carpenter, "Are you aware that on January 17, 1997, the defendant was offered a haircut and refused, saying that his attorney did not want him to get one?"

That, of course, left the impression that du Pont's hermitlike appearance—he hadn't shaved or gotten a haircut in more than a year—was nothing more than a defense ploy. But Bergstrom, at a sidebar conference, said he had a good reason for wanting du Pont to keep his hair long— and it had to do, again, with drugs.

Drug residue shows up in strands of hair. Hair, which grows about a centimeter each month, can be a month-by-month scientific marker for the presence of drugs in the body. Evidence of cocaine found in strands closer to the scalp, for instance, would indicate recent use, while residue found at the end of the strand would show drug use further in the past.

"The reason I told this defendant not to have his hair cut is because I wanted to obtain a hair sample," Bergstrom told Jenkins during sidebar. And it was only in the last two days, he said, that results had come back from the laboratory. "I don't give a damn if he shaves his head from this point on."

Later, Bergstrom would make his point before the jury that the lab results were negative.

Following Carpenter to the witness stand was Sandy Deveney, a security investigator for a Philadelphia-area corporation and du Pont's longtime friend. He told more tales from Foxcatcher, including one about a horse found dead in the pasture with a large hole in its side. Du Pont was certain it had been shot, Deveney said—shot by a Satanic cult that originated in the Virginia town of Orange, where Montpelier was located. That's where du Pont's father, William, had grown up, and one of du Pont's recurrent delusions was that his father was head of the Church of Satan.

In fact, Deveney said, he investigated the incident and discovered the horse had fallen on the ice, broken three ribs, and one rib had penetrated the heart. Du Pont, he said, was much relieved when he learned that.

McGettigan ignored the horse. But he did ask about Deveney's dog.

"You have a drug dog, don't you?"

"Yes, I do."

"Is that the same drug dog that the defendant told you to keep away from him?"

"It's the only drug dog I've ever had."

"The same one he told you to keep away from him?"

"Correct."

"And that's because you were aware of the defendant's drug problem, weren't you?"

"I had suspicions."

Deveney, in fact, had more than suspicions. In late 1995 he attended a meeting among a group of people who knew du Pont, including law-enforcement authorities, to discuss arresting the man suspected of supplying du Pont with cocaine.

"You attributed much of the defendant's behavior to his drug problem, isn't that correct?"

"It was my conclusion, yes."

The man to whom Deveney referred was a regular visitor to Foxcatcher, although wrestlers said he had no apparent job function. Although he was never called to testify, the man admitted to McAndrews he had not worked on the estate since March 1994, yet continued to receive a salary from du Pont. Du Pont also was cosigner of a ninety-thousand-dollar loan for his frequent guest and when the man defaulted, du Pont's stock, posted as collateral, was taken by the bank.

At least two people, McAndrews said, told him that they had purchased drugs from the same man, and one said he had introduced the man to du Pont for the purpose of getting du Pont drugs.

The alleged supplier could have cleared things up, but he balked at testifying, and, in the end, McAndrews and McGettigan didn't pursue him. They felt they had enough testimony from others to make their point.

The defense got to its star witness—psychiatrist Phillip Resnick—on Day 6. By that point, Resnick had spent a total of eleven hours with du Pont, more than any other medical expert. He cited what he called a "mountain of evidence" in concluding that du Pont was legally insane when du Pont killed Schultz.

That evidence, Resnick testified, showed that du Pont had an irrational but intense fear of being assassinated by Schultz. In du Pont's mind, Resnick said, Schultz was a terrorist who had to be killed; to du Pont, the killing was a "justifiable act of war."

"We see a building crescendo of fear," Resnick said, using a chart titled "Chronology of Critical Events" to pinpoint events leading up to the shooting, from the October 1995 arson to the day before the murder, when du Pont told wrestler Tony DeHaven that he feared for his life.

Resnick also narrated an edited version of the March

5, 1996, taped interview he and Robert Sadoff had with du Pont. That was when du Pont proposed the theory that his double committed the murder.

In addition, Resnick supported Carpenter's theory that du Pont had a "sudden clarification." But Resnick used a different phrase: "abrupt crystallization."

What caused the crystallization was impossible to say— although he couldn't discount the possibility that Pat Goodale had said something in the car ride to the Schultz house. It was just one more swipe the defense took at Goodale—and that led Pat Meehan to take a swipe at the defense.

"They have to do something to create a villain some- where where there is no villain," he said.

Resnick's testimony was spread out over three days. After he was finished, Bergstrom called a surprise witness, Michael David Parriski from West Virginia. A firearms dealer, he was questioned for just a couple of minutes. But that was all it took to make Bergstrom's point.

"Mr. Parriski, I would like to direct your attention, sir, to February of 1996," Bergstrom said. "And at that time did you receive a request regarding a .50-caliber machine gun?"

"Yes, I did."

"And do you know who that request came from?"

"It came from the Savannah Lane Shooting Associa- tion."

"And did you ultimately receive in your possession a .50-caliber machine gun?"

"Yes, I did."

"And about when did you receive the gun?"

"I received the gun on April 19, 1996."

"And for how long a period of time did you maintain possession of that weapon?"

"I maintained possession of the weapon until Novem- ber 25, 1996."

"What did you do with it on November 25, 1996?"

"I transferred the machine gun to Savannah Lane Shooting Association."

"And do you know whether or not one Patrick Goodale works for the Savannah Lane Shooting Association?"

"Yes."

"He does work there, does he not?"

"He works for the Savannah Lane Shooting Association."

That, Bergstrom hoped, would settle the mystery of what happened to the machine gun du Pont had wanted for his armored personnel carrier—and, of course, cut more of Goodale's credibility.

Bergstrom then called Robert Sadoff, one more psychiatric voice to bolster the argument that du Pont was insane when he shot Schultz.

But what about du Pont's actions after the killing, McAndrews wondered, when he held police at bay for forty-eight hours and repeatedly asked for his lawyer? Sadoff said they were in keeping with his delusions. Du Pont was in a predicament, he said, that he believed had to be solved on an international level. The local police were irrelevant in that context, pesky gnats to be swatted away in favor of ambassadors, presidential pardons, and intervention from world leaders.

McAndrews then turned to drugs.

"You can not be certain that the defendant did not obtain and use controlled substances in prison, can you?" McAndrews asked.

"I would be very surprised if he did," Sadoff answered.

Did you know, McAndrews asked, that du Pont had approved five cash transactions of $7,500 each to a man prosecutors implied was du Pont's drug supplier while the millionaire was in prison awaiting his murder trial?

"I didn't know that."

Wochok objected and asked for a sidebar. There he complained that McAndrews left the inference that du Pont was getting drugs in jail. Jenkins said she wouldn't allow any information from the alleged supplier unless it came from him—and he refused to testify.

So McAndrews dropped that line of questioning. When he finished with Sadoff, the defense rested, five days after it began.

At the beginning of their rebuttal, prosecutors went right back to the drugs, calling four wrestlers in a row who alluded to du Pont's drug use. That forced Bergstrom, in his daily few minutes with reporters, to try to put it in perspective.

"I don't believe we've heard any evidence whatsoever that there was any drug use anywhere near the time of the offense, and I don't think you will, either," he said.

The last of the four wrestlers called was Dan Chaid. Bergstrom tried to rattle him with some tough questions, especially about a spat with his fiancée in which Bergstrom all but accused the brawny Chaid of choking and slapping her. But Chaid maintained his composure—and he remained cool even when he admitted that investigators told him he was suspected of setting the fires at Foxcatcher in October 1995.

One of the fire investigators, State Trooper Nicholas Saites, followed Chaid to the stand and inadvertently provided the greatest moment of comic relief in the trial.

Saites said he met with du Pont in the mansion and found him fascinating; he enjoyed hearing about du Pont's international travels.

"And is one of the things he told you that he did while traveling was purchase nuclear weapons from the Slavic countries and give them to the United States?" Bergstrom asked.

"Yes, he told me that."

"And, of course, you believed that?"

Not right away, Saites answered. But he became convinced it was true. For one thing, one of du Pont's employees had told Saites that du Pont was worth $3.5 billion.

"And as Mr. du Pont was explaining this to me, I'm thinking, okay, sure," said Saites. "I looked over at Mr. Wochok and he's looking at me and he's nodding his head 'yes' and I'm thinking, okay, you know, $3 billion will get you a lot of things. And if one's a half million dollars, I mean, to a man that's got $3 billion, and he told me specifically, 'I want to do some good with my money.' And I thought, well, you know, that'll do it. That's about as good as it gets."

"So you sort of bought into the idea that he was going over to these Eastern Bloc countries buying nuclear weapons and then giving them to the United States?"

"I wasn't under the impression he does this on a daily or weekly basis. It's just something that can and could and does occur."

"Just sort of something," Bergstrom said, "that you do every now and then, maybe at Christmastime or Thanksgiving, go over to, you know, the Balkans, for example, and you buy nuclear arms and you bring them to the United States. Is that it?"

"I'm not sure," Saites said seriously, "what special holiday would be appropriate to give a nuclear weapon as a gift."

The laughter had just died down when Bergstrom asked, "How about Armistice Day?"

"Armistice Day would be good," said Saites.

Although he didn't show it during the trial, Mc-Gettigan—always intense—was particularly galled whenever Bergstrom elicited a chuckle from the jury. A murder trial, he believed, was no place for any joking at all.

As humorous as the exchange was with Saites, Bergstrom knew that he would soon be facing a witness who would be dead serious in trying to rip apart the insanity defense. John O'Brien was one of two prosecution psychiatrists, and from his testimony during the competency hearing in September it was no secret where he stood.

Before O'Brien took the stand—the last witness on Friday, February 7—Bergstrom asked Jenkins at sidebar to strike from the record all testimony of drug use, claiming it was too remote in time from the killing, especially the one eyewitness report from 1988. But McAndrews argued that the defense itself had raised issues of du Pont's change in behavior at that time. Plus, he said, it related directly to the diagnosis of paranoid schizophrenia. Jenkins agreed.

Bergstrom did get a promise from McAndrews, though, that O'Brien would not bring up the name of the alleged supplier, whose shadow, the defense felt, seemed to be hovering over the trial.

But Jenkins also denied a motion by Bergstrom to disqualify O'Brien, based on his involvement in the December 1992 evaluation of du Pont. So Bergstrom tried his best to cast his own doubts on O'Brien's ability. Each expert witness is questioned about qualifications by both sides; usually it's brief, consisting of a synopsis of experience. But Bergstrom practically queried O'Brien on every line of his resume. His desire, of course, was to plant the seed of doubt in the jury's mind.

O'Brien, himself, had no doubt about du Pont. Though conceding he was mentally ill, he believed it was cocaine, not mental illness, that set in motion the events that ended with Dave Schultz's death.

He acknowledged that du Pont did suffer from some delusions, but he refused to label him a paranoid schizophrenic. Du Pont's odd behavior and beliefs, he testified, were "more consistent with substance abuse than with a psychological disorder."

Many of his delusions—people in the walls, secret tunnels, spying activities—dissipated when he was presented with evidence to the contrary. A paranoid delusion, O'Brien said, wouldn't go away so easily. What du Pont had were "paranoid concerns or paranoid ideas." He said when he interviewed du Pont he noticed a "wry smile" that he felt was noteworthy. The smile, O'Brien testified, came when du Pont talked about the Nazi flag or his imagined Eastern European roots, indicating that du Pont was teasing, "or amused by what he was saying."

He felt du Pont was making a conscious attempt to be found not guilty by reason of insanity. Du Pont's diagnosis, he said, was complex. But he summarized it this way: "a cocaine-induced psychotic disorder with delusions."

"I think it is possible that he is a paranoid schizophrenic," O'Brien said, "but I don't regard that as one of the highest possibilities."

"Do you have an opinion as to whether the defendant, when he fired three shots into David Schultz, understood the nature and quality of that act?" McAndrews asked.

"Yes, I do. My opinion is with reasonable medical certainty that he did know the nature and quality of his acts. He shot a gun that's very difficult to shoot unless you know how to shoot well. And shot it in such a way to indicate an intent to kill. And in my opinion there is no question that he understood the nature and quality of his acts, meaning that he was shooting a gun and was killing an individual or attempting to kill."

There is nothing he heard or saw in the records, O'Brien said, "that would indicate an inability on his part to formulate the specific intent to kill"—a key component for the jury to find du Pont guilty of first-degree murder.

During cross-examination by Bergstrom, O'Brien said he could not be sure that du Pont didn't have access to cocaine while in prison.

"He's still being visited by or was visited by the person who was supplying him," he said.

Bergstrom was stopped in his tracks.

"Your Honor, I object. Move to strike. May I see you at sidebar?"

Jenkins did strike the statement from the record. But she refused Bergstrom's request for a mistrial. Bergstrom eventually elicited the concession from O'Brien that there was no hard evidence during the trial that du Pont used drugs in the months leading up to the murder.

Bergstrom also presented the hair-analysis report completed on a fifteen-centimeter strand of du Pont's hair; no evidence of cocaine was found. Noting the length of du Pont's strand, Bergstrom asked whether the test results "indicated that in the last fifteen months, from the time the hair was taken, that John du Pont had no cocaine."

"It could indicate that, yes," O'Brien said. However, O'Brien testified that with the passage of time, the test is less sensitive.

Afterward, Bergstrom tried again to downplay the drug issue.

"This is not a drug case," he said. "This is a case about mental illness. I'm hopeful that the jury will focus on the evidence, on the relevant issues."

In some ways, O'Brien, who was on the stand for three days, was a warm-up for the prosecution's cleanup hitter: Park Dietz. Dietz was one of the best-known forensic psychiatrists in the country, renowned for the amount of material he would review and his methodical way of processing the information. He had been involved in many of the most high-profile criminal cases in the country. Besides the Hinckley trial, Dietz worked on cases involving Milwaukee mass murderer Jeffrey Dahmer; the Menendez brothers in California, convicted of killing their parents; Susan Smith, who admitted driving her two young boys into a lake in North Carolina; and Robert Chambers of the preppy murder case in New York. At the same time he was working on the du Pont case, he was also retained in the case of the Unabomber, Ted Kaczynski.

Dietz was able to do a number of things. For one, he deflated the defense idea that du Pont was concerned about the "bazooka"—the bottle rocket launcher— Schultz had made with his son. Dietz said when he asked du Pont about it, du Pont was perplexed. "I never heard about it until I was in prison," he told Dietz.

Dietz said that du Pont denied ever using drugs, and said he did nothing more than drink socially. That, Dietz pointed out, clearly was a lie.

And he said du Pont was also lying when he claimed he could not remember the shooting.

"He didn't say he had amnesia or that he forgot," Dietz said. "He recalled going to the car with Pat Goodale and yet he denied recollection of taking the weapon with him. Well, if he had one of the mental experiences that causes a piece of memory to be missing, he should be missing the whole piece. And if he remembers going to the car with Pat Goodale and driving around the property looking for storm damage, then he would also remember that he took the weapon with him—particularly, as it turns out, because he took an unusual weapon with him, not his usual weapon. And so I thought it was very significant that he told me he didn't remember it when I'm confident that he must."

The prosecution was scoring points.

Dietz was emphatic that du Pont suffered from a psychotic disorder. But he was reluctant to called it paranoid schizophrenia for two reasons, he said. One, he couldn't rule out recent drug use, even in prison. Two, he wasn't satisfied that du Pont's mental problem was not something else: bipolar disorder, or manic-depressive illness.

"The reason that remains a concern is that Mr. du Pont had the onset of his psychotic symptoms as far as I know in 1988 after the death of his mother, which is late for schizophrenia, not impossible, but late in life for the onset of schizophrenia," Dietz said. "More commonly, one would expect a mood disorder, like bipolar disorder, to have its onset at that age."

But the biggest bomb Dietz lobbed at the defense was this: when du Pont got into the car with Pat Goodale, he didn't take the smaller, .38-caliber handgun, a weapon he had carried so often that the blue sheen from the surface had worn off. He took what Dietz called the "Dirty Harry" gun, the .44-caliber Smith & Wesson.

That, said Dietz, was tremendously significant.

"First, it confirms that he knew that something unusual was his purpose on January 26 of 1996," Dietz said. "He was taking a more powerful gun. In fact, he was taking the gun that was made famous in the Dirty Harry movies as the most powerful handgun in the world.

"And in taking that gun, we can know with certainty that the defense theory of an abrupt crystallization is incorrect. He did not have an abrupt crystallization in the car with Pat, and he didn't have some acute change while in the car with Pat, which is the language used by the three defense doctors."

Du Pont, Dietz said, was not insane. Not only did he kill Schultz, but he knew it was wrong. And Dietz had twelve specific reasons for coming to that conclusion, including du Pont pointing the gun at Goodale in the car (to "neutralize" him); fleeing when Nancy Schultz shouted that the police were coming ("shows an appreciation of wrongfulness"); immediately trying to reach Wochok when he returned to the mansion ("indicates that he knows that what he's done is wrong"); and asking for a presidential pardon after his arrest.

"He would not need a presidential pardon if he had done something good or neutral," Dietz said. "He would only want a presidential pardon if he knew that he had done something wrong.''

He refuted Resnick's claim that du Pont believed killing Schultz was "justifiable." And he also discounted the theory that du Pont feared Schultz as a deadly agent connected to an international conspiracy.

Instead, Dietz noted the conference call among wrestling officials and wrestlers in November 1995—initiated by Chaid—to talk about removing du Pont from USA Wrestling.

"He had tried and failed many times to accomplish great things as an athlete himself," Dietz said. "And at Foxcatcher he had put together a world-class program with outstanding athletes, and he had been a sponsor of the governing bodies; he had important influence in those bodies, and this had been very much John du Pont's identity as the head coach of Team Foxcatcher in all of its glory.

"And to have people talking about removing him from power and even calling his family about his erratic and dangerous conduct was a tremendous threat to his identity, to his stature. That's the conspiracy, I believe.''

Dietz said he found nothing in the record that showed du Pont ever feared Schultz. The killing, he said, "stemmed from growing animosity that the defendant harbored towards David Schultz." That animosity could be traced back to New Year's Eve, 1994, when he fired Schultz. He was envious of Schultz's stature among the wrestlers, and would not make him coach when Greg Strobel left. He was bothered by Schultz's friendship with Valentin Jordanov. He was incensed by his relationship with Dan Chaid.

Dietz pointed to numerous incidents in the month prior to the murder that indicated du Pont's anger at Schultz: not plowing the Schultz driveway, not allowing Schultz to travel to Colorado, withdrawing his invitation to Christmas dinner, blaming Schultz for the "baseball bat" incident, which left him injured and unable to wrestle.

The prosecution punctuated Dietz's clinical analysis by playing the dramatic 911 tape on which Nancy Schultz pleaded for an ambulance as her husband lay dying in the driveway. It was clearly an attempt to blunt the weight Bergstrom placed on Nancy's description of du Pont as "insane." Dietz testified that her words came at such an emotional time that they shouldn't in any way be viewed as a diagnosis.

Nancy and Jeanne St. Germain, Dave Schultz's mother, left their seats as the scratchy, three-minute recording filled the quiet courtroom, riveting the jurors who wore headsets and the spectators who cocked their heads toward the courtroom speakers.

Although Nancy did not hear the tape, she later had no trouble recalling her feelings at that time.

"I'm sure what was expressed is my emotion at watching my husband die in front of me that day," she said. "It was a horrible, horrible day."

Park Dietz was the final and most powerful witness for the prosecution. When he stepped down, the district attorney was finished. That left the defense with the option of presenting testimony in a phase of the case called sur-rebuttal, literally "above rebuttal." In effect, the defense had a chance to get in the last word; to do that Bergstrom put on his fourth psychiatrist, Paul Appelbaum.

Appelbaum downplayed the importance of cocaine, saying that du Pont's symptoms were apparent before his drug use and continued after he was arrested and supposedly not taking the drug. He said Dietz and O'Brien failed to recognize the importance of the fact that du Pont's delusions changed or lessened in intensity. Both factors are typical of paranoid schizophrenics, he said.

That du Pont fled to his home after the killing and believed Georgia Dusckas, his assistant, could hold off the police simply by refusing them entrance to the house was gravely misinterpreted by Dietz and O'Brien as signs that du Pont knew what he did was wrong, Appelbaum insisted.

"If Mr. du Pont had been trying to escape because he had done something wrong, driving to his house and staying there until the police arrived would have been the last thing to do," he said. "It is not a great way to escape after committing a murder."

Perhaps the most persuasive evidence that du Pont was out of touch with reality, he said, was taking Pat Goodale on the ride to the Schultz house. Who but an insane person, Appelbaum asked, would bring an eyewitness to a murder?

He believed, he said, that du Pont was permeated with a fear of Schultz at the moment he pulled the trigger.

Even when he put a bullet in Schultz's back? McGettigan asked on cross-examination.

"I don't think that I or anybody else knows precisely what was in his head at that moment," Appelbaum said. "I wish I did, but I don't."

Appelbaum also had a completely different view of the relationship between du Pont and Valentin Jordanov—a view that came after a forty-five-minute interview with the Bulgarian wrestler. Jordanov told him he didn't feel he was treated any differently than other wrestlers who had been du Pont's favorites. And he didn't believe du Pont was jealous of his friendship with Schultz.

"He really painted a very different picture from the things we have heard here in the courtroom," Appelbaum said.

What about the "abrupt crystallization" theory? McGettigan wanted to know. Didn't you say, he asked Appelbaum, that two weeks before the shooting du Pont had identified Schultz as the source of his woes?

"That would seem to be at odds, would it not, with an

abrupt crystallization on the drive to the Schultz residence?''

''I don't know what to say about abrupt crystallizations,'' Appelbaum said. ''It's not my theory and . . .''

''Dr. Appelbaum,'' interrupted McGettigan, ''feel free to reject it.''

He asked one more question and was done. Jenkins asked Bergstrom if he had anything else.

''No,'' he said. ''Fini.''

After forty-three witnesses and thirteen days, testimony in the trial of *Commonwealth vs. John E. du Pont* was over. It was Thursday, February 13. Because Monday was President's Day, Jenkins decided to give jurors off on Friday, too, giving them a four-day weekend before they would be sequestered.

Closing arguments came on Tuesday morning. Bergstrom went first; he said he had never before seen a more attentive jury. And then he talked for seventy-two minutes.

''You can read this record and you can pore over it until your eyes go blind,'' he said, ''and you will not find a rational reason for this killing and you will not be able to justify why in God's name one would take an eyewitness to a killing.

''You have to look at this record, you have to look at this evidence, not as we are, as rational people, but you have to look at this evidence through the prism of psychosis. It's not just looking through a glass darkly, it's looking through a shattered glass darkly. The pieces don't fit together.''

He likened du Pont's paranoia to ''having a nightmare every waking moment of your life.''

He attacked Goodale with a passion. ''Patrick Goodale's a liar and a thief,'' he said. ''It's that simple.''

If the jury agreed and called Goodale's credibility into question, Bergstrom said, it then had to question the words Goodale attributed to du Pont after the first shot was fired at Schultz: "You got a problem with me?" It followed, then, that the whole idea of du Pont's anger at Schultz had to be questioned.

"Some of you are going to wonder until you go to your grave, 'What was it that Patrick Goodale said to John du Pont in that car on that day?' He won't tell you now. He'll never tell you."

Bergstrom asked jurors to remember what he had asked at the beginning of the trial: put aside the fact that du Pont had enormous wealth.

"Who among you, who among you would come down and trade places with him, a man with no wife, a man with no children, a man with no family, a man with no friends. Who among any of you would come down and change places with him? There isn't a person on this planet that would trade places with him, as sick as he is and the life that is ahead of him."

He argued that du Pont wasn't angry at David Schultz. Nor did he hate him, Bergstrom said.

"But he was fearful of Dave Schultz. And that fear was not based on reality. So that's the hard part. We're used to things that we can touch and see and get our arms around. We're not used to delusions. We're not used to psychosis. We're not used to madness."

Finally, alluding to the female figure of Justice, he said, "I ask you in the name of that woman that we must all bow to, to find John du Pont not guilty by reason of insanity. Because it is the right verdict."

But McGettigan, in his closing, immediately raised this question: was it really madness that drove him to put three bullets into Dave Schultz?

No, he said, it was most definitely anger.

Sure, he hired people to put razor wire in the walls and dig trenches. "But his anger," McGettigan said, "his anger he dealt with personally."

Using charts that the jury saw during testimony, McGettigan took jurors again through events and incidents before, during, and after the shooting. They clearly showed du Pont was aware he had committed a crime and tried to get out of paying for it, McGettigan contended.

He called Bergstrom's attack on Goodale "unwarranted abuse," and scoffed at the "abrupt crystallization" theory.

"They had to erase the words that you know were said and try to conjure up a conversation which you know didn't occur."

Du Pont, McGettigan said, simply thought he could get away with murder.

"An arrogant person took the most arrogant act a human being can take, that is, take upon themselves what only God should do, and that's separate a soul from body. He controlled everything in his life. And then he took a human life because of that."

The record in the case is voluminous, McGettigan said at the end of his one-hour, twenty-two-minute summation.

"But the record is one word shy, and it's a word that only you can add. It's a word that says what the evidence and the law say is the right thing. And it's a word that holds a murderer responsible. It's a word that does the right thing. It's a word that does justice.

"And the word is 'guilty.' "

Twenty

After listening to nearly three hours of closing statements, and Judge Jenkins's long explanation of the charges, the jurors were led to the windowless deliberation room behind the courtroom. Each was handed a verdict slip, a short questionnaire that was to be used as a guide.

"Do you find that the defendant, John E. du Pont, shot and killed David Schultz?" read question Number 1.

"Do you find that the defendant, John E. du Pont, is not guilty because he was legally insane at the time he shot and killed David Schultz?" was Number 2.

Depending on their answers, jurors were directed to other questions. For example, if they answered "Yes" to Number 2, that was the end. If they answered "No" they then moved on to question Number 3:

"What is your verdict on the charge of criminal homicide by murder in the first degree? Not guilty. Guilty. Guilty but mentally ill."

There were two more options: third-degree murder, and voluntary manslaughter.

For Bert Allen, Juror Number 18, the decision was easy: du Pont, he said, was guilty of first-degree murder, but mentally ill.

"You use a .44 Magnum and you're either going to

hunt for bear or you're going to kill someone," Allen said.

Abrupt crystallization?

"Ridiculous," said Allen.

"I think he knew what he was doing at the time, that he knew he was killing a man and that it was wrong. I think he thought about it. I think he went to kill Dave Schultz."

Allen's comments should have made prosecutors jump for joy—except for one factor: Allen's vote didn't count.

An alternate, he had been dismissed following closing arguments. But he was happy to talk to reporters, who were seeking some clue as to how the jury might sift the evidence.

Allen said the last shot that du Pont fired into Schultz figured heavily into his thinking.

"That third shot in the back when he was laying on the ground put a cap on it, in my opinion," Allen said.

He also felt du Pont's scraggly appearance was a ploy to enhance his chances of being found not guilty by reason of insanity.

Du Pont, he said, "will get what he deserves." And he had confidence in the twelve men and women with whom he had spent the last month.

"They will do the right thing," he said.

Toward that quest, the jury spent about two and a half hours in deliberations on that first afternoon before heading to the hotel. They took a quick poll just to see where everyone stood. There was apparently a wide array of opinions. This was not going to be easy.

Nancy Schultz, meanwhile, stood outside the courthouse, schmoozing with reporters, who she had gotten to know very well. Now living in California, she had spent much of the past month in a motel while her son and daughter stayed with her brother on the West Coast. It had taken a toll on everyone, she said. She had with her a school assignment written by her seven-year-old daughter Danielle:

"My name is Danielle Schultz. My daddy was shot last year, and now my mom lives in court and I live with my uncle. Sometimes I see my daddy, but I know it's my imagination. I miss him and tears come down my face. I miss my mom and I hope she's all right."

"I want to see justice done," Nancy said, "and then go back home to be a mom to my kids."

Justice, though, was slow-moving.

On the second day, jurors asked Jenkins to review the criteria for first- and third-degree murder, and voluntary manslaughter. It seemed to indicate to courtroom observers that the insanity defense had failed.

First-degree murder, Jenkins said, meant there was specific intent to kill. Specific intent, however, did not require a long period of planning; intent could be formed just seconds before the killing.

Third-degree murder did not require premeditation, but would be the proper verdict if the jury found there was a reckless disregard for the fact that du Pont's act could result in death.

Voluntary manslaughter covered a killing in which the defendant had a sincere, if mistaken, belief that he was in imminent danger of being killed and believed the killing was justified.

Jurors also sought a map of the Foxcatcher estate and charts that both the defense and prosecution had used to outline their theories about what drove du Pont to murder. They got the map, but Jenkins decided that providing the charts would violate rules on jury material.

In addition, they heard portions of testimony of Pat Goodale—specifically, the half hour between his meeting with du Pont and the killing. The jurors also reviewed part of Park Dietz's testimony.

When the jury came back for a third day, it again had

Jenkins explain the degrees of homicide. She spent twenty minutes going over it again.

The concepts were difficult to understand, she said. She told jurors not to hesitate to seek further clarification if they still were confused.

The vigil kept by Schultz's relatives began to wear on them. But David Schultz's parents said they had no choice but to be patient.

"It's hard being away from home," said his mom, Jeanne St. Germain, who lives in Oregon. "But it's very important to be here to show everyone that there's somebody important to all of us who can't be here. I'm here for David."

"The fact that we're all together and able to be gentle and nurturing has been important," said Philip Schultz, Dave's dad.

He said he felt no need for revenge. "What I feel toward Mr. du Pont is great pity. He didn't seem to be able to make any connections in his life."

But he did want to see him sent to jail.

"I would like that. I think John needs to be by himself for a long time."

On Friday evening at seven-fifteen the jurors sent a note to Jenkins; they wanted another clarification of first-degree murder. Jenkins told them that would be the first order of business when they returned on Saturday. They also listened again to testimony from Nancy Schultz, Goodale, and Steve Shallis, the Newtown Township police officer who was first to arrive at the crime scene. Shallis, of course, had reported that Goodale indicated nothing was said by du Pont before he pulled the trigger.

By the time they returned to the hotel on Friday night, jurors had spent about twenty hours mulling a verdict and several more hours in the courtroom to rehear testimony or to have Jenkins answer questions. There was some hint of disagreement, too, when raised voices were heard through the jury-room door.

By Saturday, the words "hung jury" were being whispered—especially after jurors returned to the courtroom so Jenkins could go over, for the fifth time, first-degree murder and voluntary manslaughter.

D.A. Pat Meehan, though, tried to sound optimistic.

"We've had to scratch and claw for every bit of progress in this case," he said. "That's going to continue right to the end, apparently.

"Whatever it is that has this particular jury hung up, they continue to try to attack it from a variety of perspectives. So I'm encouraged that we're going to get a result."

Indications that there would not be a verdict on Saturday came throughout the day as relatives dropped off suitcases with clothes for jurors. The wife of one, carrying a large valise, joked that she was planning on taking a Las Vegas vacation in mid-March—with or without her husband.

As the day wore on, it was not at all certain that her husband would make it.

Just before being dismissed on Saturday evening, however, the jury asked Jenkins for writing materials, including an easel and marker pens. As jurors later recalled, that marked a turning point.

"We wrote down what we all remembered and hung it up, and, let me tell you, it worked," said Jessie Rodgers, a retired waitress, who at seventy-two was the oldest member of the panel. "You could see it. It opened everybody's eyes. All I can say is it was just like a little miracle. It cleared all of our minds."

"It helped to keep the focus on the facts," added Richard Kady, fifty-four, a phone-company technician. "Not on what somebody's opinion was."

But opinions still differed enough to prevent a unanimous vote. So back to the hotel jurors went, anticipating a day off on Sunday.

For Nancy Schultz, Sunday would be a day of rest, too.

"I've had so many people here for me," she said. "If I was just sitting around thinking and rethinking about all that has happened, I'd go stir-crazy. But I've had all these people for support and to talk to and to keep everything on an even keel."

Jurors spent nine hours on Monday, February 25—Day 6—in the deliberating room. One encouraging sign: they asked no more questions of Jenkins. It was a full day of uninterrupted work.

There was a feeling among lawyers on both sides, though, that at least one juror had his or her feet firmly planted and would not budge, making a unanimous verdict impossible.

But experts on the jury process who were familiar with the du Pont case were not surprised that nearly a week had gone by with no verdict.

"You have this incredible collision of assumptions, beliefs, and convoluted legal language, convoluted legal concepts, and convoluted psychiatric concepts," said Steven Penrod, a professor of law and psychology at the University of Nebraska. "It's not at all surprising that they're struggling."

Nor was it surprising, he said, that jurors repeatedly asked Jenkins the same questions.

"Jurors have a tough time understanding legal instructions," he said.

"I don't mean to suggest jurors or laypeople are stupid. But instructions are full of legal gobbledygook. Lawyers and judges, I think, have difficulty appreciating how Byzantine the conceptual matters embedded in the instructions really are. It's not everyday stuff."

One juror, John Flaherty, later endorsed Penrod's opinion. The difference between first- and third-degree murder and manslaughter caused confusion that was hard to overcome.

"I know people might think, after we asked that something be read five times, 'What the heck don't they understand?' " said Flaherty, a thirty-eight-year-old computer technician. "But we just didn't want to miss something. I thought, 'Let them think I'm stupid.' It was too important for our decision."

Flaherty also said something surprising: the insanity defense was never completely set aside.

"It was mentioned every day," he said. The reason jurors didn't ask Jenkins about it also was simply explained: they all felt they understood it.

"The three options of murder were fairly complex," Flaherty said. "The concept of insanity was straightforward."

Jenkins, meanwhile, was mulling her options, including what was called a "modified Allen charge." That was a nearly century-old rule giving a judge a little leeway in nudging a jury toward a conclusion. Under the charge, Jenkins could have told jurors that it was unlikely a more competent jury could be found and that, to the extent that they didn't compromise their consciences, they should try harder to reach a decision.

In fact, lawyers for both sides met with Jenkins on Monday to discuss whether she should approach the jury and get some feel for the status of the deliberations. But she decided not to. Despite the hard time it was obviously having, the jury had not yet indicated it was at an impasse.

"They have been a very conscientious jury throughout the trial," Meehan said. "They paid a great deal of attention to the issues, and they seem to be bringing that same work ethic to the deliberations on this matter.

"When you have a jury working this hard the indication is that they're making some progress, they're getting closer, and they don't want to quit. They seem to be a group analyzing the issues and going back and piecing things together.''

Then, on Tuesday, February 25, the last piece fell into place.

At about four-fifteen, there was activity around the deliberation room. Figures could be seen moving past the frosted glass of the door; a hand from inside knocked on the glass. Immediately, one of the court officers, sitting outside, poked his head in. A few seconds later, he emerged and walked toward the courtroom.

There was a verdict.

It took less than an hour to get everyone assembled. The courtroom, half-empty during much of the trial, was packed. Courthouse workers, done for the day, scurried to Courtroom 1 as word spread throughout the building. For television reporters, it couldn't have come at a better time; they would be able to break into the 5 P.M. newscast with live broadcasts.

Just after five, du Pont was wheeled in. None of his relatives was in the courtroom.

"All rise," said court officer Bill Lyons as Jenkins entered the courtroom.

Even du Pont—wearing his blue Foxcatcher outfit—stood up on his injured leg.

"Ladies and gentlemen," Jenkins said, looking at the jury, "have you reached a verdict?"

"We have, your honor," said foreman Peter Coary, a forty-seven-year-old train conductor.

Jenkins's court clerk stood facing the jury and read from the verdict slip.

"Do you find that the defendant, John E. du Pont, shot and killed David Schultz?"

"Yes," said Coary.

"Do you find that the defendant is not guilty because he was legally insane at the time he shot and killed David Schultz?"

"No."

"What is your verdict on the charge of criminal homicide by murder in the first degree?"

"Not guilty."

Nancy Schultz gave a slight shudder, and shook her head from side to side.

"What is your verdict on the charge of criminal homicide by murder in the third degree?"

"Guilty," said Coary, "but mentally ill."

It was 5:09 P.M. John Eleuthère du Pont was now a convicted murderer.

Du Pont showed no emotion. But Tom Bergstrom did. As soon as he heard the verdict he slapped the defense table hard, took off his glasses, and began rubbing his face as his eyes moistened. Jenkins asked him if he wanted the jury polled. It took him fifteen seconds before he could mutter "Yes" in a cracked voice.

Du Pont leaned to Terry Wochok. "So it's third-degree," he said. Wochok, though, couldn't be sure if the meaning had registered. As the jurors slowly filed out of the room, du Pont turned to Bergstrom. "Thank you," he said.

Then, for the first time since his trial began, du Pont declined the wheelchair. Slowly, with a slight limp, he walked out of the courtroom, and into an uncertain future.

Reporters and other onlookers quickly filed into a meeting room of the courthouse, set up to handle a press conference for the defense and prosecutors. Television lights illuminated a bank of microphones where Bergstrom, Terry Wochok, and Joseph Labrum stood.

"I'm pleased with the verdict, frankly," Bergstrom said. "It could have been a lot worse. This was a case with little winners. It's tragic for the Schultz family, it's tragic for du Pont."

Meehan said he, too, was happy with the outcome, but

called it a "shallow victory because it came at the loss of a great person.

"It's a shame because over the last month we saw a tremendous amount of resources, especially of a psychiatric nature, that was available to this man, and many people who alleged to be his friends," Meehan said. "And it's tragic there wasn't some intervention before the killing of David Schultz because the criminal justice system was left to pick up the pieces."

Wochok was optimistic that du Pont would one day return to his beloved Foxcatcher.

"Early on we hoped he would be able to spend at least some time at home sometime in his life," he said. "At least that possibility exists at this time."

Somewhat lost in the hoopla surrounding the murder charge was this fact: du Pont was also found guilty but mentally ill of simple assault for pointing a gun at Patrick Goodale. However, the jury found du Pont not guilty of the same charge of pointing his gun at Nancy Schultz as she stood in the doorway of her house.

Nancy, who got into the habit of joking and talking with reporters off the cuff, was subdued as she read from a prepared statement. She thanked jurors "for their commitment to seeking out the truth and coming to the conclusion of guilt. It is comforting to know that du Pont is not above the law and he must be held responsible for David's murder."

Later on, outside the courthouse, Jeanne St. Germain—who had been the most vocal in wishing for a first-degree conviction and as harsh a sentence as possible—was unable to speak through her sobs; Philip Schultz, though, said he had come to personal closure over the loss of his son and had even been able to forgive du Pont.

But, he said, he felt certain that accountability did not end for du Pont in Courtroom 1.

"There is a human justice system, and there is another

justice system that perhaps goes beyond our understanding,'' he said. ''I think John is going to have to live in the prison he created for himself on the day he killed David.''

Du Pont was returned to Norristown State Hospital, where he would remain until his sentencing in early May. Bergstrom hosted a party that night for the defense team at his house. The next day he went to see du Pont.

Du Pont looked at Bergstrom, and said, ''You know, I guess the jury is right about my mental illness.''

''It was,'' said Bergstrom later on, ''the first glimmer that he's starting to grasp the burden he has.''

Epilogue

Jeanne St. Germain stared at John du Pont, her gaze like a dagger, her voice shaky, her finger pointing.

"I want you to look me in the eye," she said.

Du Pont looked back without expression.

"You tell me why my son is dead. All I want from you is the one thing you can't give me: my son's life.

"You are less than nothing to me, a hateful, festering thorn in my side."

It was May 13, 1997. Sentencing Day for du Pont.

Nearly three months had passed since Judge Patricia Jenkins listened to a jury pronounce du Pont guilty of murder. Now it was time for her to decide his punishment.

Gone was the scraggly, long gray hair and full beard. Du Pont, on a steady dose of antipsychotic medicine for eight months, was clean-shaven, his hair cut to collar length. His teeth had been fixed, and he no longer wore a stone face. In fact, he talked frequently with his lawyers.

The prosecution, of course, wanted the stiffest sentence allowed by law: forty years. McGettigan and McAndrews made sure to remind Jenkins about that third bullet fired into Dave Schultz's back.

And to point out the impact Schultz's death had on

those close to him, they called a string of witnesses still mourning the fallen Olympian.

None was as powerful as his mother.

Since her son had been killed, Jeanne St. Germain's rage had been building. Throughout the trial, her frustration mounted; when the jury decided on third-degree murder rather then first-degree, no one in Schultz's family took it harder than she.

At last, the diminutive woman with short salt-and-pepper hair was able to give public voice to her seething anger. And she wasted no words.

"He is a self-absorbed, arrogant, narcissistic bully accustomed to buying his way out of trouble," St. Germain said.

"A lot has been said about why John du Pont might have done this. I believe it was a wretched stew made up of envy, jealousy, anger, possessiveness, a need to control."

Her son, she said, "made John aware of his own smallness, of what he was not and could never be.

"David had the love and respect of countless people, something John could not buy at any price."

She brushed aside the defense's trial-long stance that du Pont had, in his delusional state of mind, perceived Schultz as a physical threat.

"David," St. Germain said, "was only ever a threat to John's ego."

In pleading for the stiffest sentence available, St. Germain made a mother's appeal, saying that her life would never be the same.

"I am broken. I have shut down," she said. "I don't know how to start my life again without him. I have lost interest in my work and my friends. The world has been ruined for me. I am very bitter."

Looking at du Pont, she said, "John, you have no idea

what you've done. You've slaughtered a great man, and that will be your legacy.''

St. Germain also asked Jenkins to order that the trophies and awards Schultz gave to du Pont be returned to the family. Jenkins agreed.

Other members of the wrestler's family followed St. Germain to the stand, including his brother, Mark, and father, Philip. Friends, including wrestler Trevor Lewis, also testified, emphasizing Schultz's contribution to people both in and out of wrestling.

Nancy Schultz talked of the devastation to her family, making sure Jenkins didn't forget her fatherless children. She told how Alexander and Danielle suffered psychologically after the murder. Her daughter, she said, had talked of suicide ''so she can go and see her father.''

''The most common question [from my children] that I have to answer is, 'When will John get out, and will he hurt us?' '' Nancy Schultz said. ''I'd like to be able to put my kids to bed at night and tell them they don't have to worry about where John is.''

Du Pont's lawyers did not have the firepower to counteract the emotional outpourings of the prosecution witnesses. They made a plea for mercy, arguing that his mental illness demanded a lower sentence. And they used a short list of character witnesses who mostly spoke of du Pont's largesse in supporting amateur sports.

Joy Hansen Leutner, the triathlete who had trained and lived at Foxcatcher for two years in the early 1990s, called du Pont a ''father figure'' who changed her life, and helped countless others.

Bergstrom also emphasized du Pont's philanthropy, particularly his one-million-dollar donation to Crozer-Chester Medical Center, where Gale Wenk—du Pont's ex-wife—had worked so long ago.

And Bergstrom did at sentencing what he had done

throughout the trial: try to shift blame from du Pont to those around him.

"Foxcatcher Farm was not a Norman Rockwell painting," he told the court. "Foxcatcher Farm was a place of razor wire and tunnel digging and mechanical trees, where people carried guns . . . where wrestlers sat and watched videos of nothing. There was a full moon at Foxcatcher every night of the week."

Not unexpectedly, during the prosecution's closing, McGettigan and McAndrews took the opportunity to rip du Pont. McAndrews, in particular, made a dramatic presentation, picking up the Smith & Wesson .44 that du Pont used to kill Schultz. When he pulled the trigger, the click could be heard throughout the courtroom.

And he finally blurted out in court the phrase he had been using privately to describe du Pont whenever he and McGettigan talked about the case.

"He is what he's been for many years," McAndrews said. "A fraud. A colossal fraud."

When McAndrews finished, Jenkins shifted her position on the bench, leaned forward and was ready to call a recess. But a short flurry of activity at the defense table stopped her.

And then the court got a surprise: du Pont wanted to make a statement.

The only time he had talked in court since his arrest had been at his arraignment a year earlier. Now he rose from his chair and spoke softly and deliberately.

"I finally concluded that on January 26, 1996, I was ill," du Pont said. "I wish to apologize to Nancy Schultz and the children for what happened and wish them all the best in the future. I wish to apologize to my friends, family, and athletes for any disappointment I might have caused them."

Du Pont's brief remarks, though, rang hollow on the side of the room where Schultz's family sat.

"Never once," McAndrews said later, "did du Pont mention Dave Schultz's name."

When court reconvened in the afternoon, it was clear Jenkins kept the Schultz children in mind as she deliberated over du Pont's punishment.

"I have to devote special attention to the victim impact on the children of David and Nancy Schultz, who have been completely helpless throughout," Jenkins said.

And then she pronounced sentence: thirteen to thirty years, one of the longest sentences for third-degree murder in recent Pennsylvania history. Even with credit for the fifteen months du Pont had already spent in jail and Norristown State Hospital, he would be at least seventy before he would ever visit his Foxcatcher estate or sleep in his forty-room mansion. And if he did get out of prison then, probation would keep him under the scrutiny of authorities until he turned almost ninety.

"There will always be, no matter how you look at it— whether you view it as a watchful eye or a helping hand— there will always be somebody viewing Mr. du Pont," she said, "making him accountable for his behavior and making him accountable to receive the treatment he needs for his mental illness."

She also sentenced du Pont to three to six months—to be served concurrently—for simple assault for aiming his gun at Goodale.

Then, in her concluding remarks, Jenkins expressed some of her own outrage over the incredible events that became part of daily life on du Pont's estate.

"He was a tyrant," Jenkins said of du Pont. "He had a cache of dangerous weapons. He used them to threaten young athletes with violence. . . . These were the horrors of life at Foxcatcher."

The Olympic athletes, she said "stayed on in this world, and I could not help but wonder day after day during the trial, and also certainly all day today: 'Why?' "

As the courtroom emptied, it was obvious both sides were disappointed.

"When there's a loss of a human life such as this," McGettigan said, "there is no term that is satisfactory."

"I was hoping for something more in the ten-year range," Bergstrom said. "On balance, I'm hopeful he'll get into a mental-health unit . . . that will give him the care and treatment he needs so he can survive the next eleven years and come out and live whatever remaining years of his life he has left in peace."

But Bergstrom's hope wouldn't materialize. Although Jenkins noted du Pont required treatment for his mental illness, she had no power to order him sent to one of the state's mental-health facilities. After undergoing evaluation by prison authorities, du Pont was shipped to Cresson State Prison in Cambria County in western Pennsylvania, a five-hour drive from Foxcatcher. A corrections department policy begun in 1996 directed that inmates be sent outside their home areas. The idea was that prisoners who behaved would be rewarded with transfers closer to home.

At Cresson, du Pont was first put in an isolated mental-health unit. He was allowed no visitors except lawyers, and had to conduct conversations with them by telephones located on different sides of a glass partition.

It was, said his lawyer Mark Klugheit, worse for him than his prison stay in Broadmeadows Prison in Delaware County.

"In Broadmeadows he was in the deepest part of his delusional state," Klugheit said. "At that point, if he spent twenty-two hours a day alone in his cell, he had whatever flights of madness there were to occupy his mind.

"At this point, he's 100 percent aware of the reality of his circumstances and very acutely aware of just how unpleasant they are."

John du Pont remains today at Cresson, where—on a

regimen of medication and psychological counseling—his situation has improved dramatically.

He is now part of the general prison population but kept alone in a single cell.

Terry Wochok flies from Philadelphia to a small airport near the prison to visit du Pont as often as possible. In prison, Wochok said, du Pont keeps track of the news, watching CNN. And the millionaire prisoner attends classes on various topics. In fact, Bergstrom said, du Pont even led one class on one of his old, favorite topics— birds, lecturing his fellow inmates on ornithological esoterica just as he did his boyhood chums years before.

His other lawyers visit du Pont at regular intervals, working on an appeal of his sentence. They are also talking with him about the numerous other court dates that will occupy du Pont for the next few years.

Like airplanes in a holding pattern, civil suits against du Pont had been stacking up since the day he was arrested. Once he was sentenced for murder, they began to land.

Foremost was Nancy Schultz's wrongful death suit filed on March 3, 1997, within a week of du Pont's conviction. That came shortly after the O.J. Simpson civil jury in California found the ex–football star liable in the deaths of Nicole Brown Simpson and Ronald Goldman, awarding their families over $33 million.

Certainly a multimillion dollar settlement was not out of the question for the Schultz family. After all, in du Pont's case, here was a murderer who could pay the bill. A detailed analysis by Assistant District Attorney Joe Grace put du Pont's worth at a minimum of $250 million. Klugheit, who was handling all the civil suits, called that figure "a gross overstatement." But he also declined to be more specific.

What he did say was that du Pont would be the one to direct how this suit was resolved.

"As a legal matter, John is presumed competent and is in a position to make a decision as to how to deal with this case," he said.

"I would expect him to seek advice and counsel from those people whose judgment he respects and to make a decision based on it. . . . I'll do my best to see that any decisions he makes are reasonable decisions that are fair to John and fair to the Schultz family."

One of the touchiest legal matters for Klugheit was worked out before it got to trial. That was the attempt by du Pont's family to have him declared incompetent to manage his affairs. The compromise, avoiding what could have been a public airing of family finances, gave final say on nearly all financial matters and medical care to three trustees: his sister, Jean Shehan, who was fourteen years older; his landscaper and longtime friend, Terry McDonnell; and Bryn Mawr Trust Company, which had long handled du Pont's assets. There were, though, two specific caveats: on significant decisions, the trustees had to consult du Pont, but were not required to honor his requests. Second, du Pont retained the right to decide what course he should take in the murder case.

Du Pont said he realized he faced an uncertain future. In the paperwork outlining the agreement, he admitted his need for help, and expressed a wish to someday return to Foxcatcher Farm. And there was this poignant request: that his extensive collection of firearms be disposed of "to prevent me and anyone else from engaging in any activity that constitutes a danger of physical harm to myself or others."

In April 1997 both sides filed into the courtroom, happy to have this business done. But Delaware County President Judge A. Leo Sereni, who was overseeing the case, balked. His goal, he said, was to be absolutely certain that du Pont's interests were attended to. And looking at the people in front of him, he wasn't so sure that was the case.

Although he mentioned no names, it was obvious to whom he referred when he called those around du Pont "severely remiss for not taking simple steps" to have him involuntarily committed years earlier. Such attempts to commit du Pont, he complained, were "feeble, rather than aggressive."

"Was it because no one within the family structure, or the professional structure, wanted to kill the goose that lays the golden egg?" he asked.

So before he would sign the agreement, he ordered yet another psychiatrist to examine du Pont. And he appointed a guardian, telling both to report back to him whether or not they felt du Pont knew what he was doing in turning over so much power to the trustees.

Six months later, they did. Du Pont, they told Sereni, was making progress, and clearly understood the agreement. Satisfied, Sereni signed it, eliminating one large legal headache.

But plenty of others remained. There was wrestler Dan Chaid's suit, claiming du Pont made terroristic threats when he pointed a gun at his chest in the gym. Du Pont answered that one with a countersuit, charging Chaid with setting the fires in October 1995 that destroyed two buildings at Foxcatcher. The arson, du Pont said in the suit, caused him "great mental anguish and humiliation."

Chaid, of course, wasn't the only wrestler going after du Pont. Four black wrestlers, three of them tossed off Team Foxcatcher, sued du Pont, alleging discrimination. The four were 1992 Olympic gold medalist Kevin Jackson, Kanamti Ruben Solomon, John Fisher, and Robert Pritchett Jr. They contend du Pont did not pay black wrestlers the same stipends that white athletes received, and that du Pont did not invite them to live rent-free on the estate.

Jackson did receive $1,000 a month in addition to $40,000 in bonuses for winning various titles, the suit says, but he was never asked to join those who lived at Foxcatcher. The suit says that in March 1995, three of the wrestlers were thrown off the team because du Pont developed an obsessive fear of the color black that became so extreme, wrestlers were ordered not to wear black clothing and a wrestling coach was told to get rid of his black Jeep.

Still another suit, by horticulturist Thomas Speer and his wife, Barbara, a part-time worker, was settled out-of-court at the end of 1997. In their lawsuit, the Speers detailed a bizarre incident in the greenhouse in October 1995. Du Pont, the suit said, fired a shot at the furnace and then pointed the gun toward Speer. According to Speer, du Pont also shot at a desk after Speer asked if he could use it. The suit says that the shooting incident, on top of other du Pont behavior, forced Speer to seek treatment for emotional distress.

Details of the settlement were kept secret.

Also secret was the agreement that ended a suit against du Pont by Larry Eastland. Eastland's suit was the legal matter that Georgia Dusckas first thought was the reason for the police descending on Foxcatcher estate in the afternoon hours of January 26, 1996.

Eastland, an Idaho developer who once ran for governor of that state, claimed in his suit that du Pont owed him $900,000 in severance pay. Eastland said his roles working for du Pont included ghostwriter, security chief, and researcher of du Pont's genealogy. He says he had an oral agreement for the severance package.

Eastland claimed he was fired by du Pont in June 1995 after—in the words of his suit—"devoting himself faithfully to du Pont" for seven years. When he worked for du Pont, Eastland said he received $300,000 a year, plus expenses. And he said he was promised a severance package of three years' salary, or $900,000, if he were let go after five years. His suit sought that severance money, plus $50,000 in unpaid wages and benefits.

The suit was withdrawn in December 1997. Neither side would discuss it.

"He decided to drop it; we agreed nobody would say anything about it and that's the end of it," said Terry Wochok.

Finally, Pat Goodale, du Pont's former security chief and an eyewitness to Schultz's murder, filed his own federal suit in late January 1998, just before the two-year statute of limitations expired. Goodale sued for assault (remember that du Pont was convicted of pointing a gun at Goodale just before shooting Schultz). Goodale further claimed in the suit that he was defamed by Thomas Bergstrom, who called him a "liar" and a "thief" during the trial.

Bergstrom stands by his comments.

"Everything I said about Pat Goodale both in and outside of court was fully and unequivocally supported by the record," he said when he learned of the suit.

Goodale seeks in excess of $100,000.

Even the car dealership that rented du Pont the Lincoln he used to drive to Schultz's house wanted a hefty chunk of money. Du Pont got the Town Car just hours before the murder but police held it for over a year, and the dealership said du Pont was responsible for $12,000 in rental fees. That, too, was resolved out of court.

However, no one was more effective in pressing du Pont for money than Delaware County District Attorney Patrick Meehan. Prosecutors wanted du Pont to pay for the two-day siege that involved scores of police officers and for the cost of pressing the commonwealth's case in court—including the psychiatric experts used against du Pont. The bill came to more than $742,000.

Bergstrom thought that was fair—up to a point. He

balked at paying the nearly $180,000 that went for McAndrews, who was brought in from his private practice to deal with the appeals that flooded the D.A.'s office. In all, the du Pont defense had filed eighty-two petitions and appeals in various court jurisdictions—ten in the first month of the case.

McAndrews called that "nothing short of overwhelming," and characterized the case as "a miserable sixteen months" and a "nasty, vicious disagreeable experience."

That might be so, Bergstrom argued in an appearance before Jenkins, but the D.A. had over thirty lawyers in the office; certainly, he said, one of them could have done McAndrews' job.

Jenkins didn't think so. She ordered du Pont to fork over the whole bill.

Du Pont's lawyers actually had their own claim for expenses, although it was a more modest request of $23,000. That, they said, was for the damage caused by police during the forty-eight-hour standoff at Foxcatcher, and included the loss of dozens of sweatshirts and other athletic gear that disappeared from the wrestling center. Terry Wochok complained the cops went on a souvenir hunt.

That complaint is still pending.

Across the country in California, Nancy Schultz continued her work with the Dave Schultz Wrestling Club from her new home in Foster City, near San Francisco. Her organization raises money to help wrestlers train and travel to competitions—the same thing du Pont did.

She has become an unofficial ambassador for the sport, picking up where her husband left off.

"It keeps me busy, and I feel it's something Dave would be happy with," she said. "And it's good for my kids to see people who they were used to seeing all the time (in Pennsylvania), people who were David's friends."

Her love of the sport wasn't diminished, she said, by the tragedy. She is on the boards of both USA Wrestling and the National Wrestling Hall of Fame.

"I love coming to wrestling events. David got me involved a long time ago and I love the sport. . . . I don't know about the rest of my life, but for a long time I'd like to stay involved."

Time, though, did little to heal the wounds of her loss.

"I guess the grief isn't so severe constantly," she said early in 1998, two years after Dave's death. "But the loneliness and the thought that I'm going to go forever without Dave because of the whim of somebody is frustrating. But the kids get stronger, and that makes me stronger."

David Schultz wasn't forgotten. On June 7, 1997, he was inducted posthumously into the National Wrestling Hall of Fame in Stillwater, Oklahoma, where he had begun his college career at Oklahoma State. A few weeks later, several hundred people gathered at the luxurious Bellevue Park Hyatt Hotel in Philadelphia for a black tie dinner to honor him. Portraits of Schultz were auctioned, including one by artist LeRoy Neiman. There were tributes from the dais, and a video commemorating his glorious athletic career. For many, it was first time since January 26, 1996 that they could celebrate the robust, gregarious, and fun-loving way Schultz had chosen to live, rather than mourn the bewildering, tragic, and senseless way he died.

On Saturday, July 5, 1997, without announcement or publicity—a tremendous contrast to the fanfare that accompanied the opening of the building—workmen gathered on the outside of the John Eleuthère du Pont Pavilion at Villanova University.

Unceremoniously, they removed his name, letter by letter, from the brick facade.

Compelling True Crime Thrillers
From Avon Books

FREED TO KILL
by Gera-Lind Kolarik with Wayne Klatt

71546-5/ $5.50 US/ $6.50 Can

GOOMBATA:
THE IMPROBABLE RISE AND FALL OF
JOHN GOTTI AND HIS GANG
by John Cummings and Ernest Volkman

71487-6/ $6.99 US/ $8.99 Can

CHARMER: THE TRUE STORY OF A
LADIES' MAN AND HIS VICTIMS
by Jack Olsen

71601-1/ $6.50 US/ $8.50 Can

DOUBLE JEOPARDY
by Bob Hill

72192-9/ $5.99 US/ $7.99 Can

FLOWERS FOR MRS. LUSKIN
by Arthur Jay Harris

78182-4/ $5.99 US/ $7.99 Can

AND THE BLOOD CRIED OUT
by Harlan Levy

73061-8/ $5.99 US/ $7.99 Can